Cracking the SAT II: Chemistry Subject Test

Cracking the SAT II: Chemistry Subject Test

THEODORE SILVER, M.D. AND
THE STAFF OF THE PRINCETON REVIEW

2001–2002 EDITION

RANDOM HOUSE, INC.
NEW YORK

www.randomhouse.com/princetonreview

Princeton Review Publishing, L.L.C.
2315 Broadway
New York, NY   10024
E-mail: comments@review.com

The Independent Education Consultants Association recognizes The Princeton Review as a valuable resource for high school and college students applying to college and graduate school.

ISBN: 0-375-76182-9
ISSN: 1076-531X

SAT II is a registered trademark of the College Board.

Editor: Rachel Warren
Production Editor: Maria Dente
Designer: Illeny Maaza
Production Manager: Robert McCormack
Illustrations by: The Production Department of The Princeton Review

Manufactured in the United States of America on partially recycled paper.

9 8 7 6 5 4 3 2 1

2001-2002 Edition

ACKNOWLEDGMENTS

The author thanks John Bergdahl, Cynthia Brantley, Jessica Brockington, Joseph Cavallaro, Ji Sun Chang, Andrew Dunn, Leland Elliott, Greta Englert, Alicia Ernst, Kristin Fayne-Mulroy, Paul Foglino, Effie Hadjiioannou, Julian Ham, Adam Hurwitz, Sung (Peter) Jung, Sara Kane, Chris Kensler, Meher Khambata, Martha Link, Illeny Maaza, Kim Magloire, Russell Murray, Jeff Nichols, John C. Pak, Dinica Quesada, Lisa M. Ruyter, Chris "short-hair" Scott, Ramsey Silberberg, Linda Tarleton, Chris Thomas, Thane Thomsen, Maria Dente, Robert McCormack, and P. J. Waters.

Special thanks to Adam Robinson, who conceived of and perfected the Joe Bloggs approach to standardized tests and many of the successful techniques used by The Princeton Review.

The editors would like to acknowledge and thank the Research and Development team of Jeannie Yoon, Jane Lacher, and Celeste Ganderson for their assistance in ensuring that our materials and techniques are up-to-date.

The editors would also like to express their deepest gratitude to Eric Payne for his extensive help. Without him, this book would not have been possible.

CONTENTS

1 INTRODUCTION 1

2 TEST STRATEGIES 5

3 SOME BASIC STUFF 19

Mass 19
Volume 20
Density 20
Pressure 21
Energy 22
Temperature and Specific Heat 23

4 ELEMENTS, ATOMS, AND IONS 29

Atoms and Elements 30
Protons, Neutrons, Electrons, The Periodic Table, Mass Number, Isotopes, Atomic Weight

5 CHEMICAL REACTIONS AND STOICHIOMETRY 37

Molecules 37
Formula Weights, Empirical Formulas, Percent Composition
The Mole 39
Chemical Reactions 42
Reaction Stoichiometry 44
Entropy 45
Enthalpy 45
Heat of formation
Spontaneity and Gibbs Free Energy 46

6 ELECTRON CONFIGURATIONS AND RADIOACTIVITY 51

Electrons and their Orbitals 51
Quantum Theory and the Heisenberg Principle, De Broglie's Hypothesis, Electron Configurations
Radioactivity 58
Alpha Decay, Beta Decay, Positron Emission, Gamma Decay, Half-life

7 THE PERIODIC TABLE AND BONDING 63

The Periodic Table 64
Chemical Families, Metals, Nonmetals, Semi-metals
More About the Periodic Table: Some Important Trends 66
Chemical Bonding—Intermolecular vs. Intramolecular, Ionic Bonds, Covalent Bonds, Metallic Bonds, Single, Double, and Triple Bonds, Bond Energies, Molecular Shapes, Polarity

8 SOLIDS, LIQUIDS, AND GASES 79

Gases 79
Ideal Gas Equation, Partial Pressure
Intermolecular Forces 85
Hydrogen Bonding, Network Solids, Hydrates

Phase Changes 86
    Phase Change and Pressure, Vapor Pressure
Energy and Phase Changes 90

9 SOLUTIONS 95
Solutions 95
Concentrations 96
Solubility and Saturation 96
    Ionic Solutes, Boiling Point Elevation, Freezing Point Depression

10 KINETICS AND EQUILIBRIUM 101
Kinetics 101
Factors that Affect Reaction Rate 102
Reversible Reactions and Chemical Equilibrium 104
Le Chatelier's Principle 106

11 ACIDS AND BASES 113
Acids and Bases 113
    Ionization of Water, Acids, Bases
Titration 119

12 REDOX AND ELECTROCHEMISTRY 125
Oxidation and Reduction 125
    Oxidation States and Oxidation Numbers, Redox Reactions
Electrochemistry 129
    Electrochemical Cells, Electrolysis

13 ORGANIC CHEMISTRY 135
Hydrocarbons 136
    Alkanes, Alkenes, Alkynes, Hydrocarbon Rings
Functional Groups 138
    Organic Reactions

14 LABORATORY 141
Safety Rules 141
Accuracy 142
Significant Figures 142
Lab Procedures 143
    Methods of Seperation, Titration, Identifying Chemicals
Laboratory Equipment 145

15 THE PRINCETON REVIEW SAT II: CHEMISTRY SUBJECT TEST I 147

16 ANSWERS AND EXPLANATIONS 167

17 THE PRINCETON REVIEW SAT II: CHEMISTRY SUBJECT TEST II 191

18 ANSWERS AND EXPLANATIONS 211

1

Introduction

This book is for students who want to raise their scores on the SAT II: Chemistry Subject Test. At The Princeton Review, we know what standardized test makers are doing. That's because we *study* their tests. We take them apart piece by piece and shred by shred. We examine them from every angle and perspective: right side up, upside down, frontward, backward, and inside out. *We know how these tests are built, and that's how we raise scores*. Stick with us, and we'll raise yours.

EXACTLY HOW WILL WE DO THAT?

Two ways. We'll

1. teach you chemistry *the way the Subject Test tests it*,

    and

2. show you how to approach the test *strategically*.

Now we'll elaborate.

POINT 1: TEACHING YOU CHEMISTRY
THE WAY THE SUBJECT TEST TESTS IT

ETS says its Chemistry Subject Test covers, among many other subjects,

◆   Gibbs free energy.

If you sat with your chemistry textbook or some other commercial book that promises to prepare you for the Chemistry Subject Test, you'd read a whole lot of material *that definitely* will *not be tested.* You'd see pictures like this:

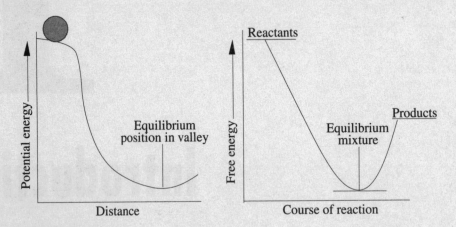

and you'd read text like this:

> We may consider free-energy change in a spontaneous reaction much as we consider the potential energy change that accompanies the rolling of an ordinary ball down a hill. The ball is driven down the hill by the potential energy within a gravitational field. By analogy, the free energy within a chemical system decreases continuously over time . . . blah, blah, blah . . . ultimately reaching a minimum. When potential energy is at a minimum, the reaction reaches its equilibrium.
>
> We might best illustrate the concept by reference to the formation of ammonia from its elements hydrogen and . . . blah, blah, blah. . . . Imagine that a particular number of moles of nitrogen react with three times the number of hydrogen atoms. The formation of ammonia will not be complete because . . . blah, blah, blah. . . . An equilibrium will be attained by the system and at equilibrium the reaction chamber will contain a mixture of . . . blah, blah, blah. . . . At that time there can be no additional spontaneous formation of ammonia because the system has reached a minimum state of free energy which . . . blah, blah, blah. . . . Free energy is a state function, and that is why . . . blah, blah, blah. . . .

The text would go on and on scaring and boring you, but offering nothing that raises your test score. You'd get so sick of it that you'd stop reading.

When *we* teach you about Gibbs free energy, we tell you exactly what you have to know to raise your test score. As we do that we drill you (in a friendly fashion) to make sure you're with us at every step. You just have to know that the symbol for Gibbs free energy is ΔG. If ΔG is negative, the reaction proceeds spontaneously in the forward direction. If it's positive, the reaction proceeds spontaneously in the reverse direction.

You need to associate:

negative ΔG with: reaction proceeds spontaneously in the forward direction

positive ΔG with: reaction proceeds spontaneously in the reverse direction

Review the few lines we've just written, starting with "You just have to know." Then answer the following two Subject Test-like questions.

<u>Directions:</u> Each set of lettered choices below refers to the numbered statements or formulas immediately following it. Select the one lettered choice that best fits each statement or formula and then fill in the corresponding oval on the answer sheet. A choice may be used once, more than once, or not at all in each set.

<u>Questions 1–2</u>

(A) Heat of formation
(B) Work
(C) Entropy
(D) Gibbs free energy
(E) Enthalpy

1. Must be negative if reaction proceeds spontaneously in forward direction

2. Must be positive if reaction proceeds spontaneously in reverse direction

The answers are both D, and you know that simply by making the associations we talked about. ETS's scoring machine doesn't look for brilliant scientists; when it scores these two questions, it just wants to see D in the little oval spaces on your answer sheet. Stick with us, and you'll end up making the scoring machines very happy.

POINT 2: STRATEGICALLY APPROACHING THE TEST

It's not enough to study chemistry the way the Subject Test tests it. You must also study Subject Test questions themselves. You should be "wise" to their design and familiar with the *techniques* that lead systematically to correct answers.

When you take the Chemistry Subject Test you won't know *all* the answers. In chapter 2 of this book we'll present eight strategies that will help you "outsmart" the Chemistry Subject Test and its writers. Then, in chapters 3 through 12, we'll show you over and over again how to use them.

Our strategies are powerful stuff. They teach you how to find right answers logically and systematically— in much the same way that a detective solves a crime. Study our strategies and you'll pick the right answers even to questions that address chemistry topics you *don't* know.

WHAT ABOUT PRACTICE AND PRACTICE TESTS?

This book is interactive. Over and over again you show us what you've learned. We don't put a long line of "drill questions" at the end of each chapter. Instead, we teach and then we test—right away—with Subject Test-type questions. We check your progress page by page, paragraph by paragraph, and we make sure you're with us every step of the way. If you're not, we help you figure out *why* you're not. And we do all of that, incidentally, in a way that makes the whole thing interesting and fun.

You might notice that our book cover is unlike most others. It doesn't promise you 4, 5, 6, or 7 full-length simulated tests. It would be easy for us to fill our pages with simulated test after simulated test. We could offer you 7, 11, or 100 tests. But we don't like that game, and we don't play it. If you test yourself repeatedly with simulated examinations you won't raise your score. You'll just prove that you can get the same score over and over again.

How about two simulated tests? Yes, of course. Chapters 13 and 14 of this book present you with two full-length tests complete with explanations that send you back to the appropriate pages of this book in case you need some quick review. But please! Don't waste your time taking unnecessary practice tests. Learn to outsmart the one test you're actually going to take on Subject Test Day.

SHOULD I BUY PRACTICE MATERIAL FROM ETS?

It's not a bad idea. If you want to take additional tests beyond the one we provide, then buy *Official Guide to the SAT II: Subject Tests*, which is published by the College Board. Take the chemistry test and see how easy it is after you've read this book. Or, if you like, take the College Board's test first. Score yourself. Then go through this book very carefully, and take the tests in the back of this book.

OUR JOB AND YOUR JOB

This book is written and published. You're holding it in your hands. That means our job is done. Your job is to read it, tackle the exercises it provides, and learn what it has to teach. We had fun doing our job, and, believe it or not, you'll have fun doing yours.

So, let the fun begin. Turn the page and start working. You'll be glad you did.

Test Strategies

The Chemistry Subject Test presents 85 multiple-choice questions and gives you one hour to answer them. You are not allowed to use a calculator on this test, but you should not need one. The test is divided into three sections, each of which contains different question types: A, B, or C. It's scored on a scale of 200–800, just like the SAT.

PART A: 20–25 QUESTIONS

Part A presents you with four to six short "matching tests" that contain a total of 20–25 questions. Each matching test gives you a list of five words or phrases lettered A through E. Then you get three to five questions, with question numbers next to them. But the questions aren't really questions. They're phrases. Your job is to match the phrase in the "question" with the word or phrase that appears in the list A through E. Forget about chemistry for a minute and see how it works.

Directions: Each set of lettered choices below refers to the numbered statements or formulas immediately following it. Select the one lettered choice that best fits each statement or formula and then fill in the corresponding oval on the answer sheet. A choice may be used once, more than once, or not at all in each set.

Questions 1–4

    (A) Red light
    (B) Swimming pool
    (C) Piano
    (D) Fire engine
    (E) Ocean liner

1. Musical instrument that involves keyboard outside and strings inside

2. Motor vehicle designed to assist in effort to extinguish flames

3. Sea vessel that carries passengers across large bodies of water

4. Water-filled pit designed for recreational or athletic activities

The answers, of course, are C, D, E, and B. You'll get about four to six of these matching tests on Part A of the Chemistry Subject Test.

PART B: 15–20 QUESTIONS

Type B questions don't ask that you decide among choices A, B, C, D, or E. Instead, they present you with some ovals set apart on the lower left corner of your answer sheet. Here's how they look:

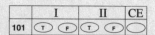

Type B questions give you two statements and put the word BECAUSE between them. You're supposed to figure out which statement is true and which is false. If both are true, you're also expected to figure out whether the word BECAUSE belongs there. Once again, forget about chemistry for a second so we can show you how the questions work. Because the ETS computers "know" they have to deal with a set of questions that do not have A, B, C, D, or E as their answer, the type B questions are numbered in a peculiar way as well. The section begins with the number 101, *even though there are only 85 questions on the whole test.*

Directions: Each question below consists of two statements, I in the left-hand column and II in the right-hand column. For each question, determine whether statement I is true or false <u>and</u> whether statement II is true or false and fill in the corresponding T or F ovals on your answer sheet. <u>Fill in oval CE only if statement II is a correct explanation of statement I.</u>

<u>I</u>   <u>II</u>

101. If one takes a shower, one gets wet   BECAUSE   the shower head releases water that falls on the individual taking the shower.

102. If one walks rapidly, one will be in motion   BECAUSE   automobiles burn gasoline.

103. A boat will sink if it fills with water   BECAUSE   it is impossible for a boat to develop a leak.

104. President Lincoln died of natural causes   BECAUSE   Lincoln was president during the Civil War.

105. Omaha, Nebraska, is the capital of the United States   BECAUSE   Omaha is the largest city in the entire world.

Question 101 should be answered like this: Both statements are true and the "because" belongs there. You get wet in a shower *because* the shower pours water on you.

Question 102 should be answered like this: Both statements are true. If you walk, you move, and automobiles do burn gasoline. But the "because" doesn't belong there. A walker doesn't move *because* automobiles burn gasoline. One statement has nothing to do with the other.

Question 103 should be answered like this: A boat will sink if it fills with water. That's true. But the second statement is false. Boats *can* develop leaks.

Question 104 should be answered like this: The first statement is false. Lincoln was murdered. The second statement is true. He was president during the Civil War.

Question 105 should be answered like this: Both statements are false. Omaha is not the capital of the United States, and it's not the largest city in the world.

Naturally these questions have nothing to do with chemistry and they're very easy. We just want you to see how type B questions work.

There are about 16 type B questions on the Chemistry Subject Test.

PART C: 40–50 QUESTIONS

Type C questions are ordinary-looking multiple-choice questions, so you already know what they're like. But let's look at one anyway.

28. Which is the formula of a compound?
    (A) HCl
    (B) He
    (C) Cu
    (D) O_2
    (E) Br_2

Naturally, the answer is A. A compound is a chemical combination of two or more elements. (We'll talk about that later.)

Now that you know what kinds of questions you'll see on the Chemistry Subject Test, let's talk about tricks and techniques. In other words, let's discuss strategies.

STRATEGY #1: STUDYING THE RIGHT STUFF IN THE RIGHT WAY

One strategy is to know what types of chemistry concepts are almost certain to show up on the test and in what *way* they'll show up. In chapters 3 through 12, we take all the subjects that are certain to appear on the test. Then we explain them in a way that's designed strictly to help you answer Subject Test questions. We want you to understand them the Subject Test way.

What topics do we cover? Everything that's sure to show up on the Chemistry Subject Test:

I. Some Basic Stuff

    A. Mass, Volume, and Density

    B. Pressure

    C. Energy and Temperature

II. Elements, Atoms, and Ions

    A. Subatomic Particles

    B. Atomic Number and Mass Number

    C. Isotopes

III. Chemical Reactions and Stoichiometry

    A. Atomic and Formula Weights

    B. Mole Concept

    C. Empirical and Molecular Formulas

    D. Writing Balanced Equations

    E. Stoichiometric Calculations

    F. Enthalpy, Entropy, and Free Energy

IV. Electron Configurations and Radioactivity

    A. Modern Atomic Model

    B. Electron Configurations

    C. Radioactive Decay and Half-Life

V. The Periodic Table and Bonding

    A. Special Families

    B. Metals and Nonmetals

    C. Periodic Table Trends

    D. Ionic, Covalent, and Metallic Bonds

    E. Shapes of Molecules

VI. Solids, Liquids, and Gases

    A. Kinetic Molecular Theory of Gases

    B. Ideal Gas Equation

    C. Intermolecular Forces

    D. Phase Changes

VII. Solutions

    A. Molarity and Molality

    B. Solubility

    C. Colligative Properties

VIII. Kinetics and Equilibrium

    A. Factors Affecting Reaction Rates

    B. Catalysts

    C. Chemical Equilibrium and K_{eq}

    D. Le Chatelier's Principle

    E. Solubility Product Constant, K_{sp}

IX. Acids and Bases

    A. pH and K_w

    B. Definitions of Acids and Bases

    C. Properties of Acids and Bases

    D. Strong and Weak Acids, and K_a

    E. Acid-Base Titrations

X. Redox and Electrochemistry

    A. Oxidation States

    B. Oxidation and Reduction

    C. Oxidizing and Reducing Agents

    D. Electrochemical Cells

    E. Electrolysis

XI. Organic Chemistry

XII. Laboratory

Look back at the list of subjects we cover. Do we address absolutely all of chemistry? No (although we do cover quite a lot). It would be a waste for us to teach you the whole science of basic chemistry since your chemistry textbook does that. Our job isn't to teach chemistry but to raise your score on the Chemistry Subject Test, and those two jobs are *not* the same. Learn what we teach and your score will go up.

STRATEGY #2: PRACTICE THE RIGHT THING AT THE RIGHT TIME

Separate from the full-length Chemistry Subject Tests in chapters 13 and 14 we present a slew of Subject Test-like questions which take you page by page through chapters 3 through 12. With these questions we check your progress page by page, sentence by sentence, idea by idea. We teach and test immediately to make sure you can take what we teach and apply it "hands on" to Subject Test-type questions. That's the only way to learn chemistry for the Subject Test.

STRATEGY #3: EASY STUFF FIRST

In each section of the Chemistry Subject Test, the easier questions tend to come first and the harder ones come later. It makes sense to begin a section and answer as many questions as you can until they start to become more difficult. Then go on to the next section and do the same. Once you've answered all of the relatively easy questions in all the sections, go back to each section and start answering the more difficult ones (although after reading this book, you probably won't find too many of them very difficult).

All questions carry the same credit: answering a hard question doesn't do you one more bit of good than answering an easy one. So you might want to pursue the test not in the order of its sections but in the order of difficulty.

STRATEGY #4: TAKE A GUESS!

When you take the Chemistry Subject Test, understand the significance of guessing. In calculating your "raw score" (from which it then derives your actual score), ETS

1. awards a full point for each question you answer correctly,

2. *deducts* $\frac{1}{4}$ of a point for each question you answer incorrectly, and

3. neither awards nor deducts credit for questions you choose not to answer at all.

Because ETS deducts $\frac{1}{4}$ of a point for any question you answer incorrectly, you definitely *should guess* at any question for which you can eliminate one of the five answer choices. After all, if you guess among five choices and lose only $\frac{1}{4}$ of a point for a wrong answer, statistical science dictates that your guess shouldn't hurt you. If you can eliminate one or more answer choices and guess among the remaining choices, statistical science dictates that your guess *should help* you.

As you read chapters 2 through 12 you'll see that all our techniques and strategies teach you to eliminate wrong choices. Use our strategies, and use guessing to your advantage.

You don't need to answer every question to get a good score on the Chemistry Subject Test. It's possible to leave 30 questions blank and still score near 600 if you do well on the questions you do answer.

STRATEGY #5: MAKING ASSOCIATIONS (TYPES A, B, AND C QUESTIONS)

Lots of Type A, B, and C questions require that you *associate* one word or phrase with another. They don't require that you understand what you're reading or what you're doing; they just require that you remember "this" goes with "that."

What are we talking about? Well, let's forget chemistry, just to make the point. You may have learned in school that Teddy Roosevelt was a "trustbuster." You might *not* know what trusts are, how he busted them, why he wanted to bust them, or why anyone cares if trusts get busted. In fact, you couldn't really understand any of that unless you had a pretty good background in law and economics, which high school students usually don't have. But you learned to associate the name Teddy Roosevelt with the phrase "trustbuster," without understanding what it was all about. If you made the association, you were able to answer a test question like this:

- Theodore Roosevelt believed in

    (A) creating trusts
    (B) destroying trusts
    (C) making trusts larger
    (D) communism
    (E) socialistic economics

Putting the name "Teddy Roosevelt" together with "trustbuster" makes you choose B, even though you don't know what you're talking about. Good! That kind of thing will get you a high score.

The same thing holds true for the Chemistry Subject Test. Lots of questions depend on your ability to associate one word or phrase with another. As it happens, chapter 11 of our presentation gives you a good Subject Test training in acids and bases. But suppose you had no idea what was meant by "pH," "acid," or "base," and you just learned to associate:

pH below 7 with: acid

pH above 7 with: base

You'd be able to answer many Subject Test questions, including:

- Which of the following solutions is most acidic?

    (A) A solution of phosphoric acid at pH 4
    (B) A solution of sodium hydroxide at pH 11
    (C) A solution of hydrochloric acid at pH 5
    (D) A solution of acetic acid at pH 6
    (E) A solution of aqueous ammonia at pH 9

Whatever else you know about acids and bases, you know that A is right because, among the listed solutions, it has the lowest pH.

Throughout our teaching of Subject Test chemistry, we show you what *associations* to make, how to make them, and how they point you to right answers on the Subject Test.

STRATEGY #6: AVOIDING THE CAMOUFLAGE TRAP (TYPES A AND C QUESTIONS)

In type A and type C questions, the test writers sometimes try to make you fall into something we call the "camouflage trap."

To understand the camouflage trap, read the two sentences below.

1. In any dynamic chemical equilibrium, the removal of any product will drive the equilibrium to the right and thus increase the concentration of any other product, while the concentration of all reactants will decrease.

2. If a dynamic chemical equilibrium is subjected to withdrawal of a product, the concentration of all reactants will diminish and the concentration of any other product will become greater.

These two statements mean exactly the same thing, but their wording is very different. Many of the words and phrases in statement 2 have the same meaning as those in statement 1, but they're disguised—they're camouflaged.

subjected to withdrawal of a product	*is camouflage for*	the removal of any product
concentration of any other product will become greater	*is camouflage for*	increase the concentration of any other product
concentration of all reactants will diminish	*is camouflage for*	the concentration of all reactants will decrease

So, What About It?

When you learn something, whether it's chemistry or anything else, you tend to learn it with certain words in mind. For instance, maybe you think of an element as "a substance that cannot be broken into any simpler substance." Fine. But if you're too attached to that particular way of thinking about it, look what happens if you try to answer this type C question:

- Which of the following best describes the characteristics of an element?

    (A) It is capable of existing in relatively simple molecular forms.
    (B) It exists only in molar quantities.
    (C) It will always react with any other element.
    (D) It is a fundamental form of matter.
    (E) It is more reactive if surrounding entropy is high.

If you're too attached to the way that you usually think about elements, you might not see the right answer even though (a) you *do* know it, and (b) it's staring you in the face. The right answer to this question is D. To say that an element is a fundamental form of matter is, more or less, to say it can't be broken into simpler substances. The words aren't the same, but the meaning *is*.

Many students who know what an element is don't answer this question correctly because they haven't thought of expressing its meaning the way it's set forth in choice D. They look quickly through the choices. They don't see anything they recognize and go into "answer-choice panic." They pick something that "sounds right"—something that has the word "simple" in it, like choice A.

That's too bad. Students who do know what they're doing nonetheless choose a wrong answer because they fall for the camouflage trap.

Here's another example from a type C question. Suppose you know that: "The average kinetic energy of gas molecules is directly proportional to the absolute temperature of the gas." (You definitely *will* know that once you finish chapters 3 through 12.) The statement means that if you add heat to a sample of gas molecules, each molecule, on average, starts bouncing around faster than it did before. But you're accustomed to stating it this way:

> The average kinetic energy of gas molecules is directly proportional
> to the absolute temperature of the gas.

If you're *married* to that statement, what's going to happen when this type C Subject Test question comes at you?

<u>Question:</u>

- What is always increased by the addition of
  thermal energy to a sample of gas in a closed
  container?

  (A) Ideal gas constant
  (B) Average speed of gas molecules
  (C) Molecular weight of gas molecules
  (D) Volume of gas sample
  (E) Volatility

You know that increased heat increases average kinetic energy, but the answer's been camouflaged.

average speed of gas molecules	*is camouflage for*	average kinetic energy
addition of thermal energy	*is camouflage for*	increasing the temperature

You're not used to thinking of increasing temperature as "addition of thermal energy," even though they're the same thing. When it comes to gases you're also not accustomed to thinking of "average speed of gas molecules" as reflecting the average kinetic energy. Even though you know your chemistry, you might not realize that the right answer to this question is B. You might decide to pick some crazy answer like A or D. Why? Because you fell into the camouflage trap.

The camouflage trap makes you miss questions just because you're too attached to a particular way of wording something. That's bad news.

But Here's the Good News:
You Can Avoid the Camouflage Trap

To avoid the camouflage trap, keep some simple rules in mind.

1. Don't take a test with blinders on your brain.

2. Remember, there's more than one way to say the same thing.

3. When you face a question and know very well that it's something you've studied and memorized, don't become unglued just because the right answer doesn't leap out at you.

4. Chill out. Realize that the right answer is probably camouflaged by words that are different from the ones you have in mind. Search for them, calmly, and all of a sudden they *will* leap out at you.

In other words, *keep an open mind.* Don't expect test makers to use *your* words. Remember: The same concept or idea can be expressed in many different ways. Keep in mind the *concepts* you know, and don't get too attached to the *words* you use to express them.

Another Way Out of the Camouflage Trap:
Translate and Work Backward

Suppose you *do* try to keep an open mind for a question and it just isn't working; the right answer isn't coming to you, even though you know your chemistry. For a type A question, here's what you do: Look through all of the choices A–E, and in your own words tell yourself what each one says. Let's try it with the set we just examined. This time, however, we'll add some more questions.

(A) Ideal gas constant:

It's the letter R in the equation $PV = nRT$. It equals about $0.082 \, \dfrac{L \cdot atm}{mol \cdot K}$

(B) Average speed of gas molecules:

It's the speed at which gas molecules are running around in a tank or container—it has to do with the energy they have. It goes up with higher temperature and down with lower temperature.

(C) Molecular weight of gas molecules:

It's the weight (expressed in amu) of a gas molecule.

(D) Volume of gas sample:

It's the space the gas sample takes up—equal to the size of the container.

(E) Volatility:

It has to do with how easily a liquid evaporates when it's sitting around, below its boiling point.

Now you've translated all of the answer choices into words that belong to *you.* Look at each of the answer choices one at a time and see which question it seems to go with.

Questions 1–4

1. Is always increased by addition of thermal energy to a sample of gas in a closed container

2. Can be related to pressure of a gas sample by the ideal gas law

3. Property associated with vapor pressure

4. Depends on formula of a gas but not its temperature

Looking at your own translations of the options A–E, does option A sound as if it goes with any of the questions? No. It looks as if A doesn't go with anything.

- How about B? If you just realize that "thermal energy" means heat, you'll realize that B goes with 1.

- How about C? Well you know (or you soon will know) that the molecular weight of a gas is calculated from its formula, so it goes with 4. The answer to 4, therefore, is C.

- How about D? Well, you know (or soon will know) that the ideal gas equation takes a sample of gas and relates temperature, volume, pressure, and the number of gas molecules in the sample. So the answer to 2 is D.

- Finally, what about E? You know that volatility expresses the degree to which a liquid evaporates even though it's below its boiling point. This is also what vapor pressure tells you. (We'll talk about vapor pressure in chapter 8.) So the answer to 3 is E.

STRATEGY #7: AVOIDING THE TEMPTATION TRAP (TYPE C QUESTIONS)

Suppose we gave this question to a 7-year-old child:

- Which of the following best expresses the effect of Gibbs free energy and the spontaneity of a chemical reaction?

  (A) When Gibbs free energy is negative, the reaction proceeds spontaneously in the forward direction.
  (B) When Gibbs free energy is negative, the reaction proceeds spontaneously in the reverse direction.
  (C) George Washington was the first president of the United States.
  (D) Gibbs free energy affects the spontaneity only of exothermic reactions.
  (E) Gibbs free energy affects the spontaneity only of endothermic reactions.

The child won't know what any of this means except that she probably *will* know that George Washington was the first president. So, she'll choose C; it's something she knows. She fell into the "temptation trap." The test writer stuck something into the answer choices that's familiar to the student. It's so familiar that the student is tempted to "go for it" even though it has nothing to do with the question.

WHAT'S THAT GOT TO DO WITH ME AND THE CHEMISTRY SUBJECT TEST?

A lot. The temptation trap rears its head, usually, on type C questions (although it can appear on type A questions, too). On the day you take the test, there will be lots of things you know and some that you don't. When you meet up with a type C question that's stumping you, you might reach out and grab an answer choice that "sounds familiar" even though it has nothing to do with the question.

Suppose you know that adding an acid to a base will always increase the hydrogen ion concentration of the solution. Now, look at this type C question.

- Which of the following will definitely occur if a quantity of acetic acid is added to a solution of potassium hydroxide at pH 11?
    - (A) The number of free protons per liter of solution will increase.
    - (B) Titration will tend to neutralize the solution.
    - (C) The acetic acid will act as a weak base.
    - (D) Acetate ion will precipitate out of solution.
    - (E) The pH will remain constant.

If the right answer to this question does not leap out at you, you might decide to make a dash for something you know. Choice B, by itself, makes a true statement with which you might be familiar. Titration between acid and base frequently does tend to neutralize a solution. You might say to yourself, quickly, quietly, and almost unconsciously: "I've heard that statement. It sounds right." But B is wrong because *it doesn't answer the question.* Choose B and you're like the 7-year-old child who chose the George Washington answer: You fall into the temptation trap. That's bad news.

BUT HERE'S SOME MORE GOOD NEWS: YOU CAN AVOID THE TEMPTATION TRAP

The temptation and camouflage traps often work together. One choice tempts you while the right choice is sitting there in camouflage.

When you find yourself running for an answer because it "sounds right"—stop. Realize you might be choosing something that doesn't answer the question. Look at the question—carefully. Then look at the answer choices to see if one of them really does answer the question in camouflage.

Now let's think about the question we just looked at. We're adding an acid to a base. We know that we'll be reducing the pH—increasing the hydrogen ion concentration. Choice A says exactly that—in camouflage. Instead of referring to hydrogen ions, it refers to free protons. Instead of referring directly to concentration, or pH, it talks about increasing the number of protons per liter of solution. The right answer is A and you knew it, but you might not have chosen it. Why? Because panic leads you straight into the temptation trap. Don't let that happen.

STRATEGY #8: DIVIDE AND CONQUER (TYPE B QUESTIONS)

Let's look again at the instructions to Part B.

Directions: Each question below consists of two statements, I in the left-hand column and II in the right-hand column. For each question, determine whether statement I is true or false and whether statement II is true or false and fill in the corresponding T or F ovals on your answer sheet. Fill in oval CE only if statement II is a correct explanation of statement I.

Now let's look at a question that has nothing to do with chemistry to show how the divide and conquer strategy works.

<table>
<tr><td>I</td><td></td><td>II</td></tr>
<tr><td>101. All persons must breathe</td><td>BECAUSE</td><td>oxygen is necessary to human survival.</td></tr>
</table>

Even though this is a simple question, let's take it through the divide and conquer strategy.

Step 1: Look at the first statement by itself, and decide whether it's true or false. Ignore the second statement. Just evaluate the first one. Is it true or false?
It's true. That means we fill in the oval marked T.
Step 2: Look at the second statement, by itself—ignoring the first statement. Is it true or false? It's true. That means we fill in the second oval marked T.
Step 3: Put the whole structure together as a single sentence and decide if it makes sense.

> All persons must breathe because oxygen is necessary to human survival.

Does it make sense? Yes. That means we fill in the oval marked CE.
Try this question:

<table>
<tr><td>I</td><td></td><td>II</td></tr>
<tr><td>102. It is unlawful to drive while drunk</td><td>BECAUSE</td><td>most automobiles in the United States are powered by internal combustion engines.</td></tr>
</table>

Step 1: Look at statement I by itself. True or false? It's true. Once again, we fill in the first oval marked T.
Step 2: Look at statement II by itself. True or false? It's true. That means we fill in the second oval marked T. Now look at the whole structure as a sentence.

> It is unlawful to drive while drunk because most automobiles in the United States are powered by internal combustion engines.

Does it make sense? No. It's nonsense. That means we do not fill in the oval marked CE.

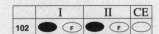

Let's do another one:

I		II
103. All Americans are exactly alike in their beliefs	BECAUSE	no foreign country has ever made a valuable contribution to civilization.

Step 1: Look at statement I by itself. True or false? It's false.
Step 2: Look at statement II by itself. True or false? It's false.

Notice that if either statement I or statement II is false, then there can be no cause and effect relationship, and you don't have to worry about the CE oval.

When it comes to the divide and conquer strategy, we use step 3 only if we find that both statements are true. If one of them is false, divide and conquer is a two-step strategy.

LET'S GET GOING

In chapters 3 through 12 we'll teach you chemistry with our own special tailored-to-the-Subject Test method. All along the way we'll ask you Subject Test-type questions. Then we'll explain the answers, showing you how to use knowledge and strategy to earn a high score.

Beating a test by cracking it open is fun. So let the fun begin.

3

Some Basic Stuff

Some Subject Test questions test only simple stuff about basic properties of matter and the way they're measured. These questions may seem difficult, but they're easy.

We'll review some basic terms: mass, volume, density, pressure, energy, temperature, and specific heat. We'll show you how these simple subjects turn into Subject Test questions that don't seem easy unless you're prepared to approach them strategically.

MASS

Let's think about a sample of matter, whether it's a hunk of solid, a glass of liquid, or a container full of gas. If we say "mass," we're talking about the *amount* of matter in a sample. What units do we use to measure mass?

1. gram (g)

2. kilogram (kg, which equals 1,000 g)

3. milligram (mg, which equals one-thous<u>andth</u> of 1 g)

For any *particular* substance, a sample of greater mass means a sample with more atoms or molecules in it. (For now, think of atoms and molecules as submicroscopic pieces of matter. We'll talk more about them later.) A sample of lesser mass means a sample with fewer atoms or molecules in it. Ten water molecules have greater mass than seven water molecules. Eight molecules of carbon dioxide have greater mass than four molecules of carbon dioxide.

For the Subject Test, there's nothing more you need to know about mass itself. It represents the quantity of matter that makes up a sample (which for any given substance relates to the number of atoms or molecules in a sample). It's measured in grams, kilograms, or milligrams.

VOLUME

Suppose we're thinking about a sample of matter—solid, liquid, or gas. If we say *volume*, we're talking about how much space the sample takes up. The Subject Test usually measures volume in one of two ways:

1. liter (L)

2. milliliter (ml, which equals one-thous<u>andth</u> of 1 L); also, 1 ml = 1 cm^3 (cubic centimeter)

When the sample is a liquid, we usually pour it into a graduated cylinder (which is really a kind of measuring cup). We read the glass where it meets the top of the liquid. Actually we don't *have* to use a graduated cylinder. We can use any kind of container that has markings on it to indicate measurements of volume.

If the sample is a solid, we can immerse it in a liquid and see how much liquid it displaces. In other words we can compare the original volume of the liquid and the volume of the solid/liquid combination, knowing that the difference will be equal to the volume of the solid.

When the sample is a gas, we only have to know the volume of its container, which will be equal to the volume of the gas since *a gas always expands to fill its container*. How do we learn the volume of the container? Well, if the volume isn't marked on the container, we can just treat the container as a solid object and find out its volume by immersing it in a liquid as we just explained.

DENSITY

We use the word density only when we're thinking about some *particular* substance, like water, lead, carbon dioxide, or ethyl alcohol, for example. Density refers to whether a given mass of the substance takes up a lot of space, as feathers do, or only a small amount of space, as lead does.

Generally, if we say "water is heavy," we mean that water has a high density. Ten kilograms of water occupy a relatively small volume—about 10 L. When we say "feathers are light," we mean that feathers have a low density. Ten kilograms of feathers occupy a relatively large volume.

How do we measure density? Since density refers to the amount of mass in a given volume, we measure it in units that reflect mass per volume. That means we might measure it in g/L, or mg/L, or kg/ml, or any other combination that represents mass per volume.

$$\text{Density} = \frac{\text{mass}}{\text{volume}}$$

If we say that substance X has a density of 2 g/ml, we're saying that 1 ml of that substance has a mass of 2 g, which means that 2 ml have a mass of 4 g, that 10 ml have a mass of 20 g, and so on.

If another substance, substance Y, has a density of 1.75 g/ml then its density is less than that of substance X. If we had samples of both substances X and Y and the two samples were of equal volume, we'd find that the X sample was of greater mass than the Y sample. Why? Because Y is less dense than X, which only means that when we think of mass per volume, we get a lower number for Y than for X.

Remember we said that gas always expands to fill its container? It's true *only* for gases; it's *not* true for solids and liquids. For a particular solid or liquid at a given temperature, a given volume always represents the same mass. Gas is different. A billion gas molecules might take up 1 ml or 1 L. A particular volume of some solid or liquid will always have the same mass at a given temperature, since mass is determined by the actual number of atoms or molecules present in a sample. *But for a gas at a given temperature, mass will not necessarily vary with volume.* We can change the volume of a gas sample, even while holding its temperature steady, simply by changing the size of its container. The number of atoms or molecules remains the same, which means the mass of the gas remains the same. But the volume has been changed, as shown in the illustration below:

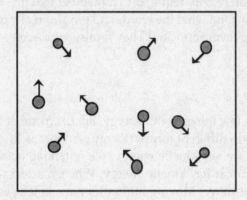
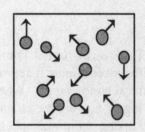

PRESSURE

When Subject Test writers say "pressure," they are talking about (1) a sample of gas in a closed container and the force with which its molecules are banging into the container walls, or (2) a solid or liquid standing in an environment, and the force with which gas in the environment is banging into the walls of the environment and everything that's in it—including the surface of the solid or liquid.

(1)   (2)

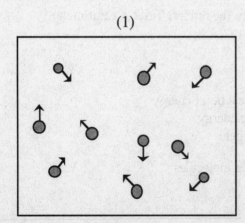
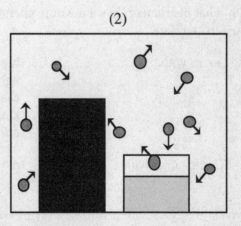

With what units do we measure pressure on the Subject Test? A few. There are torr, millimeters of mercury (mmHg), and atmospheres (atm): 1 torr and 1 mmHg are exactly the same, and 760 torr (or 760 mmHg) = 1 atm.

With what instruments do we measure pressure on the Subject Test? Two: (1) the barometer and (2) the manometer.

Learn to associate:

Pressure with:	torr
	mmHg
	atm
	barometer
	manometer

When we say you should *associate* one thing with another, we mean you should remember to think of them as "going together"—the way you associate night with darkness and winter with cold. For lots of Chemistry Subject Test questions, you're only required to remember that one word or phrase goes with another—even if you don't understand what the words and phrases really mean. When we present you with our association lists, take them seriously! They'll raise your score.

ENERGY

For the Subject Test, you do have to know a few things about energy. First, remember that energy can wear several different costumes; it appears in different forms. Energy can exist as heat, light, kinetic energy, or chemical bond energy. When we say kinetic energy, we're talking about the fact that things are moving. A moving bus, train, or car has kinetic energy. When we deal with chemistry, we're usually thinking about *molecules* that move. Moving molecules have kinetic energy. As molecules move faster they have higher kinetic energy.

With what units do we measure energy on the Subject Test? Three:

1. calorie (cal)

2. joule (J)

3. kilojoule (kJ, which equals 1,000 J)

One calorie (1 cal) equals slightly more than 4 J.

With what instrument do we measure energy on the Subject Test? A calorimeter.
Learn to associate:

Energy with:	heat
	light
	chemical bond energy
	kinetic energy
	calorimeter
Kinetic energy with:	moving molecules

TEMPERATURE AND SPECIFIC HEAT

We can measure all forms of energy including heat energy, in calories. So heat is measured in calories. You might then want to know: What's temperature?

Temperature is not exactly a measure of heat. You can't necessarily say that something at a higher temperature contains more heat than something else at a lower temperature. Temperature, however, reflects heat content. If a particular sample of a substance experiences an increase in temperature, then you can say that particular sample has experienced an increase in heat content. So what exactly does temperature measure? Temperature indicates the average kinetic energy of molecules in a sample. Since kinetic energy is associated with motion, as the molecules in a sample move faster, the temperature of that sample increases.

For some substances, a large addition of heat will have only a small effect on its temperature. For others, even a small addition of heat will have a big effect on its temperature. If this seems strange, relax. We'll tell you why this is so.

Think for a minute about people and their reactions to pain. Some people can take a lot of pain and they'll hardly show it. Others will complain loudly even about small amounts of pain. If we're looking at one person and we see that he reacts more strongly to a first painful stimulus than to a second, we can probably conclude that the first stimulus was more painful than the second. But we can't do that if we're comparing two people. By comparing the degree to which two different people respond to pain, you can't tell how much pain each is feeling. Why? Because different people have different capacities to "absorb" pain without expressing it.

The same goes for substances. Different substances differ in their capacity to absorb heat without expressing a significant increase in temperature. When we think of a particular substance and the extent to which the addition or removal of heat increases or decreases its temperature, we are talking about its specific heat.

Here's an equation that puts these pieces together:

$$q = mc\Delta T$$

q equals heat, m equals mass, c equals specific heat, and ΔT is equal to the difference between final and initial temperatures. (The symbol "Δ" means change, or difference.)

For example, it takes 1 calorie of heat to raise the temperature of 1 gram of water by 1 °C. So we say that the specific heat of water is 1 cal/g–°C. The specific heat of carbon is 0.033 cal/g–°C. It takes 0.033 calorie to raise the temperature of 1 gram of carbon by 1°C. Specific heat measures a substance's ability to "take the heat" without showing too much of an increase in temperature.

Now suppose you take a sample of water and a sample of carbon and both samples have the same mass—say 40 g. Then suppose you add equal amounts of heat—200 calories—to each sample. Using temperature change as its voice, the carbon will "scream" about the heat increase much more "loudly" than the water will.

$$\Delta T = \frac{q}{mc}$$

$$\Delta T_{carbon} = \frac{(200 \text{ cal})}{(40 \text{ g})\left(.033\dfrac{\text{cal}}{\text{g} - °\text{C}}\right)} = 151.5 \text{ }°\text{C}$$

$$\Delta T_{water} = \frac{(200 \ cal)}{(40 \ g)\left(1\dfrac{cal}{g-{}^{\circ}C}\right)} = 5 \ {}^{\circ}C$$

Carbon will increase in temperature by 151.5° C. Water will increase in temperature by only 5 °C. Why? Because the specific heat of water is roughly 30 times that of carbon. When it comes to "taking the heat" without showing an increase in temperature, water is approximately 30 times better than carbon. So when we add 200 calories of heat to 40 g of carbon, we get a 151.5 °C increase in temperature. When we add the same 200 calories to 40 g of water, we get an increase of only 5 °C.

Similarly, if we have equal masses of water and carbon and we want to raise the temperature of each sample by the same amount, we'll have to put about 30 times more heat into the water than we have to put into the carbon.

What goes for temperature increase also goes for its decrease. If we take heat away from water, the temperature will decrease by a relatively small amount. If we take the same amount of heat away from carbon it will decrease by a relatively large amount. By what factor will the two substances differ in their temperature decrease? By a factor of roughly 30, just as they do for temperature increase when we add heat.

We've been talking about temperature in °C, and when we think of specific heat, that's the right way to think of temperature. But, for the Subject Test, you also need to know about another temperature scale: K (degrees Kelvin). The Kelvin scale is also called the "absolute temperature" scale. How do you convert °C to K?

$$K = {}^{\circ}C + 273.$$
$$\text{So, } 0 \ K = -273 \ {}^{\circ}C$$
$$0{}^{\circ}C = 273K$$

Learn to associate:

Temperature with: °C and K
average kinetic energy

Specific heat with: the extent to which addition or
removal of heat will affect
temperature

cal/g–°C

And remember, when it comes to heat content, temperature is a *reflection* of, but <u>not</u> a direct *measure* of, heat content. Heat content is <u>not</u> measured in °C. It's measured in calories, joules, or kilojoules.

How the Subject Test Tests You on This

For these simple subjects, as for others, the Subject Test writers sometimes make their questions look more difficult than they are by catching you off guard and steering you off course. They might, for instance, use the camouflage and temptation traps.

Now try these ten Subject Test-type questions:

QUESTION TYPE A

(A) Volume
(B) Temperature
(C) Density
(D) Pressure
(E) Mass

1. Is a quantity that allows one to calculate mass if density is known

2. Always varies with the number of molecules present in a sample of a particular substance

3. Can be expressed as kilograms per liter

4. Is a measure of the average kinetic energy of a substance's molecules

QUESTION TYPE B

<u>Directions:</u> Each question below consists of two statements, I in the left-hand column and II in the right-hand column. For each question, determine whether statement I is true or false <u>and</u> whether statement II is true or false and fill in the corresponding T or F ovals on your answer sheet. <u>Fill in oval CE only if statement II is a correct explanation of statement I.</u>

I   II

103. If the density of a solid substance and its volume are both known, mass can be calculated

    BECAUSE

    for any substance, the relationship between mass and volume varies directly with sample size.

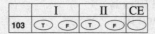

104. For any substance, solid, liquid, or gas, mass increases as volume increases

    BECAUSE

    density represents mass per volume.

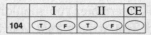

105. If substances X and Y have specific heats of 0.2 cal/g-°C and 0.6 cal/g-°C, respectively, then 10 g of substance X has less heat content than 10 g of substance Y

    BECAUSE

    a substance with a relatively low specific heat will, when heated, experience less change in its temperature than a substance with a relatively high specific heat.

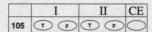

26. Two solid objects are of equal volume, but object A has density = X, and object B has density = (0.5)(X).

    Which of the following is true concerning objects A and B?

    (A) Objects A and B are of equal density.
    (B) Object B has twice the density of object A.
    (C) Objects A and B are of equal mass.
    (D) Object A has one half the mass of object B.
    (E) Object A has twice the mass of object B.

33. The specific heat of a substance is approximately 0.5 cal/g–°C. If 30 calories of heat are absorbed by 15 g of the substance at 30 °C, its temperature will become

    (A) 19 °C
    (B) 32 °C
    (C) 34 °C
    (D) 60 °C
    (E) 90 °C

38. Ten grams of oxygen gas are in a rigid 5 L vessel. If 2 g of oxygen gas are added to the vessel and temperature is kept constant, which of the following characteristics of the gas will increase?

    I. Mass
    II. Density
    III. Pressure

    (A) I only
    (B) III only
    (C) I and II only
    (D) II and III only
    (E) I, II, and III

LET'S LOOK AT THE ANSWERS

Question 1: The question talks about calculating mass if density is known, but you shouldn't be tempted to choose "mass" as the answer just because that word appears in the question. That would be falling for the temptation trap. Furthermore, you shouldn't choose "density" just because it appears in the question. The Subject Test writers *want* you to do this—that way you'll answer incorrectly. To answer correctly, you have to think carefully about what the words mean, and you must not rush to an answer simply because the question contains a word that reminds you of something in the answer choices.

Let's work through this together. If you're given a sample of some substance and you know the density of the substance, what additional knowledge would allow you to calculate the mass? If you know its density, then you know the ratio of mass/volume. Therefore if you also were provided with the sample's volume, you could figure out its mass. That's why A is right.

Question 2: You're asked to determine which quantity or property *always* varies with the number of atoms or molecules in a given sample of a substance. You have the knowledge to answer this question, but the wording might throw you.

Think about what you know. Mass measures quantity of matter. That means that for any sample of a particular substance, mass always varies with the number of atoms or molecules present within a sample. More molecules of substance X have a greater mass than fewer molecules of substance X— *always*.

What about volume, temperature, density, and pressure? Volume measures the space a sample will occupy. The volume of any substance may vary as the number of molecules of that substance is varied. The volume, however, *does not have to* change with the number of molecules. This is most clear with gases: a rigid container (with fixed volume) may hold vastly different amounts of the same gas. That's because gases are very expandable and very compressible. The volume of even solids and liquids *does not have to* change with changes in the number of molecules; since these can expand or contract somewhat when heated or cooled and could therefore keep the same volumes in spite of a small change in amount of the substance.

Changing the amount of a substance does not necessarily raise its temperature.

By remembering the formula for density $(d = m/v)$ we see that density may remain the same even with an increase or decrease in number of molecules (mass) of a substance, if the volume is changed in direct proportion to the change in mass. This is most obvious with gases, but since densities of solids and liquids are described at certain temperatures, we know that temperature can affect the density of solids and liquids a bit.

Pressure on a solid or liquid, however, remains the same, regardless of the number of molecules of the substance. Pressure of a gas will change with an increase or decrease in mass, *but only if* the volume of the container holding that gas is not at the same time increased or decreased.

So A, B, C, and D are wrong. E is right.

Question 3: The units of kilograms per liter mean that we are measuring mass per volume. That's density. So C is correct.

Question 4: Remember to associate temperature with average kinetic energy. That's what it measures. B is right.

Question 103: This is a type B question, so we divide and conquer! You examine each statement separately and determine whether it's true or false.

Start with the first statement, ignoring the second. Is it true? Yes it is, even though camouflage might at first prevent you from realizing it's true. But because

$$\text{density} = \frac{\text{mass}}{\text{volume}}$$

simple algebra lets you calculate mass if you know both density and volume.

$$\text{mass} = (\text{density})(\text{volume})$$

The first statement is true. Look at statement II by itself, and decide whether it's true or false. Don't let words camouflage the message. What does the statement mean? For a bigger piece of some substance the relationship between mass and volume is different than it is for a smaller piece of that same substance. That's certainly false. For any substance, the relationship between mass and volume is given by density. Density does not change with sample size for solids and liquids.

Question 104: Here's another type B question. Divide and conquer. Look at the first statement on its own. Is it true? Be careful. For solids and liquids, volume can be increased somewhat by heating (and then expanding) the substance, even while keeping the mass constant. The volume of a constant amount (mass) of gas can be increased by heating or cooling the gas, or by simply placing the gas in a different-sized container. Therefore the statement is false.

Look at the second statement. Does density represent mass per volume? Yes, it does. The second statement is true. Since one of the statements is false, you can skip over the CE oval and move on to the next question.

Question 105: Divide and conquer. Since we do not know the temperature of X or Y we cannot say which 10 g sample has more heat content. So statement I is false.

Consider statement II. A substance with a relatively low specific heat is like the person with a relatively low pain threshold. Such a substance will respond strongly (by a relatively large temperature change) to the addition of heat just as the person with a low pain threshold will respond strongly to the experience of pain. So statement II is false. Skip the CE oval and move on.

Question 26: Don't even look at the answer options until you really understand the situation that's been described. You've got two objects. They're the same volume but one has half the density of the other. Since

$$\text{density} = \frac{\text{mass}}{\text{volume}}$$

you know that the object with lesser density has one half the mass of the object with greater density. Look for an answer choice that tells you that.

Object A has the greater density so it should have twice the mass of an equal volume of Object B. That's why E is right.

Question 33: Remember $q = mc\Delta T$? Substituting into it gives

$$30 \text{ cal} = (15 \text{ g})(0.5 \text{ cal/g–°C}) \, \Delta T$$

Solve for ΔT. You'll get 4 °C. This is the increase in temperature. So if the substance was at 30 °C it is now at 34 °C. That's choice C.

Question 38: Adding more oxygen gas will certainly increase the mass of the gas sample. Therefore statement I is true.

Since density is the ratio of mass per volume, increasing mass while maintaining the same volume will increase this ratio and, therefore, increase the density of the gas. Statement II is also true.

Pressure is a measure of the force per unit area with which gas molecules collide with the walls of the vessel. More gas in the same volume means more collisions and, therefore, greater pressure. So statements I, II, and III are true. E is the answer.

Notice that even if you don't know if all the statements are true, you can make a really good guess with just a little knowledge on this type of question. Just knowing that statement I is true allows you to eliminate choices B and D, and by knowing that statement II is also true, you can rule out choice A. At this point, you have a 50% chance at choosing the right answer even if you know nothing about pressure!

4

Elements, Atoms, and Ions

A solid understanding of matter—how it consists of elements that are built from atoms—is critical for grasping the chemistry that appears on the Subject Test. We'll focus on matter in this chapter.

ATOMS AND ELEMENTS

Here's a periodic table. You will be provided with a periodic table when you take the SAT II: Chemistry test. The vertical columns are called groups. The horizontal rows are called periods. The symbols represent elements.

PERIODIC TABLE OF THE ELEMENTS

1 H 1.0																	2 He 4.0
3 Li 6.9	4 Be 9.0											5 B 10.8	6 C 12.0	7 N 14.0	8 O 16.0	9 F 19.0	10 Ne 20.2
11 Na 23.0	12 Mg 24.3											13 Al 27.0	14 Si 28.1	15 P 31.0	16 S 32.1	17 Cl 35.5	18 Ar 39.9
19 K 39.1	20 Ca 40.1	21 Sc 45.0	22 Ti 47.9	23 V 50.9	24 Cr 52.0	25 Mn 54.9	26 Fe 55.8	27 Co 58.9	28 Ni 58.7	29 Cu 63.5	30 Zn 65.4	31 Ga 69.7	32 Ge 72.6	33 As 74.9	34 Se 79.0	35 Br 79.9	36 Kr 83.8
37 Rb 85.5	38 Sr 87.6	39 Y 88.9	40 Zr 91.2	41 Nb 92.9	42 Mo 95.9	43 Tc (98)	44 Ru 101.1	45 Rh 102.9	46 Pd 106.4	47 Ag 107.9	48 Cd 112.4	49 In 114.8	50 Sn 118.7	51 Sb 121.8	52 Te 127.6	53 I 126.9	54 Xe 131.3
55 Cs 132.9	56 Ba 137.3	57 La* 138.9	72 Hf 178.5	73 Ta 180.9	74 W 183.9	75 Re 186.2	76 Os 190.2	77 Ir 192.2	78 Pt 195.1	79 Au 197.0	80 Hg 200.6	81 Tl 204.4	82 Pb 207.2	83 Bi 209.0	84 Po (209)	85 At (210)	86 Rn (222)
87 Fr (223)	88 Ra 226.0	89 Ac† 227.0	104 Unq (261)	105 Unp (262)	106 Unh (263)	107 Uns (262)	108 Uno (265)	109 Une (267)									

*	58 Ce 140.1	59 Pr 140.9	60 Nd 144.2	61 Pm (145)	62 Sm 150.4	63 Eu 152.0	64 Gd 157.3	65 Tb 158.9	66 Dy 162.5	67 Ho 164.9	68 Er 167.3	69 Tm 168.9	70 Yb 173.0	71 Lu 175.0
†	90 Th 232.0	91 Pa (231)	92 U 238.0	93 Np (237)	94 Pu (244)	95 Am (243)	96 Cm (247)	97 Bk (247)	98 Cf (251)	99 Es (252)	100 Fm (257)	101 Md (258)	102 No (259)	103 Lr (260)

WHAT'S AN ELEMENT?

An element is a substance that can't be broken down into a simpler substance by a chemical reaction.

Now, what exactly is an **atom**? Suppose you have a spoonful of some element—carbon, for instance. The smallest, tiniest, teeniest "piece" of carbon in the spoonful is one atom of carbon. So, what's an atom? When you're talking about an element, it's the smallest piece there is. When it comes to any element, there's nothing smaller than one atom of that element.

Associate:

Element with: can't be broken into anything simpler
without losing its identity

Atom with: smallest piece of any element

How an Atom Is Made: Protons, Neutrons, and Electrons

At the center of every atom is a nucleus. What's in the nucleus? Two things: **protons** and **neutrons**. Every proton has a charge of +1, and neutrons have no charge at all. Because protons and neutrons comprise the nucleus of an atom, they are sometimes referred to as **nucleons**. What's outside the nucleus? One thing: electrons. Every electron has a charge of –1.

For now, consider that, in an atom, the number of electrons is equal to the number of protons. The charges inside and outside the nucleus are balanced. The atom is electrically neutral.

Sometimes it happens that in an atom loses or gains one or more electrons. When that happens the number of electrons outside the nucleus is not equal to the number of protons inside. The atom isn't electrically neutral anymore and we call it an **ion**. If the atom loses one or more electrons, it has fewer negative charges than positive charges, and we call it a positively charged ion, or **cation**. If the atom gains one or more electrons, it has more negative charges than positive charges. We call it a negatively charged ion, or **anion**. When we say "ion," we're talking about an atom that has lost or gained one or more electrons. It's charged—positively if it loses electrons, negatively if it gains them.

The Numbers on the Periodic Table

For the Subject Test, you have to know about some of the numbers you see on the periodic table.

Atomic number

Look at any element on the periodic table. There's a whole number above the element's symbol in its box. That number is the element's **atomic number**. It tells you how many protons are in the nucleus of one atom of that element. The number of protons in the nucleus of an atom makes the atom "what it is." Oxygen, for instance, has the atomic number 8. That means an atom of oxygen has 8 protons in its nucleus. If somehow we could take a proton away from an oxygen atom, it would have only 7 protons in its nucleus and it wouldn't be an oxygen atom anymore. It would be a nitrogen atom, because any atom with 7 protons in its nucleus is nitrogen.

What if an oxygen atom loses an electron but not a proton? Well, so long as the atom has 8 protons in it, it's oxygen. If it has only 7 electrons, then it's a positively charged oxygen ion. If it has 9 electrons, it's a negatively charged oxygen ion. But if the atomic number—the number of protons in the nucleus—doesn't change, the element doesn't change either: It's still oxygen.

The atomic number is very important. It tells you how many protons are in the atom's nucleus and that tells you what the atom is. The number of protons determines the identity of an element.

Associate:

    Atomic number with: number of protons in nucleus
                                       identity of element

Mass Number, Isotopes, and Atomic Weight

We said before that an atom has two things in its nucleus: protons and neutrons. Each proton has a positive charge and each neutron is neutral. But both protons and neutrons have mass. Electrons have practically no mass. So, an atom's mass is approximately equal to the mass of its protons plus the mass of its neutrons.

A proton and a neutron each have mass of roughly 1 atomic mass unit (amu), and an atom's **mass number** is equal to the sum of its protons and its neutrons.

Does the number of protons always equal the number of neutrons? Definitely not. We've said that in an atom the number of protons equals the number of electrons. But this says nothing about neutrons. Most carbon atoms, for instance, have 6 neutrons in their nuclei. A few have 8. All have 6 protons in their nuclei, so they all have the atomic number 6, and they're all carbon. But they can differ in number of neutrons.

If two atoms of the same element differ in the number of neutrons in their nuclei, we call them **isotopes**. A carbon atom that has 6 neutrons and a carbon atom that has 8 neutrons are isotopes. Both are carbon atoms (because both have 6 protons in their nuclei), but they're isotopes of each other because they've got different numbers of neutrons in their nuclei.

Let's think about isotopes and mass number. Since an atom's mass number is equal to the sum of its protons and its neutrons, two different isotopes of the same element will have different mass numbers. For instance, the carbon atom with 6 neutrons in its nucleus has a mass number of 6 protons + 6 neutrons = 12 amu. And, because its mass number is 12, we call it carbon-12. The carbon atom with 8 neutrons in its nucleus has a mass number of 6 protons + 8 neutrons = 14 amu. And, because its mass number is 14, we call it carbon-14.

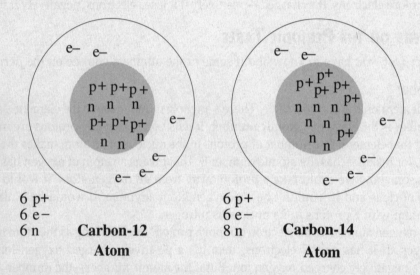

By the way, mass number doesn't appear on the periodic table. Why not? Because for any element, there's no such thing as one mass number. As we've just learned, different isotopes of the same element have different mass numbers.

—But—

Chemists have figured out, roughly, the degree to which each isotope of each element tends to occur on the Earth. So, for each element, they've figured out a sort of "average" mass number, which for each element represents the average of the mass numbers of all isotopes as they occur on the Earth. That average number is called **atomic weight.** For each element a number for atomic weight *does* appear on the periodic table, just below the element's symbol. When we want to know the mass of an atom of a particular element then, for practical purposes, we use the number for atomic weight that appears on the periodic table.

Associate:

Neutrons with: isotopes; two atoms of the same element are isotopes if they differ in the number of neutrons in their nuclei

Mass number with:	number of protons plus number of neutrons
	isotopes: two isotopes of an element have different mass numbers because they differ in number of neutrons
Atomic weight with:	average of mass numbers for all isotopes of an element as they occur on the Earth

Now try these Subject Test-type questions.

QUESTION TYPE A

(A) Atom
(B) Ion
(C) Neutron
(D) Proton
(E) Electron

4. The smallest representative particle of helium

5. Gain or loss creates positively or negatively charged ion, respectively

6. Particle responsible for positive nuclear charge

7. Isotopes of uranium always differ in their number of this particle

8. Their number in the nucleus determines an element's atomic number

QUESTION TYPE B

Directions: Each question below consists of two statements, I in the left-hand column and II in the right-hand column. For each question, determine whether statement I is true or false <u>and</u> whether statement II is true or false and fill in the corresponding T or F ovals on your answer sheet. <u>Fill in oval CE only if statement II is a correct explanation of statement I.</u>

<u>I</u>		<u>II</u>
105. The periodic table does not report mass numbers	BECAUSE	a mass number can be assigned to one isotope of an element, but not to an element in general.

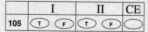

106. Addition of an electron to an atom creates a positively charged ion

BECAUSE

every electron carries a negative charge.

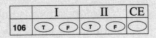

	I	II	CE
106	T F	T F	◯

QUESTION TYPE C

27. Two different sodium atoms or ions may differ in all of the following ways EXCEPT

    (A) the number of electrons outside their nuclei
    (B) the overall charge they carry
    (C) their mass numbers
    (D) the number of neutrons in their nuclei
    (E) the number of protons in their nuclei

28. Two isotopes of the same element will always differ in

    (A) mass number but never in atomic number
    (B) atomic number but never in mass number
    (C) charge outside but never inside their nuclei
    (D) nuclear charge but never in overall charge
    (E) the number of electrons outside their nuclei but never in the number of neutrons inside their nuclei

OKAY? LET'S LOOK AT THE ANSWERS

Question 4: Helium is an element and the smallest piece of an element that exists is an atom of that element. That's why A is right.

Question 5: You know that every electron carries a charge of –1. You know that an atom becomes (1) a positively charged ion when it loses an electron(s), or (2) a negatively charged ion when it gains an electron. That's why E is right.

Question 6: Whatever is responsible for positive nuclear charge must be found in the nucleus. That narrows our choices down to C and D—neutrons and protons. Now which particle carries a positive charge? Protons do. So the answer is D.

Questions 7: Don't be fooled by the mention of uranium. It's just another element. You know that isotopes of the same element never differ in their number of protons, could differ in their number of electrons, but must differ in their number of neutrons. That's why C is correct.

Question 8: The atomic number of an element depends on the number of protons in that element's atoms. So the answer must be D.

Question 105: This is a type B question. Divide and conquer! Evaluate the first statement without looking at the second. Decide whether it's true or false. Answer? It's true. The periodic table reports atomic weights, but not mass numbers. So the first statement is true.

See if the second statement, by itself, is true or false. Is it true that a mass number can be assigned only to a single isotope of an element but not to an element in general? Yes. Mass number = number of protons + number of neutrons. Different atoms of the same element may vary as to the number of neutrons they contain. That's what makes them isotopes.

Both statements are true. Now see if this sentence makes sense: "The periodic table does not report mass numbers because a mass number can be assigned to one isotope of an element, but not to an element in general." It does, so fill in the oval marked CE.

Question 106: Divide and conquer. Look at the first statement on its own. Decide whether it's true or false. Electrons are negatively charged. If we add an electron to an atom we get a negatively charged ion. It's false.

Now look at the second statement. Is it true? Yes. Electrons are negatively charged. The first statement is false and the second is true.

Question 27: You know the answer. Don't fall into the camouflage trap. The atomic number represents the number of protons in the nucleus and it tells us what the atom or ion is. Any sodium atom or ion must have, in its nucleus, the same number of protons as any other, otherwise it's not sodium.

A and B are wrong because different sodium ions might carry different charges depending on how many electrons they've gained or lost. C and D are wrong because different isotopes of sodium will differ in the number of neutrons in the nucleus. That means their mass number will differ. But all sodium atoms or ions must have 11 protons in their nuclei. That's why E is right.

Question 28: You know what creates isotopes: a difference in number of neutrons. Two different isotopes of the same element might differ in the number of electrons outside the nucleus. They must differ in their mass numbers since they have different numbers of neutrons. They can't differ in the number of protons in their nuclei, or they wouldn't be isotopes of the same element. B, C, D, and E are wrong. A is right.

5

Chemical Reactions and Stoichiometry

Don't be intimidated by this chapter's title. A chemical reaction is simply a process that may change one or more substances into different substances. Stoichiometry enables us to determine the amounts of substances consumed or produced in chemical reactions.

MOLECULES

As we mentioned in Chapter 4, an atom is the smallest piece of an element. Atoms of one element often attract each other or atoms of a different element. If this attraction is strong enough a chemical bond can result. (We'll discuss bonding in chapter 7.) Certain types of bonds join two or more atoms into units called **molecules**.

Everybody knows the formula of water—it's H_2O. The formula H_2O means that two hydrogen atoms and one oxygen atom are bonded together into an individual unit. This unit is a water molecule and a drop of water has trillions and trillions of water molecules. So what's the smallest unit of water that exists? It's one molecule of water.

DIATOMIC MOLECULES

When a molecule consists of just two atoms (whether they're from identical or different elements), it's called a **diatomic molecule**. Some elements exist as diatomic molecules at room temperature and atmospheric pressure. For example, a sample of oxygen in air consists of many tiny O_2 units. Each unit is a diatomic oxygen molecule. There are seven important elements that exist as diatomic molecules: hydrogen (H_2), nitrogen (N_2), fluorine (F_2), oxygen (O_2), iodine (I_2), chlorine (Cl_2), and bromine (Br_2). Try to remember:

Oh, I Have Nice Closets For Brooms

SOME MORE ABOUT ATOMS AND MOLECULES: FORMULA WEIGHTS, EMPIRICAL FORMULAS, AND PERCENT COMPOSITION

You know that when two or more atoms bond together, they form a molecule. For the Subject Test you need to fool around with some simple atom–molecule math.

1. Formula Weight: For any molecule, we calculate the formula weight by adding up the atomic weights of all the atoms in the molecule. It's easy. Let's take hydrogen peroxide: H_2O_2. The molecule has

- 2 hydrogen atoms, and the atomic weight of hydrogen is 1 amu. That gives us 2(1).

- 2 oxygen atoms, and the atomic weight of oxygen is 16 amu. That gives us 2(16).

    2(1) + 2(16) = 34.

So, the formula weight for H_2O_2 is 34 amu.
Let's figure out the formula weight for sulfuric acid: H_2SO_4. The molecule has

- 2 hydrogen atoms, and the atomic weight of hydrogen is 1 amu. That gives us 2(1).

- 1 atom of sulfur, and the atomic weight of sulfur is 32 amu. That gives us 1(32).

- 4 atoms of oxygen, and the atomic weight of oxygen is 16 amu. That gives us 4(16).

    2(1) + 32(1) + 4(16) = 98.

So, the formula weight for H_2SO_4 is 98 amu.

2. Empirical Formula: An empirical formula shows the ratio of atoms within a molecule. For instance, we know that the molecular formula for hydrogen peroxide is H_2O_2. And if you look at that formula, you see that there's one hydrogen atom for every oxygen atom. The molecule contains hydrogen and oxygen atoms in a ratio of 1:1. Hydrogen peroxide's empirical formula, therefore, is HO.

To find an empirical formula from a molecular formula, first find the largest whole number that will go evenly into all of the subscripts in the molecular formula. Then you just divide each subscript by that number. In the case of H_2O_2, that number is 2. Dividing each subscript by 2, we get HO.

Ethane has the molecular formula C_2H_6. So, what is its empirical formula? Take a look at the molecular formula. What's the largest whole number that goes evenly into 2 and 6? It's 2. So, we divide both subscripts by 2 and we get an empirical formula of CH_3.

How about water (H_2O)? The biggest whole number that will divide evenly into 2 and 1 is 1. So the empirical formula is the same as the molecular formula: H_2O.

3. Percent Composition: The Subject Test writers may ask you to determine something called a "percent composition." Here's an example: What is the percent of oxygen by mass in hydrogen peroxide, H_2O_2?

All you need to do is find the mass in amu of all of the oxygen atoms in the molecule and compare it to the total formula weight. As shown earlier the two oxygen atoms in H_2O_2 each weigh 16 amu. So the mass due to oxygen is 2 (16) or 32 amu. The formula weight of H_2O_2 is 34 amu. So the percent of oxygen by mass in H_2O_2 is $\frac{32}{34} \times 100\%$ or roughly 94%. That means the percent of hydrogen by mass in H_2O_2 is about 6%.

THE MOLE

What's a mole? It's a number, like a dozen or a gross. Dozen, as you know, means 12. Gross means 144. Mole means 6.02×10^{23}. The number 6.02×10^{23} is known as Avogadro's number.

We said earlier that atomic mass is measured in something called atomic mass units (amu). The mass of a helium atom is approximately 4 amu. Because people are accustomed to dealing with mass in grams, someone wanted to know how many atomic mass units were in 1 gram, and the answer turned out to be 6.02×10^{23}. There are 6.02×10^{23} atomic mass units in 1 gram.

Now think about what that means. If for any element we take a sample whose mass in grams is numerically equal to its atomic weight in amu, the sample has 1 mole of atoms in it. If we take a substance whose mass in grams is numerically equal to twice its atomic weight in amu, we have two moles of atoms. If we take a substance whose mass in grams is numerically equal to three times its atomic weight in amu, we have three moles of atoms. It's as simple as that.

Helium's atomic weight is 4 amu. So, 4 g of helium contains 1 mole (6.02×10^{23}) of helium atoms. Eight grams of helium contain 2 moles of helium atoms. Carbon's atomic weight is 12 amu. So, in 12 g of carbon there is 1 mole (6.02×10^{23}) of carbon atoms. In 36 grams of carbon there are 3 moles of carbon atoms. Got it?

How many moles of oxygen *molecules* are in 64 g of oxygen gas? Remember, oxygen consists of tiny O_2 units. Each O_2 molecule has a mass of roughly 2(16) or 32 amu, so 1 mole of O_2 molecules would have a mass of 32 g. Thus in 64 g of oxygen gas, there are 2 moles of oxygen molecules. Now how many moles of oxygen *atoms* would be present in this 64 g sample? Think. Each O_2 molecule is made up of two oxygen atoms. So if the sample contains 2 moles of oxygen molecules, it contains 4 moles of oxygen atoms.

Mass Composition to Empirical Formula: Now that you know what an empirical formula is, we want you to know how to figure out an empirical formula from its percent composition. The Subject Test writers might tell you that some unknown substance is analyzed, and it turns out by mass to contain approximately 75% mercury and 25% chlorine. Then you'll be asked to take the percent composition and figure out the unknown substance's empirical formula.

Here's how you do it.

- Imagine, first, that you have 100 g of the substance, and then think in moles.

- If you have 100 g of the substance and it's 75% mercury by mass, then you've got 75 g of mercury, right? Since the atomic weight of mercury is about 200 amu (which means there are 200 g in 1 mole of mercury atoms), you've got $\frac{75}{200}$ mole = 0.375 moles of mercury atoms in a 100 g sample.

- If you have 100 g of the substance and it's 25% chlorine, by mass, then you've got 25 g of chlorine. Since the atomic weight of chlorine is about 35 amu (which means there are 35 g in 1 mole of chlorine atoms), you've got $\frac{25}{35}$ = 0.700 moles of chlorine atoms in the 100 g sample. (Note: When finding moles of a diatomic element such as chlorine in a *compound*, use its atomic weight, *not* its formula weight, as a diatomic molecule in the calculation.)

- If you've got 0.375 moles of mercury atoms and 0.700 moles of chlorine atoms, then the ratio of chlorine to mercury atoms is $\frac{0.700}{0.375}$ (which is close to 2:1), which means the empirical formula is $HgCl_2$. That's the way it's done.

Now go back and review everything we've told you about molecules and moles. Then, answer these Subject Test-type questions.

QUESTION TYPE A

(A) N_2O
(B) $C_6H_{12}O_6$
(C) SO_3
(D) NO
(E) N_2O_5

6. Is a diatomic molecule

7. Has a formula weight of approximately 108 amu

8. Has an empirical formula that is different from its molecular formula

9. Composition is approximately 60% oxygen by mass

QUESTION TYPE B

Directions: Each question below consists of two statements, I in the left-hand column and II in the right-hand column. For each question, determine whether statement I is true or false and whether statement II is true or false and fill in the corresponding T or F ovals on your answer sheet. Fill in oval CE only if statement II is a correct explanation of statement I.

	I		**II**

102. Chlorine is an element   BECAUSE   chlorine exists as unbonded atoms at room temperature and atmospheric pressure.

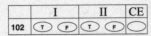

103. One mole of HBr has greater mass than one mole of NO₂   BECAUSE   the mass of a molecule of HBr is greater than the mass of a molecule of NO₂.

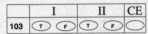

QUESTION TYPE C

27. The formula for calcium nitrate is $Ca(NO_3)_2$. What is its approximate formula weight?

   (A)   64 amu
   (B)   164 amu
   (C)   240 amu
   (D)   310 amu
   (E)   380 amu

48. An unknown substance is found to have a composition of 9% magnesium and 91% iodine by weight. The empirical formula for the substance is:

   (A) MgI
   (B) Mg_2I_2
   (C) Mg_2I
   (D) MgI_2
   (E) Mg_3I_2

GOT ANSWERS? LET'S CHECK THEM OUT

Question 6: "Diatomic" means two atoms, so a diatomic molecule consists of two atoms bonded together. Don't be fooled by choice A. O_3 is ozone and it is a "triatomic" molecule. Among the choices, only nitrogen monoxide (NO) contains just two atoms per molecule. Never mind that the atoms are from different elements. It's still a diatomic molecule. So the answer is D.

Question 7: First eliminate the obvious losers: by inspection you know that N_2O and NO are nowhere near 108 amu. Cross them out. Then you'll need to do some atom-molecule math. Use the periodic table to find the atomic weight of each element in the compounds. Then multiply this mass by the number of that kind of atom in the molecule. Sum the mass contributions from each element to get the formula weight. When you do so for choice E you'll get: 2(14 amu) + 5(16 amu) = 28 amu + 80 amu = 108 amu. E is your answer.

Question 8: Look at the ratios between different types of atoms. If the ratio can be put in terms of smaller whole numbers then the formula is <u>not</u> an empirical formula. Check out choice B. In this molecule the ratio of carbon to hydrogen to oxygen is 6:12:6. If we divide this ratio by 6 we'll get the simpler (though still equivalent) ratio of 1:2:1. So the empirical formula of $C_6H_{12}O_6$ is CH_2O. Since molecular and empirical formulas differ, this must be the answer.

Question 9: Here, proceed as you did in question 7. If you are comfortable with your intuitive sense of relative molecular weights, you should be able to eliminate choices A and E without calculation. Then, after you get the formula weight for each choice, compare it to the contribution due to oxygen. Look at choice C. The formula weight of SO_3 is 32 amu + 3(16 amu) = 80 amu. Oxygen's percent of the composition by mass is $\frac{48}{80} \times 100\%$ or 60%. So C is right.

Question 102: Type B—divide and conquer! Look at the first statement. Is it true or false? Of course it's true. Chlorine is an element. What about statement II? It's false. Remember that chlorine exists as diatomic molecules at room temperature and atmospheric pressure.

Question 103: Divide and conquer. Consider statement I. One mole of HBr contains the same *number* of molecules as one mole of NO_2—6.02 × 10²³ molecules. But that doesn't necessarily mean 6.02 × 10²³ HBr molecules weigh the same as 6.02 × 10²³ NO_2 molecules. Do ten paper clips weigh the same as ten elephants? Certainly not. Use the periodic table. One molecule of HBr has a mass of about 1 amu + 80 amu, or 81 amu. One molecule of NO_2 has a mass of about 14 amu + 2(16 amu), or 46 amu. So one molecule of HBr has greater mass than one molecule of NO_2. And one mole of HBr would thus have greater mass than one mole of NO_2. So statement I is true.

What about statement II? Well, we've already had to consider it and it's also true.

Now does this sentence make sense?: "One mole of HBr has greater mass than one mole of NO_2 because the mass of a molecule of HBr is greater than the mass of a molecule of NO_2." It sure does. So fill in the oval marked CE.

Question 27: You have to calculate the formula weight of $Ca(NO_3)_2$, and you know exactly how to do it. Calcium's atomic weight is 40 amu, nitrogen's is 14 amu, and oxygen's is 16 amu. That means the formula weight = 40 + 2(14 + 3(16)) = 40 + 2(14 + 48) = 40 + 28 + 96 = 164 amu. B is right.

Question 48: You're given a substance's mass composition and you have to figure out its empirical formula. So, you imagine that you have 100 g and you think in moles:

♦ you've got 9 g of magnesium and once you see that magnesium's atomic weight is 24 amu, that means you have $\frac{9}{24}$ = 0.375 moles of magnesium atoms.

♦ you've got 91 g of iodine and once you see that iodine's atomic weight is 127 amu, that means you have $\frac{91}{127}$ = 0.717 moles of iodine.

♦ the ratio of iodine atoms to magnesium atoms is $\frac{0.717}{0.375}$, which is very close to 2:1

That means the empirical formula is MgI_2, and that's why D is right.

CHEMICAL REACTIONS—HOW MOLECULES ARE FORMED, UNFORMED, AND REFORMED

You know that atoms or ions or molecules can get together and react. The result? In the starting substances, bonds break. Free atoms then form new bonds with one another to form new molecules. The starting substances are called reactants. They are changed into new substances—that have compositions and properties—that we call products. This is a chemical reaction. When we want to write about a chemical reaction we write a chemical equation, like this one:

$$C_3H_8(g) + 5O_2(g) \rightarrow 4H_2O(l) + 3CO_2(g)$$

What's this equation telling us? Well, two things. On a molecular level this equation means that 1 molecule of propane (C_3H_8) and 5 molecules of molecular oxygen react to form 4 molecules of water and 3 molecules of carbon dioxide. It's also telling us that 1 mole of C_3H_8 reacts with 5 moles of O_2 to form 4 moles of H_2O and 3 moles of CO_2. This equation also indicates the state of each reactant and product: (*s*) means solid, (*l*) means liquid, and (*g*) means gas.

CHEMICAL EQUATIONS MUST BE BALANCED

Look again at the chemical equation we just presented:

$$C_3H_8(g) + 5O_2(g) \rightarrow 4H_2O(l) + 3CO_2(g)$$

Notice that all of the elements are "in balance." How can you tell? For each element on the left side of the equation, multiply the coefficient in front of the substance that element is in by the element's subscript. Any number that doesn't appear is assumed to be 1. For oxygen, in $5O_2$, there are $5 \times 2 = 10$ oxygen atoms. Now do the same for the right side of the equation. In $4H_2O$ there are $4 \times 1 = 4$ oxygen atoms. In $3CO_2$ there are $3 \times 2 = 6$ oxygen atoms. So there are $4 + 6 = 10$ oxygen atoms on the right side. Since there are also 10 oxygen atoms on the left side, oxygen is in balance. Check to see that carbon and hydrogen are also in balance. They are. There are 3 carbons on the left and 3 carbons on the right. There are 8 hydrogens on the left and 8 hydrogens on the right. For each element that participates in the reaction, the total number of atoms on the left must equal the total number on the right. Then the equation is balanced.

When it comes to balancing equations, the Subject Test writers will show you about five unbalanced equations and, in their way, ask you to balance them. Here's what the question will look like:

$$\ldots C_2H_4(g) + \ldots O_2(g) \rightarrow \ldots CO_2(g) + \ldots H_2O(l)$$

When the equation above is balanced, and all co-efficients are reduced to lowest whole-number terms, which of the following would be the coefficient for CO_2?

(A) 1
(B) 2
(C) 4
(D) 5
(E) 6

Fortunately, these questions are easy to answer if you use the "plug-in" balancing strategy. Start with choice A, and put the number 1 in front of CO_2. (Don't be afraid to write as much as you want in your test booklet. Scribble and do whatever you want. Your test booklet belongs to you and nobody cares what you write in it. Only your answer sheet is scored.) Now, if we have a 1 in front of CO_2, we end up with 1 carbon on the right. Yet we have at least two carbons on the left, so we know that 1 is not the answer.

Let's try choice B. Put a 2 in front of CO_2 and see what happens. We have 2 carbons on the right and 2 on the left. Good. We have 4 hydrogens on the left, so let's try putting a 2 in front of the H_2O. That gives us a total of 6 oxygens on the right and 2 on the left. Let's put a 3 in front of O_2 on the left so we have a total of 6 oxygens on the left.

Now, what have we got? 2 carbons on right and left, 4 hydrogens on right and left, and 6 oxygens on right and left. The equation is in balance, and B is right. So, when the Subject Test asks you to perform a balancing act, use the plug-in balancing strategy. It can't fail.

REACTION STOICHIOMETRY

Sometimes Subject Test questions want you to determine *how much* of a product is formed or a reactant is consumed by a chemical reaction. These are stoichiometry questions. When you attack a stoichiometry problem, remember to always work from a balanced equation. The coefficients in front of each species indicate the mole ratio between any two species. Consider for the next few pages the reaction between ammonia gas and oxygen, which yields nitrogen monoxide and water:

$$4NH_3(g) + 5O_2(g) \rightarrow 4NO(g) + 6H_2O(l)$$

Now see what we mean about coefficients.

- For every 4 moles of ammonia that are consumed, 5 moles of molecular oxygen are also consumed.

- For every 5 moles of oxygen that are consumed, 6 moles of water are produced.

- For every 4 moles of ammonia that are consumed, 4 moles of nitrogen monoxide are produced. In other words, the mole ratio of ammonia consumption to nitrogen monoxide production is 1:1.

You can compare any two species in a balanced equation in this manner. How do you put these ratios to use? Take a look: If 2 moles of ammonia are consumed, how many moles of water are produced?

From the balanced equation, we see that for every 4 moles of ammonia that are consumed, 6 moles of water are produced. So the ratio of ammonia to water is 4:6 or, simplifying, 2:3. Thus, two moles of ammonia will react completely to produce 3 moles of water.

A few Subject Test questions begin by giving you data on the amounts of two reactants that are mixed together. Remember that reactants will combine according to their mole ratio. So if we mix together amounts of two reactants that are not in their stoichiometric mole ratio, one reactant will be consumed first. When this happens the reaction will stop, leaving some of the excess reactant unreacted.

Consider this question: If 34 g of ammonia and 32 g of oxygen are combined, how many grams of nitrogen monoxide will be produced?

The formula weight of NH_3 is 17 amu. Thus 1 mole of NH_3 has a mass of 17 g and 2 moles have a mass of 34 g. So we have 2 moles of ammonia. How many moles of oxygen do we have? Since the formula weight of O_2 is 32 amu, one mole of O_2 has a mass of 32 g. So our actual mole ratio of ammonia to oxygen is 2:1. However from the balanced equation given earlier in this section, we see that the ratio of ammonia consumption to oxygen consumption is 4:5. In keeping with this stoichiometric ratio, 2 moles of ammonia would react with 2.5 moles of oxygen. But we have only 1 mole of oxygen. Thus we will run out of oxygen before all 2 moles of ammonia have reacted. For this reason oxygen in this problem is called a **limiting reactant**. Once a limiting reactant is gone, the reaction will end. So 1 mole of oxygen actually reacts. Since 4 moles of nitrogen monoxide are produced for every

5 moles of oxygen that react, $\frac{4}{5}$ moles, or 0.8 mole, of nitrogen monoxide is produced when 1 mole of oxygen is reacted. The formula weight of NO is 30 amu. So 1 mole of NO has a mass of 30 g. The mass of 0.8 mole of NO is (0.8 mole)(30g/mole), or 24 g.

ENTROPY

Now hear this: The universe is fundamentally lazy. Everything in the universe is happier when it's in a low-energy state. Everything tends toward states of low energy. Low-energy states are more stable than high-energy states. That's such a fundamental principle that we'll ask you to repeat it. Fill in the blank lines:

_____energy states are more stable than _____energy states.

Because the universe is lazy, it's also fundamentally disordered. When we talk about disorder we think **entropy** and use the symbol S. Everything tends toward maximum entropy. When we talk about a chemical reaction and the difference between entropy of the products and entropy of the reactants, we use the symbol ΔS. If ΔS is negative, the reaction has lost entropy; the products are more "orderly" than the reactants. If ΔS is positive, the reaction has gained entropy; the products are less "orderly" than the reactants.

Entropy is really a very *complex* concept, but for Subject Test purposes it's a very *simple* concept. When you see the word entropy, think "disorder," and realize that because the universe is lazy, it tends toward maximum entropy. All things in the universe are more stable when they're in (1) states of low energy and (2) states of high entropy. DON'T FORGET THAT.

Learn to associate:

Entropy with:	disorder, randomness
Stability with:	low energy high entropy

ENTHALPY: EXOTHERMIC REACTIONS, ENDOTHERMIC REACTIONS, AND HEATS OF FORMATION

Because the universe tends toward low energy, it likes chemical reactions that release energy—reactions that set energy free—leaving the products of the reaction in an "energy state" that's lower than that of the reactants. When we talk about the energy states of reactants or products, we say **enthalpy**, and we use the symbol H. High enthalpy means high-energy state. Low enthalpy means low-energy state. When referring to how enthalpy changes in a reaction, we use ΔH. So, the universe likes reactions in which enthalpy moves from higher to lower values—reactions in which ΔH is negative, which means they give away energy when they happen. These reactions are called **exothermic** and the universe is happy about them. If, on the other hand, enthalpy of products is greater than enthalpy of reactants, then ΔH is positive. These reactions are called **endothermic**, which means they require the addition of energy to occur, and the universe isn't so crazy about them.

Learn to associate:

Exothermic with:	ΔH is negative, enthalpy decreases
Endothermic with:	ΔH is positive, enthalpy increases

THIS IS A GOOD TIME TO TALK ABOUT A THING CALLED "HEAT OF FORMATION"

Every compound has a heat of formation, which refers to the amount of heat that's released or absorbed when one mole of the compound is formed from its elements. When we talk about heat of formation, we use the same symbol we use for enthalpy change but we put a little "f" on it: ΔH_f. Let's consider gaseous carbon dioxide's (CO_2) heat of formation:

$$C(s) + O_2(g) \rightarrow CO_2(g); \quad \Delta H_f = -393 \text{ kJ/mol}$$

The negative sign means heat is released; this is an exothermic reaction. We're saying that when 1 mole of $CO_2(g)$ is formed from its elements ($C(s)$ and $O_2(g)$), 393 kilojoules (kJ) of energy are released. Naturally, the universe likes that since it likes things to move from high- to low-energy states.

On the Subject Test, by the way, for all *elements*, the heat of formation is zero. That means that for C, Ni, Cl_2, O_2, H_2 and N_2—or any other elemental atom or molecule—the heat of formation is zero.

For the Chemistry Subject Test you'll also want to know that for any reaction, the heats of formation of all the products minus the heats of formation of all the reactants is equal to ΔH *for the whole reaction*. The test writers might show you a reaction and give you heats of formation for all of the reactants and products. Then they'll ask you to figure out ΔH for the whole reaction.

That's simple to do. Add up the heats of formation for all of the products and then all of the reactants, multiplying each by its "number" (coefficient) from the balanced equation and you've got ΔH for the reaction. Remember this: ΔH_f (reaction) = ΔH_f (products) – ΔH_f (reactants), and that the heats of formation of all elements are zero.

Here. Look at this reaction:

$$C_6H_{12}O_6(s) + 6O_2(g) \rightarrow 6CO_2(g) + 6H_2O(l)$$

Suppose you're told that the heat of formation for:

- $C_6H_{12}O_6(s)$ is –1,273 kJ/mol

- $H_2O(\ell)$ is –286 kJ/mol

- $CO_2(g)$ is –393 kJ/mol

(ΔH_f for $O_2(g)$, of course, is 0.)
ΔH for the whole reaction is equal to:

$$\Delta H_f(\text{products}) - \Delta H_f(\text{reactants})$$

So, let's do it.

$\Delta H_f(\text{products}) = 6(-393) + 6(-286) = -4,074 \text{ kJ}$

$\Delta H_f(\text{reactants}) = -1,273 \text{ kJ} + 0\text{kJ} = -1,273\text{kJ}$

So, ΔH for the whole reaction = $(-4,074) - (-1,273) = -2,801$ kJ. ΔH for the whole reaction is negative, which means the reaction is exothermic. The universe likes that.

SPONTANEITY AND GIBBS FREE ENERGY

In chemistry, spontaneous does not mean fast. A spontaneous reaction is one that will occur at a given temperature without the input of energy. It may be fast or slow, but if it's spontaneous just leave it alone and it will happen. Even though the universe isn't crazy about endothermic reactions, sometimes endothermic reactions do occur spontaneously. Why? Because, as we said, the universe likes entropy—disorder. If a particular reaction is endothermic on the one hand (ΔH is positive), but creates greater disorder on the other (ΔS is also positive), the universe is willing to consider it. If the disorder that the reaction creates exceeds the energy it requires, then the reaction may occur spontaneously, even though it's endothermic. Similarly, if a reaction creates order instead of disorder, it may occur spontaneously so long as it's exothermic and the negative enthalpy change exceeds the negative entropy change.

What decides whether a reaction will or won't occur spontaneously? The overall combination of ΔH and ΔS. A negative ΔH tends to mean that a reaction will occur spontaneously, and a positive ΔH tends to mean that it won't. On the other hand, a positive ΔS tends to mean that a reaction will occur spontaneously, and a negative ΔS tends to mean that it won't. The overall combination of ΔH and ΔS is called "Gibbs free energy," or ΔG. The actual formula for ΔG is $\Delta G = \Delta H - T\Delta S$. ($T$ is temperature in degrees Kelvin.)

- If for some reaction at a given temperature, ΔG is negative, then that reaction occurs spontaneously as it is written.

- If ΔG is positive, then that reaction occurs spontaneously at that temperature in the opposite direction from how it's written.

- If ΔG is 0, the reaction is in "equilibrium." (We'll discuss equilibrium later.)

Learn to associate:

Gibbs free energy, ΔG, with:	combination of enthalpy change (ΔH) and entropy change (ΔS)
Negative ΔG with:	spontaneous reaction in the forward direction
Positive ΔG with:	spontaneous reaction in the reverse direction

Review everything we've talked about since our last set of Subject Test-type questions. Then answer this set of questions.

QUESTION TYPE A

(A) Gibbs free energy
(B) Heat of formation
(C) Enthalpy change
(D) Entropy
(E) Kinetic energy

6. Value that determines whether reaction is spontaneous

7. Quantity that determines whether reaction is exothermic or endothermic

8. Indicates the degree of disorder of a system

Question Type B

Directions: Each question below consists of two statements, I in the left-hand column and II in the right-hand column. For each question, determine whether statement I is true or false <u>and</u> whether statement II is true or false and fill in the corresponding T or F ovals on your answer sheet. <u>Fill in oval CE only if statement II is a correct explanation of statement I.</u>

I		II

105. If a reaction is exothermic it always proceeds spontaneously   BECAUSE   the universe favors a negative enthalpy change.

	I	II	CE
105	T F	T F	

106. Ice melting into water is an endothermic process   BECAUSE   heat must be absorbed by ice if it is to melt.

	I	II	CE
106	T F	T F	

Question Type C

28.   ....$C_2H_4(g)$ + ...$O_2(g)$ → ....$CO_2(g)$ + ...$H_2O(l)$

If the equation for the reaction above is balanced using the smallest possible whole-number coefficients, then the coefficient for oxygen gas is

(A) 1
(B) 2
(C) 3
(D) 4
(E) 5

50. $2Na(s) + Cl_2(g) \rightarrow 2NaCl(s) + 822$ kJ

How much heat is released by the above reaction if 0.5 mole of sodium reacts completely with chlorine?

(A)   205 kJ
(B)   411 kJ
(C)   822 kJ
(D) 1,644 kJ
(E) 3,288 kJ

56. $2Al(s) + Fe_2O_3(s) \rightarrow Al_2O_3(s) + 2Fe(s)$

If 80 grams of Al and 80 grams of Fe_2O_3 are combined, what is the maximum number of moles of Fe that can be produced?

(A) 0.5
(B) 1
(C) 2
(D) 3
(E) 4

LET'S SEE HOW YOU DID

Question 6: You know to associate Gibbs free energy with the question of whether a reaction will or will not proceed spontaneously. That alone is enough to tell you the answer. (But if you want to understand it a little better, remember that a reaction is spontaneous if the overall combination of enthalpy change—energy change—and entropy change is adequate to "satisfy" the universe. Even an endothermic reaction—a reaction in which energy is consumed—can proceed spontaneously if it's accompanied by a large enough increase in entropy. The overall combination of energy change and entropy change is known as Gibbs free energy, which is represented by the formula $\Delta G = \Delta H - T\Delta S$ (where T is the temperature in degrees Kelvin). A is right.

Question 7: You should associate enthalpy with the words "exothermic" and "endothermic." Those words are all about whether a reaction releases energy (which the universe tends to like) or consumes energy (which the universe tends not to like). The word <u>enthalpy</u> represents enthalpy change. If enthalpy change is negative, the reaction is exothermic. If it's positive, the reaction is endothermic. That's why C is right.

Question 8: Remember to always associate entropy with disorder. That's what it measures and that's why D is correct.

Question 105: We're into type B. Divide and conquer! Check out the first statement on its own. Is it true? No. The mere fact that a reaction is exothermic does not guarantee it will occur spontaneously. We get spontaneity only if the combination of energy and entropy makes the universe happy. So the first statement is false.

Does the universe favor a negative enthalpy change? Yes. Generally speaking, it likes exothermic reactions. So the first statement is false and the second is true.

Question 106: Divide and conquer. Evaluate the first statement by itself. True? False?—True! For ice to melt into water, it must absorb heat. Since melting involves a net absorption of energy (heat), it is an endothermic process.

What about statement II? Of course your own experience tells you it is true. Ice must absorb heat to melt. Now put both statements together: "Ice melting into water is an endothermic process because heat must be absorbed by ice if it is to melt." Does it make sense? Absolutely. So fill in the CE oval.

Question 28: Starting with A, let's plug in choices. If the coefficient for O_2 is 1, then there are two oxygen atoms on the left. Since we are starting with at least 3 oxygen atoms on the right, this is too small. Now try B. If the coefficient for O_2 is 2, we have 4 oxygen atoms on the left. Putting a 2 in front of H_2O gives 4 oxygen atoms on the right. However, now we cannot balance carbon without upsetting the oxygen balance. So B is also wrong. What about C? If the coefficient for O_2 is 3, then we have 6 oxygen atoms on the left. Putting a 2 in front of CO_2 and H_2O gives 6 oxygen atoms on the right. So far, so good. Notice that putting a "1" in front of C_2H_4 puts carbon and hydrogen in balance, so the answer is C.

Question 50: Notice that the consumption of 2 moles of Na will release 822 kJ of heat. What happens if only 0.5 mole of Na is consumed? Since 0.5 is only 25% of 2, only 25% of 822 kJ of heat will be released. As you can see, choice A is about one quarter of 822 kJ. The other choices are too big. The answer is A.

Question 56: When information about more than one reactant is given, brace yourself for a limiting reactant question. The stoichiometric mole ratio of Al to Fe_2O_3 is 2 to 1. An actual mole ratio that exceeds 2 to 1 indicates Fe_2O_3 is limiting, and vice versa if the ratio is less than 2 to 1. Time for a little math. The atomic weight of one aluminum atom is roughly 27 amu. This means one mole of Al has a mass of about 27 grams. So 80 grams of Al represent nearly 3 moles. The formula weight of Fe_2O_3 is 160 grams. Thus, we have approximately 0.5 mole of Fe_2O_3. So the actual mole ratio of Al to Fe_2O_3 is roughly 3 to 0.5 (or 6 to 1). This makes Fe_2O_3 the limiting reactant. It will get used up first and end the reaction. Notice from the balanced equation that for every 1 mole of Fe_2O_3 consumed, 2 moles of Fe are produced. So 0.5 mole of consumed Fe_2O_3 corresponds to 1 mole of produced Fe. The answer is B.

6

Electron Configurations and Radioactivity

Chemical reactions involve interactions between the electrons of atoms. So to understand how and why atoms react we need to know something about electron configurations—which describe how electrons are arranged in atoms. Radioactivity involves changes that occur within an atom's nucleus.

ELECTRONS AND THEIR ORBITALS

QUANTUM THEORY AND THE HEISENBERG PRINCIPLE

A guy named Niels Bohr thought electrons orbited the nucleus the way planets orbit the sun. He invented the Bohr model of the atom. But the Bohr model is wrong. For the Subject Test, you have to know that electrons definitely do *not* circle the nucleus as planets circle the sun. Electrons do not orbit. Instead, they exist in things called **orbitals**.

Just as a room is a region in a house where a person may be found, an orbital is a region in an atom where an electron may be found. Rooms come in a variety of sizes and shapes, and so do orbitals. A collection of orbitals with roughly similar sizes constitutes an **energy shell**. Electrons that are farther from the nucleus have greater energy than those that are closer. Therefore, electrons in the orbitals of larger energy shells have greater energy than those in the orbitals of smaller energy shells. Each energy shell is designated by a whole number, so we have the 1st (smallest energy shell), 2nd, 3rd energy shell, and so on.

Shape is another important characteristic of orbitals. There are four significant types of orbital shapes. Orbitals that have the same shape in a given energy shell comprise a **subshell**. An *s* subshell always consists of one spherical orbital. A *p* subshell always consists of three dumbbell-shaped orbitals. The *d* and *f* subshells contain five and seven oddly-shaped orbitals, respectively. Any orbital, regardless of size and shape, can hold a maximum of two electrons.

So what's an orbital? The Subject Test writers expect you to associate the word orbital *not* with an orbit, but with something called a "probability function." An orbital describes the "likelihood that an electron will be in a particular location." Also remember that an orbital is not an orbit but is, instead, a probability function, and this has something to do with the quantum theory. It also has something to do with the Heisenberg principle. What's the Heisenberg principle? Well, for the Subject Test, it means this: When it comes to an electron, we can't know both its position and its momentum at the same time.

Associate:

Bohr model with:	the incorrect idea that electrons orbit the nucleus in true orbits, as planets orbit the sun
Electron orbitals with:	probability function
	quantum theory
	Heisenberg principle
Heisenberg Principle with:	the fact that electrons are located in orbitals, not orbits
	the fact that one cannot know an electron's position and velocity at the same time

HERE'S ANOTHER WEIRD THEORY YOU DON'T HAVE TO FULLY COMPREHEND: DE BROGLIE'S HYPOTHESIS

We think of electrons as little tiny dots of negative charge, right? According to De Broglie, we can also think of them as waves of electromagnetic radiation. In fact, according to De Broglie, everything can be thought of as a wave or as a particle.

Associate:

De Broglie's Hypothesis with: the idea that everything can be thought of as a
wave or as a particle

ELECTRON CONFIGURATIONS (WE DO IT THE EASY WAY)

For the Subject Test you'll have to be able to figure out electron configurations. Here's how:

1. The Subject Test will give you a periodic table. First, draw these brackets
   on it:

PERIODIC TABLE OF THE ELEMENTS

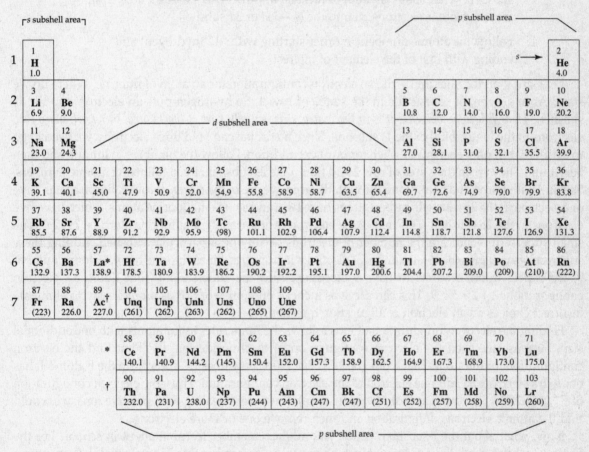

2. Each (horizontal) row of the periodic table corresponds to an energy shell.
   For example, atoms of carbon, C, (row **2**) have outer electrons in the **2nd**
   energy shell; atoms of sodium, Na, (row **3**) have outer electrons in the **3rd**
   energy shell, and so on.

3. When determining which subshell to fill be aware of what area and row you are in. Then remember this:

◆ An element in the s area of row n puts outer electrons into the **n**s subshell.

◆ An element in the p area of row n puts outer electrons into the **n**p subshell.

◆ An element in the d area of row n puts outer electrons into the $(\mathbf{n}-1)d$ subshell.

◆ An element in the f area of row n puts outer electrons into the $(\mathbf{n}-2)f$ subshell.

How does this work? Consider an atom of phosphorus, P, (row 3). It's in the 3rd row and in the p area. So its outer electrons are put into the $3p$ subshell. What about an atom of nickel, Ni, (row 4)? It's in the d area. That means its outer electrons go into the $(4-1)d$ or $3d$ subshell.

4. Follow the atomic numbers in order starting with "1" (hydrogen) and ending with that of the element of interest.

Let's put it all together and write an electron configuration for an atom of fluorine. Where do we start? At hydrogen, of course. It's in the s area of row 1. So hydrogen puts an electron into the $1s$ subshell. *Though helium looks like it is in the p area, it is actually part of the $1s$ area.* Now we have two electrons in the lone orbital of the $1s$ subshell. Since no orbital can hold three electrons, we need to go to a different (higher energy) subshell for our next addition. Follow the numbers to lithium and then beryllium. They are in the s area of row 2 and fill up the $2s$ subshell. Keep following atomic numbers. Starting with boron and continuing through fluorine, we are in the p area of row 2. Boron atoms have one electron in the $2p$ subshell, carbon atoms have two, and so on—to fluorine atoms, which have five electrons in the $2p$ subshell. This makes the electron configuration of a fluorine atom $1s^2\, 2s^2\, 2p^5$. The small superscripts indicate the number of electrons occupying a particular subshell. Adding these superscripts will give the total number of electrons in a species. Since fluorine has the atomic number 9, we expect fluorine atoms to have 9 electrons. Add the superscripts from fluorine's electron configuration: $2 + 2 + 5 = 9$. This can serve as a check on your work or as a quick way to eliminate incorrect choices on an electron configuration question.

Finding the electron configuration of ions follows the same rules as for atoms with one additional step. Suppose we need the electron configuration of the fluoride ion, F^-. First find the electron configuration for the atom. That would be $1s^2 2s^2 2p^5$. Now, how does F^- differ from the F atom? It has one extra electron. So add one electron to the electron configuration. Thus, the electron configuration of F^- is $1s^2 2s^2 2p^6$ (the same as that of a neon atom). If we were dealing with positive ions, we would find the atomic electron configuration and then remove one or more electrons.

Now, what about the f subshell, which you might remember learning about in school? For the Subject Test you don't have to know much about it. Just remember this: If an element has an atomic number greater than 57, some of its electrons are in the f subshell, which is another way of saying they're in f orbitals. So, element number 76, osmium (Os), has electrons in the f subshell. So do gold (Au), samarium (Sm), and terbium (Tb).

ELECTRON CONFIGURATIONS AND THE STABLE OCTET

Look at element number 10, neon (Ne). Its electron configuration is $1s^2\, 2s^2\, 2p^6$. Neon's configuration has one 1 notation and two 2 notations. It has no 3 notations or 4 notations, so the two 2 notations (indicating the 2nd energy shell) reflect its "outermost shell."

Take a look now at neon's outermost shell: $1s^2 2s^2 2p^6$. Count the electrons in the 2nd shell: $2 + 6 = 8$. The fact that neon has 8 electrons in its outermost shell means that it has a stable octet.

Examine element number 18, argon (Ar), and look especially at its outermost shell, which is the 3rd shell: $1s^2\ 2s^2\ 2p^6\ \mathbf{3s^2 3p^6}$. Notice, once again, that argon has a "stable octet." That is, it has eight electrons in its outermost shell. The same is true for

- krypton (Kr): $1s^2\ 2s^2\ 2p^6\ 3s^2\ \mathbf{4s^2}\ 3d^{10}\ \mathbf{4p^6}$

- xenon (Xe): $1s^2 2s^2\ 2p^6 3s^2\ 3p^6\ 4s^2\ 3d^{10}\ 4p^6\ \mathbf{5s^2}\ 4d^{10}\ \mathbf{5p^6}$

- radon (Rn): $1s^2\ 2s^2\ 2p^6 3s^2\ 3p^6\ 4s^2\ 3d^{10}\ 4p^6\ 5s^2\ 4d^{10}\ 5p^6\ \mathbf{6s^2}\ 4f^{10}\ 5d^{10}\ \mathbf{6p^6}$

All the elements just mentioned are **noble gases**, or **inert gases**. They're very stable. They don't like to react with anything or change themselves in any way. They're very happy the way they are. Why? Because the stable octet makes atoms happy. Atoms are happy to have 8 electrons in their outermost shell. Helium [He, atomic number 2] is also very happy. It, too, is an inert gas even though it has only 2 electrons in its outermost shell.

By the way, when we talk generally about the electrons in an atom's outermost shell, we say "valence electrons." So, another way of saying "stable octet" is to say "8 valence electrons." All of the noble gases have 8 valence electrons. Beryllium, on the other hand (Be, atomic number 4)—$1s^2 2s^2$—has 2 valence electrons. Oxygen—$1s^2 2s^2 2p^4$—has 6 valence electrons.

Associate:

Valence electrons with:	number of electrons in outermost energy shell
Stable octet with:	8 valence electrons very stable atom or ion noble gases

Now review the material on electrons, electron configurations, and the stable octet, and try some Subject Test-type questions.

QUESTION TYPE A

(A) Bohr model
(B) De Broglie's hypothesis
(C) Heisenberg principle
(D) Quantum theory
(E) Atomic theory

9. Provides that all matter may be considered as a wave

10. Views electrons in true orbits around nucleus

11. Considers that one cannot know position and velocity of electron at same moment

QUESTION TYPE B

Directions: Each question below consists of two statements, I in the left-hand column and II in the right-hand column. For each question, determine whether statement I is true or false and whether statement II is true or false and fill in the corresponding T or F ovals on your answer sheet. Fill in oval CE only if statement II is a correct explanation of statement I.

I		II
105. The Bohr model of the atom is inaccurate	BECAUSE	an element may exist as several isotopes, each with a different number of neutrons in the nucleus.

	I	II	CE
105	T F	T F	◯

106. Krypton is an extremely unstable atom	BECAUSE	an atom with 8 electrons in its outermost shell tends toward great stability.

	I	II	CE
106	T F	T F	◯

QUESTION TYPE C

31. The electron configuration $1s^2 2s^2 2p^6 3s^2 3p^6 4s^2 3d^7$ represents an atom of the element

    (A) Br
    (B) Co
    (C) Cd
    (D) Ga
    (E) Mg

32. The electron configuration for an atom of the element Tc is

    (A) $1s^2 2s^2 2p^6 3s^2 3p^6 3d^{10} 4s^2 4p^5 5s^2 5p^6$
    (B) $1s^2 2s^2 2p^6 3s^2 3p^6 3d^{10} 4s^2 4p^3 5s^2 4d^5$
    (C) $1s^2 2s^2 2p^6 3s^2 3p^6 3d^{10} 4s^2 4p^3$
    (D) $1s^2 2s^2 2p^6 3s^2 3p^6 3d^{15}$
    (E) $1s^2 2s^2 2p^6 3s^2 3p^6 3d^{10} 4s^2 4p^6 5s^2 4d^5$

33. A neutral species whose electron configuration is $1s^2 2s^2 2p^6 3s^2 3p^6 3d^{10} 4s^2 4p^6 4d^{10} 5s^2 5p^6$ is

    (A) highly reactive
    (B) a positively charged ion
    (C) a noble gas
    (D) a transition metal
    (E) a lanthanide element

Okay? Let's Look at the Answers

Question 9: You may be tempted to pick E, but don't. Atomic theory is associated with a fellow named Dalton and says that all elements are composed of atoms. It preceded the ideas expressed in choices A–D by at least 100 years. For the Subject Test, you're not asked to fully understand the De Broglie hypothesis. You're just supposed to associate it with the statement that "matter can be conceived of as waves, and waves can be conceived of as matter." So B is right.

Question 10: You learned that Bohr incorrectly believed that electrons circled the nucleus in true orbits, the way planets circle the sun. So A is right.

Question 11: You're not supposed to truly understand the Heisenberg principle. You're just supposed to associate it with the idea that one cannot, at any one moment, know an electron's position and velocity. So C is right.

Question 105: We've got a type B question. Divide and conquer! Evaluate the first statement on its own, and decide whether it's true or false. Is it true that according to the Bohr model electrons circle the nucleus in true orbits? Yes, it is.

Now, look at the second statement by itself. Is it true? Yes. Now let's find out if the sentence makes sense. "The Bohr model of the atom is inaccurate because an element may exist as several isotopes each with a different number of neutrons in the nucleus." The sentence is ridiculous. The second statement has nothing to do with the first. The Bohr model is inaccurate because electrons occupy orbitals, not orbits. Both statements are true, but they have nothing to do with each other.

Question 106: We divide and conquer. Evaluate the first statement by itself and decide whether it's true or false. Is it true that krypton is an unstable atom? No, it is not true. Krypton is a very stable atom. Why? Because it has a stable octet in its outermost shell.

Now look at the second statement and evaluate it on its own. Is it true or false? It's true. Atoms with 8 electrons in their outermost shell are stable. The first statement is false and the second is true.

Question 31: Here you're given the configuration and asked to identify the element. The easiest way to answer is to add up the electrons in the configuration. You'll find that the sum is 27. Since the question asks about an *atom*, and not an *ion*, this means the answer is Co, with atomic number 27. So, B is right.

Question 32: Here you're given the element and asked to identify the electron configuration. Following our system shows you that E is right. If you have trouble putting together an electron configuration, you can also arrive at the answer by testing each answer choice. See which answer choices have superscripts that add up to the atomic number of Tc, which is 43. Then eliminate the other answer choices.

Question 33: Do it the easy way. Count up the superscript numbers. They add up to 54. Look on the periodic table and see that element 54 is xenon. Xenon, as you can see from the table, is a noble gas. It's as simple as that.

RADIOACTIVITY

LET'S TALK ABOUT NUCLEI: RADIOACTIVITY AND HALF-LIVES

Nuclei, as you know, are made of protons and neutrons. For some atoms, the combination of protons and neutrons makes the nucleus unstable. It "decays"—on its own—spontaneously. As it decays, it emits things called "radioactive particles." Radioactive particles include alpha (α) particles, beta (β) particles, and gamma (γ) rays. Radioactive particles have lots of energy in them. And if you think about it, that makes sense: A radioactive nucleus is trying to become more stable. Greater stability means lower energy. As it becomes more stable, the radioactive nucleus loses energy.

As a radioactive atom decays—emitting α or β particles and γ rays—it actually changes its identity and turns into something else. It turns into either:

(1) another isotope of the element it originally was or (2) another element with another atomic number.

Some nuclei hold together better than others. Here's another way of saying that: Some nuclei are stable and some are unstable. The unstable ones have a tendency to break apart, and this breaking apart is radioactivity. Unstable nuclei are radioactive.

Why are some nuclei unstable? For the Subject Test, you only have to know that the instability has something to do with the combination of neutrons and protons. Some combinations of neutrons and protons just don't get along too well, and the nucleus in which they're located thus becomes unstable. So what do unstable nuclei do about their unhappy situation? They try to become more stable by altering their particular mix of protons and neutrons. This altering process is called nuclear decay. For the Subject Test, you can think this: When an unstable nucleus undergoes nuclear decay, it's radioactive and it gives off radioactivity. A **Geiger counter** is used to detect and measure radioactive particles.

You should know about four kinds of radioactive decay:

RADIOACTIVE DECAY TYPE 1: ALPHA DECAY

An alpha particle consists of 2 protons and 2 neutrons. When a nucleus gives off an alpha particle, it reduces its atomic number by 2 and it reduces its mass number by 4. Since the atom changes its atomic number, it actually turns into a different element. After all, atomic number is the basis of an atom's identity. If you have an atomic number of 6, then you're carbon and that's all there is to it, even if you used to be oxygen, with an atomic number of 8.

And another thing about alpha particles: since an alpha particle consists of 2 protons and 2 neutrons, it's actually the same thing as a helium-4 nucleus, and it's often symbolized that way: $_2^4\text{He}$. The 4 represents the mass number, and the 2 represents the atomic number (number of protons).

RADIOACTIVE DECAY TYPE 2: BETA DECAY

When a nucleus decides that it will become more stable by reducing its neutron to proton ratio, it takes a neutron and turns it into a proton. The atomic number goes up by 1, since there's an extra proton, but the mass number remains the same. (We lost a neutron, but we gained a proton, so we have no net change in the mass number.) When an atom decides to undergo beta decay it emits a beta particle. A beta particle is identical to an electron. It is symbolized as $_{-1}^{0}e$. So what's beta decay?

- neutron is converted to proton

- beta particle (which is an electron) is emitted

- atomic number goes up by 1; mass number stays the same

RADIOACTIVE DECAY TYPE 3: POSITRON EMISSION

When a nucleus decides that it will be more stable by increasing its neutron to proton ratio, it takes a proton and converts it to a neutron. The atomic number goes down by 1, and the mass number remains the same. When a nucleus undergoes positron emission, it emits a positron. What is a positron? Well, it's a positively charged particle, but it's not a proton. It has the same mass as an electron, but it carries a positive charge. Somehow or other when a proton is converted to a neutron, this positron thing is created. A positron is symbolized as $_1^0e$.

- proton is converted to neutron
- positron is emitted
- atomic number goes down by 1; mass number stays the same

RADIOACTIVE DECAY TYPE 4: GAMMA DECAY

We should also mention gamma rays, which are electromagnetic radiation. Radioactive nuclei often emit gamma rays, which are high-energy particles with the symbol $_0^0\gamma$ together with alpha particles, beta particles, or positrons. When nuclei emit alpha or beta particles, they are sometimes left in a high energy state, but when they emit gamma rays, they become relaxed.

HALF-LIFE

You should know everything we just said about radioactive decay, and you should also know about the speed of radioactive decay. The speed of radioactive decay is called a half-life. If we start with 1,000 g of a radioactive substance and its half-life is 1 year, then

- after 1 year we'll have 500 g of the original sample left.
- after another year we'll have 250 g of the original sample left.
- after another year we'll have 125 g of the original sample left.
- after another year we'll have 62.5 g of the original sample left.
- after another year we'll have 31.25 g of the original sample left.
- after another year we'll have 15.625 g of the original sample left.

And so on. That's how half-lives work.
Associate:

Radioactive decay with:
    unstable nuclei
    spontaneous process
    emission of α and β particles, positrons,
      and γ rays
    half-lives
    alteration of atom's identity

Now review everything we've said about radioactive decay and half-lives and try some Subject Test-type questions.

Question Type A

    (A) Alpha decay
    (B) Beta decay
    (C) Positron emission
    (D) Gamma decay
    (E) Electron capture

14. Often accompanies other radioactive processes

15. Causes an atom to reduce its atomic number by 2
    and its mass number by 4

16. Occurs when a neutron is converted into a proton
    in a nucleus

Question Type B

	I		II

107. Radioactive elements can emit   **BECAUSE**   radioactive elements have
     alpha particles, beta particles,   extremely stable nuclei.
     and gamma rays

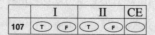

108. If a radioactive sample with a   **BECAUSE**   one half of 100% is 50%, and
     half-life of 40 years decays for   one half of 50% is 25%.
     80 years, 25% of the original
     sample will remain

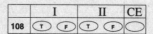

Question Type C

$$^{222}_{86}\text{Rn} \rightarrow ^{218}_{84}\text{Po} + ^{4}_{2}\text{He}$$

39. The radioactive decay shown above is an example
    of

    (A) positron emission
    (B) gamma ray emission
    (C) alpha decay
    (D) beta decay
    (E) ionization

$$^{131}_{53}\text{I} \rightarrow\ ^{131}_{54}\text{Xe} +\ ^{0}_{-1}\text{e}$$

40. The radioactive decay shown above is an example of
    (A) positron emission
    (B) gamma ray emission
    (C) alpha decay
    (D) beta decay
    (E) ionization

TIME FOR SOME ANSWERS

Question 14: As we said earlier, the emission of gamma rays generally accompanies other forms of radioactive decay. So D is right.

Question 15: In order to reduce atomic number by 2, an atom must lose 2 protons. In order to reduce its mass number by 4, it also loses a total of 4 nucleons (protons or neutrons). If the atom loses 2 protons, then it also loses 2 neutrons to make a total loss of 4 nucleons.

  The atom loses 2 protons and 2 neutrons. That's the description of alpha decay, so A is right.

Question 16: Beta decay—which involves the emission of an electron—has the effect of converting a neutron into a proton. Positron emission and electron capture (a decay process that you don't need to know for the Subject Test) have the effect of converting a proton into a neutron. So beta decay is the answer. That's choice B.

Question 107: Divide and conquer. The first statement is true. The second statement is false.

Question 108: Divide and conquer. The first statement is true. If an element decays for one half-life, half of the original sample remains. If it decays for two half-lives, one quarter of the original sample remains. The second statement is also true. Since 25% of the original sample remains, 75% has decayed. The answer depends on whether the whole sentence makes sense. Does it? Yes. Fill in oval CE.

Question 39: Look what's happening. An atom of Rn (radon) with an atomic number of 86 and a mass number of 222 undergoes a change. What happens to it? All of a sudden it's a different element, Po (polonium), with an atomic number of 84 and a mass number of 218. It lost two protons and that's how it lost 2 points in its atomic number. It also lost 2 neutrons, which is how it lost, altogether, 4 points of mass number. This Rn atom has undergone alpha decay. In fact, you can see that an alpha particle—that helium-4 nucleus—has been emitted as a part of the whole process. We're dealing with alpha decay, and that's why C is right.

Question 40: To begin with, you can see that an electron has been emitted, so that's one way to know, right away, that we're dealing with beta decay. You can also see that the atom of I (iodine) has turned into something else—xenon—by increasing its atomic number from 53 to 54. But its mass number stays the same. So, it looks like a neutron was turned into a proton. That's beta decay for sure, and D is right.

The Periodic Table and Bonding

When it comes to scoring high on the Subject Test the periodic table may well be your best friend. Why? Well, for one, it will be there for you on Test day. Second, it can help you answer quite a few Subject Test questions. We just saw how to use the periodic table to figure out an atom's electron configuration. Now we'll take a look at how it can help us predict how atoms will bond.

THE PERIODIC TABLE

1																	18
1 **H** 1.0																	2 **He** 4.0
3 **Li** 6.9	4 **Be** 9.0											5 **B** 10.8	6 **C** 12.0	7 **N** 14.0	8 **O** 16.0	9 **F** 19.0	10 **Ne** 20.2
11 **Na** 23.0	12 **Mg** 24.3											13 **Al** 27.0	14 **Si** 28.1	15 **P** 31.0	16 **S** 32.1	17 **Cl** 35.5	18 **Ar** 39.9
19 **K** 39.1	20 **Ca** 40.1	21 **Sc** 45.0	22 **Ti** 47.9	23 **V** 50.9	24 **Cr** 52.0	25 **Mn** 54.9	26 **Fe** 55.8	27 **Co** 58.9	28 **Ni** 58.7	29 **Cu** 63.5	30 **Zn** 65.4	31 **Ga** 69.7	32 **Ge** 72.6	33 **As** 74.9	34 **Se** 79.0	35 **Br** 79.9	36 **Kr** 83.8
37 **Rb** 85.5	38 **Sr** 87.6	39 **Y** 88.9	40 **Zr** 91.2	41 **Nb** 92.9	42 **Mo** 95.9	43 **Tc** (98)	44 **Ru** 101.1	45 **Rh** 102.9	46 **Pd** 106.4	47 **Ag** 107.9	48 **Cd** 112.4	49 **In** 114.8	50 **Sn** 118.7	51 **Sb** 121.8	52 **Te** 127.6	53 **I** 126.9	54 **Xe** 131.3
55 **Cs** 132.9	56 **Ba** 137.3	57 **La*** 138.9	72 **Hf** 178.5	73 **Ta** 180.9	74 **W** 183.9	75 **Re** 186.2	76 **Os** 190.2	77 **Ir** 192.2	78 **Pt** 195.1	79 **Au** 197.0	80 **Hg** 200.6	81 **Tl** 204.4	82 **Pb** 207.2	83 **Bi** 209.0	84 **Po** (209)	85 **At** (210)	86 **Rn** (222)
87 **Fr** (223)	88 **Ra** 226.0	89 **Ac†** 227.0	104 **Unq** (261)	105 **Unp** (262)	106 **Unh** (263)	107 **Uns** (262)	108 **Uno** (265)	109 **Une** (267)									

	58 **Ce** 140.1	59 **Pr** 140.9	60 **Nd** 144.2	61 **Pm** (145)	62 **Sm** 150.4	63 **Eu** 152.0	64 **Gd** 157.3	65 **Tb** 158.9	66 **Dy** 162.5	67 **Ho** 164.9	68 **Er** 167.3	69 **Tm** 168.9	70 **Yb** 173.0	71 **Lu** 175.0
*	58 Ce 140.1													
†	90 **Th** 232.0	91 **Pa** (231)	92 **U** 238.0	93 **Np** (237)	94 **Pu** (244)	95 **Am** (243)	96 **Cm** (247)	97 **Bk** (247)	98 **Cf** (251)	99 **Es** (252)	100 **Fm** (257)	101 **Md** (258)	102 **No** (259)	103 **Lr** (260)

We've already seen that elements are arranged on the periodic table from left to right in order of increasing atomic number (except, of course, for the *f* area elements, which are alone at the bottom). We've also noted that the periodic table can be divided into four regions: the *s*, *p*, *d*, and *f* areas. By arranging elements in both of these ways, two important ideas emerge:

1. Elements in the same horizontal row, also called a **period**, put electrons into the same energy shells.

2. Elements in the same vertical column, also called a **group**, generally share similar chemical and, sometimes, physical properties.

Let's look at these ideas a little closer, one at a time.

The first period consists of just hydrogen and helium. Both of these elements put electrons into the first energy shell. Since the first energy shell consists of one 1*s* orbital, it can hold only two electrons. So lithium (Li) puts an electron into the second energy shell. So, too, do Be, B, C, N, O, F, and Ne. These elements make up the 2nd period and they fill up the 2nd energy shell. Third-period elements from sodium (Na) to argon (Ar) fill up the 3rd energy shell. Now you may ask: what about an element in the *d* area, like iron (Fe)? Doesn't iron have valence electrons in the 3*d* subshell of the *third* energy shell? Well, it does. But iron also places two electrons into the 4*s* subshell. So it is an element in the 4th period that puts electrons into the 4th energy shell.

CHEMICAL FAMILIES

Valence electrons are the most important electrons in an atom. Why? Because valence electrons can participate in bonds. Since chemical reactions involve bond breaking and bond making, the behavior of valence electrons is responsible for all the chemical reactions you see, from the souring of milk to the burning of rocket fuel. Thus, it makes sense that if two elements have atoms with the same number of valence electrons, they will react similarly. And in general, this is just what happens. We mentioned that the atoms of elements (except helium) in the extreme right-hand column of the periodic table have 8 valence electrons. Do they share similar reactivities? Yes. These elements (including helium) are all typically unreactive. Because they share a similar unreactive nature these elements can be considered part of the noble gas family. A **family** is a collection of elements from the same vertical group that share similar chemical properties. Not surprisingly, the elements of a particular family will have the same number of valence electrons.

There are other important families of elements. The atoms of elements in the extreme left-hand group on the periodic table all have one valence electron (in an *s* subshell). All of these elements (except hydrogen), from lithium (Li) to francium (Fr), also share much in common. Chemically, they are all extremely reactive. (A piece of potassium, for example, will produce a violent reaction if placed into water.) Physically, they are shiny, grayish-white metals. However, they melt more easily than the metals you are used to seeing, like iron or copper. They also tend to have lower densities than the more common metals. Due to their similarities, the elements in the first column, from lithium (Li) to francium (Fr), are called the **alkali metals**.

The elements of the group to the right of the alkali metals from beryllium (Be) to radium (Ra) constitute another family—the **alkaline earth metals**. The atoms of alkaline earth metals have two valence electrons. They are less reactive than the alkali metals but more reactive than common metals like iron and copper. They look a lot like alkali metals. Because of their highly reactive nature, elements of the alkali and alkaline earth families are also collectively known as the **active metals**.

The group of elements alongside the noble gases make up another important family of elements—the **halogens**. The halogens are quite distinct physically: fluorine (F) and chlorine (Cl) are greenish-yellow, toxic gases, bromine (Br) is a brown liquid at room temperature and iodine (I) is a grayish-purple solid. So what makes these elements a family? They each consist of atoms with seven valence electrons and this gives rise to similar chemical properties. All of the halogens are very reactive.

In addition to names like "alkali metals" or "halogens," all groups are indicated by a combination of a Roman numeral and a letter. For instance, the alkali metals group is designated IA. The alkali earth metals group is IIA. The groups in the *d* area all have a designation that ends in a "B." You will not be responsible for these groups on the Subject Test. To the right of the *d* area, designations ending in "A" resume. The group containing aluminum is IIIA, and so on up to VIIA (the halogens) and VIIIA (the noble gases). Notice that for the "A" groups, the Roman number represents the number of valence electrons found in an atom of elements for that group. So a lithium atom (IA) has one valence electron, a carbon atom (IVA) has four valence electrons, and an iodine atom (VIIA) has seven valence electrons.

Metals, Nonmetals, and Semi-Metals

All elements can be classified as either a **metal**, **nonmetal**, or **semi-metal** (also referred to as a **metalloid**). Metals share certain physical characteristics. They are usually shiny. Metals are generally good conductors of heat and electricity. Many metals are said to be **malleable**. This means they can be hammered into thin sheets like aluminum foil. Metals are also often **ductile**, which means that they can be drawn into wire. Copper, for example, is ductile. With the exception of mercury (a liquid), all metals are solid at room temperature. While these characteristics are noteworthy, there is one chemical characteristic that, above all else, makes an element a metal. Metals tend to *give up electrons* when they bond. Roughly 75% of the elements are considered to be metals. Metals can be further divided into active and **transition metals**. The reactive metals of the *s* area are classified as "active." The rest are transition metals. Transition metals are quite different from active metals. They are generally harder, more difficult to melt, and less reactive than active metals. Transition metals include those elements of the *d* and *f* areas. Many of the elements that come to mind when we think of metals are transition metals: iron, copper, gold, and silver. Many compounds that contain a transition metal are intensely colored. For instance, many copper compounds (not the element itself) are blue. The blue color results from the copper compound absorbing the right combination of visible wavelengths so that the visible light reflected from the copper compound appears blue.

Nonmetals are elements that tend to *gain* or *share electrons* when they bond. This distinguishes them from metals. Nonmetals are usually poor conductors of heat and electricity. Some nonmetals like sulfur (S) and phosphorus (P) are solids at room temperature. Unlike metals, they are dull, brittle, and melt easily (though diamond, which is composed of the nonmetal carbon, is an exception to these rules). A few nonmetals such as oxygen (O) and fluorine (F) are gases. The nonmetal bromine (Br) is a liquid at room temperature. So the physical properties of nonmetals vary considerably.

Semi-metals, or metalloids, typically have some of the physical characteristics of metals and some of nonmetals. For instance, silicon (Si) is shiny like a metal, but brittle like a nonmetal. Appropriately enough, semi-metals can be found in between metals and nonmetals on the periodic table.

The diagram below summarizes key families and regions on the periodic table:

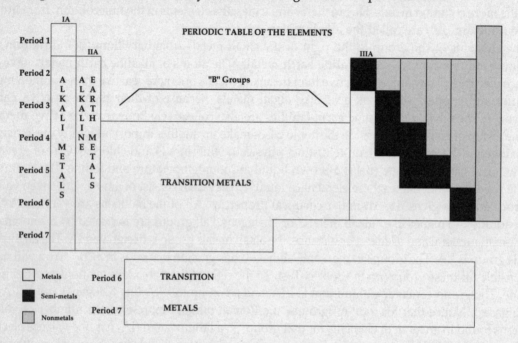

MORE ABOUT THE PERIODIC TABLE:
SOME IMPORTANT TRENDS

The Subject Test will want you to know about four important trends associated with movement along the periodic table.

1. Ionization Energy: The atom's nucleus is positively charged and that's what keeps the negatively charged electrons in their orbitals; the nucleus holds on to the electrons. If you want to take an electron away from an atom and create a positively charged ion, you have to supply energy. For any atom, the amount of that energy is called the ionization energy. As you move from left to right across the periodic table, ionization energy generally increases: It gets harder and harder to pull an electron off of the atom. As we move from top to bottom through a column (group), ionization energy decreases.

Also, each successive removal of an electron from an atom requires significantly higher ionization energy. This increase becomes much more dramatic once you have removed all of an atom's valence electrons. The ionization energy required to remove an inner (non-valence) electron from an atom is incredibly high because inner electrons are strongly attracted by an atom's nucleus. So for an atom with two valence electrons like magnesium (Mg), the energy needed to remove a third electron (its 3rd ionization energy) is very high.

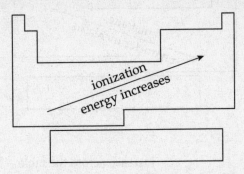

2. Electronegativity: Electronegativity refers to the amount of "pull" that an atom's nucleus exerts on another atom's electrons when it gets itself involved in a bond. Atoms of different elements typically have different electronegativities. As we move across the periodic table from left to right, electronegativity increases (just like ionization energy). Also, as we move down a column (group) on the periodic table, electronegativity decreases.

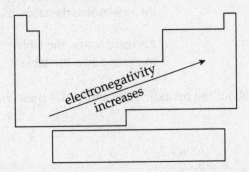

3. Atomic Radius: We can imagine atoms to be roughly spherical. The nucleus is at the center of the sphere. Electrons move about in orbitals within the sphere. Every sphere has a radius—the distance from the center to the edge. The larger the atom, the greater the radius of the atom is. As we move across the periodic table from left to right, atomic radius decreases. As we move down a group, atomic radius increases.

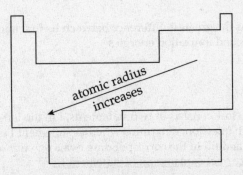

4. Metallic Character: Metallic character is a measure of how much an atom likes to give up electrons and form a positive ion. As we move from left to right across a period, metallic character decreases. As we move from top to bottom down a group, metallic character increases.

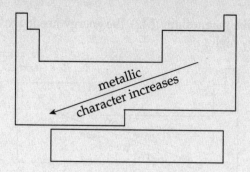

Associate:

Ionization energy with: increase across the table
decrease down the table

Electronegativity with: increase across the table
decrease down the table

Atomic radius with: decrease across the table
increase down the table

Metallic character with: decrease across the table
increase down the table

Review what we've said about the periodic table and tackle these Subject Test-type questions:

QUESTION TYPE A

(A) Na
(B) Ca
(C) Mn
(D) F
(E) Ne

11. Is an alkaline earth metal

12. Regularly forms bonds by receiving electrons

13. Has the greatest difference between its first and
second ionization energies

QUESTION TYPE B

Directions: Each question below consists of two statements, I in the left-hand column and II in the right-hand column. For each question, determine whether statement I is true or false and whether statement II is true or false and fill in the corresponding ovals on your answer sheet. Fill in oval CE only if statement II is a correct explanation of statement I.

	I	II

I   II

109. Only an atom's valence electrons can participate in bonding   BECAUSE   an atom's inner electrons are held too tightly to be shared or transferred.

	I		II		CE
109	T	F	T	F	⬭

110. Potassium has greater metallic character than iron   BECAUSE   potassium has a higher melting point than iron.

	I		II		CE
110	T	F	T	F	⬭

QUESTION TYPE C

39. Which of the following metals is most reactive?

   (A) Sodium, Na
   (B) Magnesium, Mg
   (C) Copper, Cu
   (D) Gold, Au
   (E) Chlorine, Cl

42. All of the following are true regarding nickel, Ni, EXCEPT:

   (A) It is malleable.
   (B) It is ductile.
   (C) It is lustrous.
   (D) It is an insulator.
   (E) It forms colored compounds.

51. Which of the following represents an ordering of the period 4 elements bromine (Br), calcium (Ca), krypton (Kr), and potassium (K) by increasing atomic size?

   (A) K, Kr, Ca, Br
   (B) K, Ca, Br, Kr
   (C) Kr, Br, Ca, K
   (D) Ca, K, Br, Kr
   (E) Br, Kr, Ca, K

IT'S TIME FOR SOME ANSWERS

Question 11: Remember that the Group IIA elements make up the alkaline earth metals. Calcium (Ca) is in this family, so B is right.

Question 12: Metals bond by *losing* valence electrons, so eliminate A, B, and C. That leaves us with fluorine and neon. They're both nonmetals. However, neon is a noble gas and as such it generally does not form bonds, but fluorine does. And it bonds by gaining electrons. D is the answer.

Question 13: The first ionization of an element involves the amount of energy needed to remove one electron from an atom. Second ionization energy deals with removing a second electron. What kind of electrons are hardest to remove from an atom? Inner shell electrons. So the answer should be an element whose atoms have only one valence electron. Why? Because removing a second electron from such an atom would involve removing an inner shell electron and thus take an enormous amount of energy. Hence there would be a great difference between first and second ionization energies. So which of the choices has atoms with one valence electron? Think Group IA elements. Sodium is one of those. So A is right.

Question 109: Time to divide and conquer. Is the first statement true or false? It's true. What about statement II? It's also true. Inner shell electrons spend more time closer to the positive nucleus than do valence electrons. Thus inner shell electrons are too strongly held to be useful in bonding. Let's see if the whole sentence makes sense: "Only an atom's valence electrons can participate in bonding because an atom's inner shell electrons are held too tightly to be shared or transferred." It certainly does. Fill in oval CE.

Question 110: Consider statement I. Does potassium have greater metallic character than iron? Remember that metallic character involves the ease with which an element's atoms can give up electrons. Potassium is much more reactive than iron and thus can be expected to give up its electrons much more readily in order to bond. So potassium does have greater metallic character, making statement I true.
Look at the second statement. Is it true or false? It's false. Potassium is an active metal and active metals tend to have lower melting points than transition metals like iron.

Question 39: Don't be fooled by choice E. Chlorine is very reactive but it's not a metal. Recall that the alkali metals are the most reactive metals. Sodium is a member of the alkali metal family. So A is correct.

Question 40: Nickel is a transition metal. We can expect it to be malleable, ductile, and lustrous (shiny). As is true of many transition metals, nickel compounds are intensely colored (usually a bright green). So eliminate A, B, C, and E. That leaves D. Nickel is a conductor of heat (and electricity) not an insulator. Pick D.

Question 51: Remember the periodic table trends. Within a period as you move from left to right, atoms get smaller. So the smallest atoms of any period 4 element belong to krypton (Kr). Eliminate any choice that does not start with Kr. That makes C the answer.

CHEMICAL BONDING—INTERMOLECULAR VS. INTRAMOLECULAR

Naturally, the Subject Test will want you to know something about bonding—how atoms get together to form molecular or ionic compounds.

You'll need to remember, first of all, that bonding usually works because each atom in the bond ends up with 8 electrons in its outermost shell. It ends up with a stable octet, and that makes each atom happy.

There are three main types of bonds:

1. the ionic bond

2. the covalent bond

3. the metallic bond

1. The Ionic Bond: When atoms in a bond give up one or more electrons to the other, this is called an ionic bond. The atom that gives up the electron becomes a positively charged ion and the one that takes the electron becomes a negatively charged ion. Positive attracts negative and the two ions attract each other. That makes the ionic bond very strong.

For example, when sodium (Na) bonds with chlorine (Cl), the sodium atom gives up its outermost electron to become Na^+ and the chlorine atom receives it to become Cl^-. The Na^+ ion has 8 electrons in its outermost shell. Its electron configuration looks like neon's.

And what about chlorine? Having gained an electron, chlorine also ends up with 8 electrons in its outermost shell. Its electron configuration looks like argon's. The result is sodium chloride: NaCl. The sodium portion is positive and the chloride portion is negative. The two ions are happy because each has a stable octet. Furthermore, one ion is positive and the other is negative. So, they attract one another and stick together. The attraction between a positive charge and a negative charge is called an electrostatic force; this force is very strong. The strength of an ionic bond comes from the electrostatic force between the positive ions and negative ions, and that's where they get their high melting points, hardness, and other physical properties. Ionic bonding is all about electrostatic force. That's what an ionic bond is all about.

For the Subject Test, think like this: *When a metal and nonmetal bond, the result is an ionic bond, which is held together by an electrostatic attraction between a positive and a negative ion.*

When an active metal and nonmetal bond, it is easy to predict the empirical formula of the resulting ionic compound if we know the identity of the elements involved. For example, suppose calcium and fluorine atoms bond. Since we have a metal and a nonmetal these atoms will form an ionic compound. Ionic compounds consist of ions. What ions will be involved? Well, calcium atoms have two valence electrons. Since calcium is a metal it will give up its valence electrons to achieve a stable octet. Since it gives up two electrons a calcium atom will become a Ca^{2+} ion when it bonds. Conversely, fluorine atoms have seven valence electrons. Since fluorine is a nonmetal it will achieve an octet by gaining electrons. So each fluorine atom gains one electron (from calcium) to form a F^- ion. To get the empirical formula of calcium fluoride, begin by writing the cation and anion (in that order) next to each other: $Ca^{2+} F^-$. Now drop the "+" and "−" signs: Ca^2F^1. Finally, take the number next to the metal and write it as the subscript of the nonmetal. And vice versa to get the subscript for the metal. Thus the empirical formula of calcium fluoride is Ca_1F_2, which we simplify to CaF_2. If magnesium and oxygen were to bond, we would get the ions Mg^{2+} and O^{2-}. This would make the empirical formula of magnesium oxide Mg_2O_2, which reduces to MgO (since the ratio 2:2 is equivalent to 1:1).

Substances that are held together by ionic bonds are inevitably solids at room temperature and atmospheric pressure. Ionic solids are characterized by their hardness, brittleness, and high melting points. Although ions are charge carriers, ionic solids cannot conduct electricity because their ions have very restricted movement. However, if an ionic solid is melted, its ions are freer to move and the substance can conduct electricity.

2. The Covalent Bond: When two nonmetals bond, the result is a covalent bond in which two atoms share electrons. By sharing electrons, each atom can achieve a stable octet. In fact, atoms come together to form covalent bonds simply because it's a way for them to obtain a stable octet.

Look how two oxygen atoms get together to form a molecule of O_2. The little dots around the oxygen atom signify oxygen's 6 valence electrons.

$$\overset{..}{\underset{..}{O}}: \quad :\overset{..}{\underset{..}{O}}$$

Now, if each atom could somehow acquire two more electrons, it would have a stable octet. So what happens?

Each atom donates a pair of electrons to share with the other. The shared pairs are attracted to the nuclei of both atoms at the same time. Each atom has, in a sense, 8 valence electrons instead of 6. Each atom is happy. The sharing keeps the atoms together, because each atom now has a full, stable octet.

$$\ddot{O}::\ddot{O}$$

The Covalent Bond That's "Polar": The two oxygen atoms that we just looked at get together and share their electrons equally. But sometimes in a covalent bond one atom tends to hog the electrons. It still shares with the other atom, but it tends to keep the electrons for more than its fair share of the time.

When do atoms hog electrons? When one atom "pulls" harder than the other. When that happens we say that atom has a greater electronegativity than the other. As you know, electronegativity increases as we move from left to right across a period. It decreases as we move from top to bottom in a column.

Think about a water molecule. It's made of two hydrogen atoms and one oxygen atom.

Each hydrogen atom has one valence electron and donates it to be shared with oxygen. The oxygen atom donates two electrons to be shared with the hydrogen atoms.

So what happens? Each hydrogen atom, basically, acquires an electron and has a configuration like helium's (which is very stable). The oxygen atom acquires two electrons and has an electron configuration like neon's (an octet).

So a water molecule can be represented as follows:

$$H:\ddot{O}:H$$

—But—

oxygen's electronegativity is greater than hydrogen's. Oxygen "hogs" the electrons it's sharing with hydrogen. The shared electrons spend more time around the oxygen than they do around the hydrogen.

The result? Each hydrogen atom, not getting its fair share of the shared electrons, has a partial positive charge; the oxygen atom, getting more than its fair share, has a partial negative charge.

When, in a covalent bond, some atoms are partially negative and others are partially positive, we say the covalent bond is polar. Sharing isn't equal. The bond is called a "polar covalent bond."

And what causes a polar covalent bond? A difference in electronegativity between bonded atoms.

3. The Metallic Bond: As you've probably guessed, a metallic bond results when two metals bond. For example, the copper atoms that make up a copper wire are attracted to each other by metallic bonds. In metallic bonding the metal atoms donate valence electrons to become cations. These valence electrons are not directly transferred to another atom as they are in ionic bonding. Instead these valence electrons move about freely throughout the sample, producing an attractive force that keeps the metal cations in place. Often the behavior of the free electrons is referred to as the "sea of mobile electrons." Because of the motions of the free electrons, metals are characteristically good conductors of electricity and heat.

Associate:

		Examples
Ionic bond with:	exchange of electrons to form stable octet; bond between a metal and nonmetal	$NaCl$, CaF_2
Covalent bond with:	sharing of electrons to form stable octet; bond between nonmetals	Cl_2, N_2

| Polar covalent bond with: | unequal sharing of electrons to form stable octet | H_2O, NH_3 |
| Metallic bond with: | sea of mobile electrons; bond between metals | Cu, Ag |

SINGLE, DOUBLE, AND TRIPLE BONDS

To this point we've considered covalent bonds in which one pair of electrons is shared between two atoms. Covalent bonds in which one pair of electrons is shared are also called **single bonds**. In the structural formula of a compound, a single bond is represented by a dash. For example, if we use dashes to indicate the single bonds in a water molecule, we get:

$$H-\ddot{\underset{..}{O}}-H$$

More than one pair of electrons can be shared between atoms in a covalent bond. If two pairs of electrons are shared, the bond is called a **double bond**. If three electron pairs are shared, it is a **triple bond**. In general, as more pairs of electrons are shared between atoms, the bond gets stronger and the distance between bonded nuclei gets shorter. The oxygen molecule we looked at earlier possesses a double bond. It can be represented by a "double dash" as follows:

$$\ddot{\underset{..}{O}}=\ddot{\underset{..}{O}}$$

As you probably figured, a triple bond, like the one in a molecule of hydrogen cyanide, is represented by a "triple dash." Take a look:

$$H-C\equiv N:$$

PREDICTING ΔH USING BOND ENERGIES

Different bonds naturally have different strengths. For instance, the bond between a carbon atom and an oxygen atom is stronger than the bond between two chlorine atoms. When a bond is relatively strong, we say its bond energy is high. Bond energy involves the amount of energy it takes to break a bond. Since a C–O bond is harder to break than a Cl–Cl bond, the C–O bond has higher bond energy than the Cl–Cl bond.

Chemical reactions are about breaking bonds in the reactants (which requires energy) and forming bonds to make products (which releases energy). If we know which bonds are to be made and which are to be broken, and we know their respective bond energies, we can estimate ΔH for the reaction.

Suppose we need to estimate ΔH for the reaction $H_2 + Br_2 \rightarrow 2HBr$, given the following bond energies:

H–H bond : 436 kJ/mol
Br–Br bond : 193 kJ/mol
H–Br bond : 366 kJ/mol

In converting H_2 and Br_2 to products, we must break 1 mole of H–H bonds and 1 mole of Br–Br bonds. This will require (1 mole) (436 kJ/mol) + (1 mole) (193 kJ/mol) = 629 kJ of energy. Notice that we form 2 moles of H–Br bonds. This will release (2 moles) (366 kJ/mol) = 732 kJ of energy. The enthalpy change for the reaction, ΔH, is equal to the net energy change, which is 629 kJ – 732 kJ = – 103 kJ. If 1 mole of H_2 and 1 mole of Br_2 react to form two moles of HBr, the reaction should release 103 kJ. (A positive ΔH would indicate a net absorbance of energy.)

MOLECULAR SHAPES

Some Subject Test questions may deal with the shapes of molecules. Although we can represent molecules in two dimensions on paper, they really exist in three dimensions. If you are given a molecular formula and asked to determine its shape, follow these preliminary steps:

1. Assume the first atom in the formula is the central atom of the structure (unless it is hydrogen, which is never a central atom).

2. Using dots to indicate the valence electrons of each atom, surround the central atom with the others, trying to give each atom an octet. Remember hydrogen needs only 2, not 8, valence electrons to be satisfied. It is important to realize that electrons shared between two atoms count toward the total for both.

Completing steps 1 and 2 will give you the structural formula of a molecule. To determine the shape of that molecule you must consider the number of sites in which valence electron pairs surround the central atom. Since electrons all have the same negative charge, they repel each other. The valence electron sites will arrange themselves around the central atom to be as far from each other as possible. There are two types of electron pair sites: those that contain electron pairs in a bond, and those that contain unbonded electron pairs (also called lone pairs). The number of total electron pair sites and number of lone pairs will dictate the molecule's shape.

Suppose we have a molecule of carbon tetrachloride, CCl_4. The structural formula of CCl_4 is as follows:

$$:\ddot{C}l: \\ | \\ :\ddot{C}l - C - \ddot{C}l: \\ | \\ :\ddot{C}l:$$

Now focus on the central carbon atom. It has four sites in which it is surrounded by electron pairs. How can these four sites move as far from each other as possible around the central carbon atom? You might be tempted to say that they should be 90° apart from each other, as the structural formula shows. But that's thinking in two dimensions, not three. The four sites can actually be 109° apart if they arrange themselves in a tetrahedron (a symmetrical, four-sided figure):

$$:\ddot{C}l: \\ | \\ :\ddot{C}l - C - \ddot{C}l: \\ | \\ :\ddot{C}l:$$

This molecular shape is called "tetrahedral."

A slightly different situation arises in a molecule of ammonia, NH_3. Ammonia's structural formula is as follows:

$$H - \ddot{N} - H \\ | \\ H$$

So there are four distinct electron pair sites around the central atom of nitrogen. Three of these sites involve bonded pairs of electrons, and one involves a lone pair. These four sites arrange themselves in a tetrahedral geometry around nitrogen. *However, when you consider molecular shape, look only at the central atom and its surrounding atoms.* For ammonia, they are arranged like so:

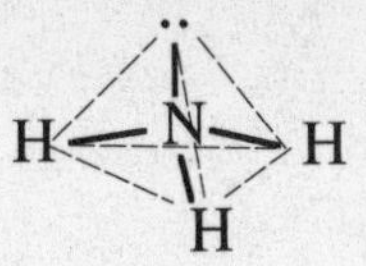

The molecular shape we have here is not exactly a tetrahedron, it's a pyramid with a triangular base. This shape is known as "trigonal pyramidal."

Check out water's molecular structure:

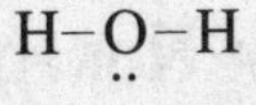

Water has four electron pair sites around the central oxygen atom. However, two of these are lone pairs, so that when we consider water's molecular shape, we get:

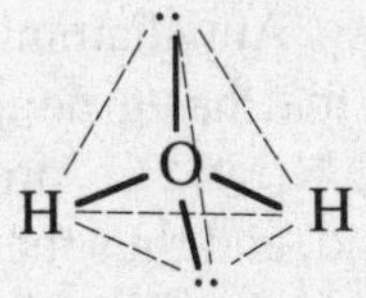

This is another variant of the tetrahedron, with two corners occupied by electron pairs. The shape is known as "bent." The angle between O–H bonds is around 105°.

The central molecule need not have four electron pair sites. If it has two, the molecule's shape will be linear, meaning that there is 180° between bonds. If it has three electron pair sites (and no lone pairs) the sites will be 120° apart and the molecule's shape is trigonal planar. "Planar" means that the shape is flat or two-dimensional. If there are three sites and one is a lone pair, the shape resembles that of the water molecule and is also called "bent."

SUMMARY OF MOLECULAR SHAPES

Number of Electron Pair Sites Around Central Atom	Number of Lone Pairs Around Central Atom	Shape	Bond Angles with Central Atom*	Example
4	0	Tetrahedral	109.5°	CCl_4
4	1	Trigonal Pyramidal	approx. 107°	NH_3
4	2	Bent	approx. 107°	H_2O
3	0	Trigonal Planar	120°	NO_3^-
3	1	Bent	approx. 116°	SO_2
2	0	Linear	180°	CO_2

*assuming atoms of the same element surround the central atom

You should also be aware of two elements that violate the octet rule. Beryllium (Be) atoms are happy with four valence electrons. When beryllium serves as a central atom, the molecule is linear. Boron (B) atoms strive to gain six valence electrons. When boron acts as the central atom in a molecule, that shape is generally trigonal planar.

$$180°$$

:$\ddot{F}$ — Be — $\ddot{F}$:

beryllium difluoride
(linear)

:$\ddot{Cl}$:

$|$ 120°

B

:$\ddot{Cl}$ $\ddot{Cl}$:

boron trichloride
(trigonal planar)

MOLECULES CAN ALSO BE POLAR OR NONPOLAR

We talked earlier about covalent bonds being polar or nonpolar depending on the electronegativity difference between the bonded atoms. Molecules can also be considered polar or nonpolar. How can you tell? If the molecule is diatomic it's easy. Any diatomic molecule that has a polar bond is polar, for example CO. Any diatomic molecule that has a nonpolar bond is nonpolar, for example, all elemental diametric molecules such as Cl_2, N_2, and O_2, are nonpolar. Otherwise there will be some electronegativity difference making the bond, and thus the molecule, polar. Molecules that consist of three or more atoms are generally polar unless the following condition is met: If the central atom has no lone pairs <u>and</u> is surrounded by atoms of one element, then the molecule is nonpolar, for example, CO_2. In effect, what happens is that the individual bond polarities cancel each other out. Imagine a tug-o-war. If both sides are pulling in opposite directions with equal strength, then there is no net movement of the rope. It's the same idea when equal bond polarities are arranged symmetrically about a central atom. So it is possible that a molecule has polar bonds but is, itself, nonpolar. Methane is an example:

H

|

H — C — H

|

H

The individual polarities from each C–H bond cancel out making the methane molecule, CH_4, nonpolar. Also note that methane satisfies our condition for being nonpolar: The carbon central atom has no lone pairs and is surrounded by atoms of one element (in this case, hydrogen).

Look back over what we've discussed since the last question set, and then try the following Subject Test-type questions.

QUESTION TYPE A

(A) Hydrogen gas, H_2
(B) Carbon monoxide, CO
(C) Potassium, K
(D) Aluminum oxide, Al_2O_3
(E) Bromine, Br_2

14. Substance held together by metallic bonds

15. Substance held together by ionic bonds

16. Consists of polar molecules

QUESTION TYPE B

<u>Directions:</u> Each question below consists of two statements, I in the left-hand column and II in the right-hand column. For each question, determine whether statement I is true or false <u>and</u> whether statement II is true or false and fill in the corresponding T or F ovals on your answer sheet. <u>Fill in oval CE only if statement II is a correct explanation of statement I.</u>

I   **II**

105. Some covalent bonds are polar   BECAUSE   atoms of different electro-
     in nature   negativities are unequal in the
                                                    degree to which they attract
                                                    electrons.

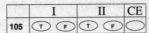

106. Most atoms are less stable   BECAUSE   both ionic and covalent bonds
     in the bonded state than   fail to provide the participating
     in the unbonded state   atoms with a stable electron
                                                    configuration.

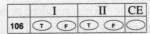

QUESTION TYPE C

56. How many single bonds are in a molecule of car-
    bon dioxide, CO_2?

    (A) None
    (B) One
    (C) Two
    (D) Three
    (E) Four

60. The geometry of a molecule of SO_2 is

    (A) linear
    (B) bent
    (C) trigonal planar
    (D) trigonal pyramidal
    (E) tetrahedral

63. What is the approximate ΔH for the reaction
    $CH_4 + Cl_2 \rightarrow CH_3Cl + HCl$ given the following
    bond energies:
    C–H bond = 410 kJ/mol
    C–Cl bond = 330 kJ/mol
    Cl–Cl bond = 240 kJ/mol
    H–Cl bond = 430 kJ/mol

    (A) +270 kJ
    (B) +110 kJ
    (C) +70 kJ
    (D) –70 kJ
    (E) –110 kJ

LET'S LOOK AT THE ANSWERS:

Question 14: Metals are held together by metallic bonds. Potassium is a metal; therefore, C is the answer.

Question 15: Ionic compounds possess ionic bonding. How can you spot an ionic compound by looking at formulas? Easy. Just find a compound composed of a metal and nonmetal. Choices A, B, and E are substances composed solely of nonmetals. Choice C represents a purely metallic substance. Aluminum oxide consists of Al^{3+} ions from the metal aluminum and O^{2-} ions from the nonmetal oxygen. So D is the answer.

Question 16: A polar molecule must contain polar covalent bonds. Of the choices, only A, B, and E involve covalent bonding. However, A and E involve diatomic molecules consisting of one element. So we know that no difference in electronegativity will arise, and these molecules will contain nonpolar covalent bonds. Carbon monoxide molecules contain different nonmetals. Thus polar covalent bonds will exist. That's why B is right.

Question 105: Type B—divide and conquer! Look at the first statement on its own, and decide whether it's true or false. Well? It's true.

Look at the second statement by itself. It's true. We know that atoms have different electronegativities.

Let's see if the whole sentence makes sense. "Some covalent bonds are polar in nature because atoms of different electronegativities are unequal in the degree to which they attract electrons." Does that make sense? What makes a polar covalent bond polar? The fact that one of the atoms in the bond "hogs" the shared electrons. That's the same as saying one atom has a higher electronegativity than the other (although the phrase "electronegativity" acts as a little camouflage). So the sentence makes sense. Fill in oval CE.

Question 106: Divide and conquer. Look at the first statement by itself. Is it true? No! We know that most atoms "like" bonds because they get to have an electron configuration that resembles a stable octet. What about the second statement? It's false. Ionic and covalent bonding do provide atoms with a stable configuration—the configuration that resembles a stable octet.

Question 56: A carbon atom has four valence electrons, and an oxygen atom has six. Using carbon as the central atom and arranging the atoms to achieve octets yields:

$$\ddot{O}::C::\ddot{O} \quad \text{or} \quad \ddot{O}=C=\ddot{O}$$

Notice that the carbon dioxide molecule consists of two double bonds, but no single bonds. The answer is A.

Question 60: Don't jump to any answers before determining the structure of SO_2. Make sulfur the central atom. Each atom has six valence electrons. Arranging atoms to obtain octets gives:

$$\ddot{O}::\ddot{S}::\ddot{O}$$

Notice there are three electron pair sites around the central sulfur atom (a double or triple bond only "counts" as one site, same as a single bond). So the central atom has three electron pair sites, one of which is a lone pair. This will result in a "bent" shape. So B is correct.

Question 63: In going from reactants to products, one mole of C–H bonds and one mole of Cl–Cl bonds are broken. So 410 kJ + 240 kJ or 650 kJ are needed for bond breaking. The reaction produces one mole of C–Cl bonds, one mole of H–Cl bonds, and three moles of C-H bonds. So 330 kJ + 430 kJ or 760 kJ are released by bond making. The net change, which is roughly equal to ΔH, is 650 kJ – 760 kJ or –110 kJ. So this reaction is exothermic. And the answer is E.

8

Solids, Liquids, and Gases

After spending a few chapters focusing on atoms, electrons, molecules, and other things we can't observe with our eyes, we'll now focus on the three states of matter: solids, liquids, and gases.

GASES

You know, of course, that gas is a state of matter, and all matter theoretically becomes gaseous if its temperature exceeds its boiling point, however high or low that boiling point may be. The Subject Test writers will certainly ask you a couple of questions about things that gases do.

Look at these gas molecules moving around in a box.

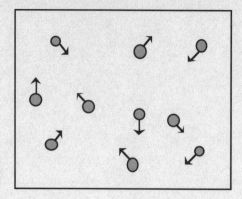

The molecules are moving, banging, and bumping against one another and against the walls of the box, in every which way. Because they bang into the walls of the box, they create pressure against the walls. When we're talking about a gas and we say "pressure," we're talking about the amount of force (which really means the amount of "bang") the gas particles are exerting on the walls of their container per unit area of the container. As we've said before, we measure pressure in torr or millimeters of mercury (mmHg) or atmospheres (atm). Each of these units represents a unit of force per area, and 760 torr = 760 mmHg = 1 atm.

The gases on the Subject Test are assumed to be "ideal gases." An **ideal gas** satisfies these conditions:

1. Its molecules do not attract or repel each other.

2. Its molecules occupy an insignificant volume compared to the volume of the container holding the gas.

No gas ever acts completely like an ideal gas. In real gases, molecules attract each other slightly, which causes them to strike the walls of their container with slightly less force than ideal gases. However, most gases (especially lighter ones like hydrogen and helium) under typical temperatures and pressures act enough like an ideal gas to make the concept useful.

When you deal with gases on the Chemistry Subject Test, you've got to know the relationships between temperature, volume, and pressure.

1. Pressure and Temperature: Suppose we start with a 3 L sample of gas at 200 K and a pressure of 900 torr. Let's say we then raise the temperature to 400 K without changing the volume of the container. What will happen? Because we doubled the temperature, the pressure will double too—to 1,800 torr. In other words, if volume doesn't change, then pressure is directly proportional to temperature in degrees Kelvin. Double the temperature (K), and you'll double the pressure.

Why is that? The increased temperature provides the gas molecules with more heat. The gas molecules take the heat and convert it to kinetic energy, which means, basically, movement. The molecules start moving faster. If they're moving faster, they're banging harder into the walls of the container, and that increases pressure. Pretty simple, right?

When you think about raising the temperature of a gas and thereby increasing the kinetic energy of its gas molecules, you should think of the **kinetic molecular theory**, which means that the kinetic energy of a gas molecule (the degree to which it's banging around all over the place) increases proportionally with temperature in degrees K.

2. Pressure and Volume: Now suppose we start with the same 3 L sample of gas at 200 K and 900 torr. Imagine, without changing the temperature, that we suddenly increased the size container to 6 L. We've doubled the volume of the gas, and we haven't changed the temperature. What happens to pressure? It goes down by one half, to 450 torr. Here's why. It's true that the gas molecules have just as much kinetic energy as they had before, but they've got twice the volume to move around in. Thus, gas molecules will hit the container walls less often—exerting half as much pressure.

So remember, when there's no change in temperature, volume and pressure are inversely proportional. Triple the volume, and you'll cut the pressure to one third of its original value. Cut the volume by one half, and you'll double the pressure.

MAKING GASES EVEN SIMPLER: THE IDEAL GAS EQUATION

The relationship between pressure, volume, amount (moles), and temperature of an ideal gas is given by the "ideal gas equation":

$$PV = nRT$$

P = pressure in atm (mmHg or torr)

V = volume in liters

n = number of moles of gas particles in the container

R = the ideal gas constant

T = temperature in Kelvin

The ideal gas equation is practically all you need to answer Subject Test questions about gases and their temperature, volume, or pressure. First of all, let's talk about R—the ideal gas constant, which is equal to $0.082 \dfrac{L-atm}{mol-K}$—but you don't have to remember that number.

Just look at the equation, and you can see that P is inversely proportional to V.

P and V are both directly proportional to T, and P and V are both directly proportional to n. Get that straight and you can't miss.

Here's another way to look at it. When you think about the ideal gas equation, think like this:

- Values on the *same* side of the equation are *inversely* proportional to each other when the other variables are held constant.

- Values on *opposite* sides of the equation are *directly* proportional to one another when the other variables are held constant.

MORE ABOUT GASES: PARTIAL PRESSURES

Sometimes the Subject Test will tell you about a container filled with more than one gas. Each gas, of course, exerts a pressure. The pressure of any one gas within the container is called its partial pressure, and all of the partial pressures add up to create the total pressure inside the container.

When the Subject Test writers tell you about a container that has different gases in it, they might ask you to figure out the partial pressure for one of them. Let's say there are 100 moles of gas in a container: 20 moles of oxygen, 30 moles of hydrogen, and 50 moles of nitrogen. Oxygen makes up

20% of the gas. That means that it will also make up 20% of the total pressure. So if you're told that the total pressure within the container is 500 torr, you know that

- oxygen's partial pressure is $(0.20)(500) = 100$ torr

- hydrogen's partial pressure is $(0.30)(500) = 150$ torr

- nitrogen's partial pressure is $(0.50)(500) = 250$ torr

  $100 + 150 + 250 = 500$ torr

If you know the ideal gas equation ($PV = nRT$) and what you've just learned about partial pressures, you'll be in good shape when the Subject Test asks you about gases.

Let's try some Subject Test-type questions.

QUESTION TYPE A

(A) Ideal gas constant
(B) Celsius temperature
(C) Kelvin temperature
(D) Partial pressure
(E) Volume

10. Is inversely proportional to moles of gas, when other variables are held constant

11. Sum for each gas in a mixture yields total for that mixture

12. Is a measure of average kinetic energy of gas molecules in a closed container used in the ideal gas equation

QUESTION TYPE B

Directions: Each question below consists of two statements, I in the left-hand column and II in the right-hand column. For each question, determine whether statement I is true or false and whether statement II is true or false and fill in the corresponding T or F ovals on your answer sheet. Fill in oval CE only if statement II is a correct explanation of statement I.

	I			II

109. If an ideal gas is located in a closed container and temperature is increased, the average speed of the molecules will always increase as well

BECAUSE

for an ideal gas, temperature and moles of gas are inversely proportional.

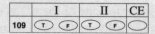

	I		II	CE
109	T F		T F	◯

110. For an ideal gas, pressure and volume have no relationship

BECAUSE

according to the ideal gas law, temperature and volume are directly proportional when other variables are held constant.

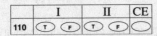

	I	II	CE
110	Ⓣ Ⓕ	Ⓣ Ⓕ	◯

QUESTION TYPE C

61. Four grams of helium are in a sealed, 2 L container. If helium were a true ideal gas, how would its behavior differ from its actual behavior?

(A) Its molecules would attract each other.
(B) Its molecules would repel one another.
(C) Its molecules would be in continuous motion.
(D) It would exert more pressure on the container walls.
(E) It would exert less pressure on the container walls.

ideal gas has no attraction!

62. A closed mixture of helium, hydrogen, and carbon dioxide gases are at a pressure of 1,200 torr in a 4 L container. There are a total of 24 moles of gas molecules in the container. If the helium concentration is 2 moles/L and the hydrogen concentration is 1.5 moles/L, which of the following expresses the approximate partial pressure of the carbon dioxide in torr?

8 He
6 H
10 CO₂

(A) $\dfrac{1}{24} \times 1200$ torr

(B) $\dfrac{2}{24} \times 1200$ torr

(C) $\dfrac{3}{24} \times 1200$ torr

(D) $\dfrac{10}{24} \times 1200$ torr

(E) $\dfrac{14}{24} \times 1200$ torr

LET'S LOOK AT THE ANSWERS

Question 10: Remember that values on the same side of the ideal gas equation are inversely proportional. In $PV = nRT$, both R and T (Kelvin temperature) are on the same side as n (moles of gas). Since R (ideal gas constant) cannot change with a change in moles, the answer must be C.

Question 11: In a mixture of gases, each will fill its container, so E cannot be right. It doesn't make sense to add temperatures to get a total temperature, so B and C are eliminated. That leaves A and D. The ideal gas constant is not something that would be summed for each gas either. So the answer is D. Recall that adding the partial pressures of a mixture gives the total pressure of that mixture.

Question 12: Don't forget that temperature is a measure of average kinetic energy. Furthermore, Kelvin temperature increases in proportion to changes in kinetic energy. So C is right.

Question 109: We're into type B, so it's time to divide and conquer. What do you think of the first statement by itself? It's true. It's basically telling you about the kinetic molecular theory.

The second statement is also true. You know it's true if you know the ideal gas law: $PV = nRT$. Temperature and pressure are on opposite sides of the equation, so they're directly proportional when other variables are constant.

Let's see if the whole sentence makes sense. "If an ideal gas is located in a closed container and temperature is increased, the average speed of the molecules will always increase as well because for an ideal gas, temperature and moles of gas are inversely proportional.

The sentence does not make sense. Both statements are true, but when they're put together the two halves have nothing to do with each other.

Question 110: Divide and conquer. How's the first statement? It's false. We know that pressure and volume do have a relationship. The ideal gas law tells us they do: $PV = nRT$.

Now, what about the second statement? It's true. Look at the ideal gas law: $PV = nRT$. Temperature and volume are on opposite sides of the equation, so they're directly proportional when other variables are constant. The first statement is false and the second is true.

Question 61: Don't fall into the temptation trap. In an ideal gas there is *no* attraction or repulsion between molecules. So eliminate A and B. Molecules are already in continuous motion in a real gas. So C shows no difference. Eliminate it. In a real gas, molecules will slightly attract each other. As a result gas molecules will strike container walls with less force than if no attraction existed. Less force means lower pressure. So pressure is less in the real situation as compared to the ideal. The question asks how the ideal case differs from the real. It differs by involving more gas pressure than in the real case. So D is right.

Question 62: This is a partial pressure question. You know the total pressure is 1,200 torr, and you know that each gas contributes to the total pressure by exerting a partial pressure according to the number of its molecules that are flying around as a fraction of all molecules flying around.

There are a total of 24 moles of molecules flying around. The helium concentration is 2 moles/L. We've got 4 L total, so there are $2 \times 4 = 8$ moles of helium molecules in the mixture. Hydrogen's concentration is 1.5 moles/L so we've got $1.5 \times 4 = 6$ moles of hydrogen molecules. $8 + 6 = 14$. Since the total number of moles of molecules—for all 3 gases—is 24, there must be 10 moles of carbon dioxide molecules in the mixture.

If there are 10 moles of carbon dioxide molecules and 24 moles of molecules total, carbon dioxide's mole fraction $= \dfrac{10}{24}$. Total pressure = 1,200 torr and carbon dioxide's pressure, therefore, is $\dfrac{10}{24} \times 1,200$ torr. So D is right.

INTERMOLECULAR FORCES

All gases, virtually all liquids at room temperature, and many solids are molecular substances; that is, they are composed of molecules. In the previous chapter we took a look at covalent bonding, which attracts atoms to each other *within* a molecule. Now we want to consider the attractive forces *between* molecules. These **intermolecular forces** are responsible for the physical properties of matter such as boiling point. Intermolecular forces typically involve the positively-charged portion of one molecule attracting the negatively charged portion of a nearby molecule. In a sample of water, the partial negative pole ($\delta-$) on one molecule is attracted to the partial positive pole ($\delta+$) on another as follows:

Intermolecular force

These forces of attraction are present between molecules throughout the water sample, holding it together.

HYDROGEN BONDING

The attractive forces that hold water together are special types of intermolecular force called **hydrogen bonds**. Hydrogen bonds occur between hydrogen [when it's bonded to a highly electronegative atom of nitrogen (N), oxygen (O), or fluorine (F)] on one molecule and a N, O, or F atom on a nearby molecule. Hydrogen bonds are stronger than most other types of intermolecular attraction. However, even the strongest intermolecular force is far weaker than a covalent or ionic bond.

SOLIDS, LIQUIDS, AND GASES

It is the relationship between a substance's average kinetic energy (how energetically its molecules are moving about) and the strength of its intermolecular forces that determine if the substance is a solid, liquid, or gas. In a solid, a substance's intermolecular forces are much stronger than the average kinetic energy of its molecules. As a result, molecules are restricted in their ability to move about. Strong intermolecular forces permit molecules to merely vibrate in place. This gives solids the characteristic "definite size and shape" associated with them.

In a liquid, intermolecular forces are still more significant than the energy of molecules. However, molecules in a liquid have enough kinetic energy to move past each other. This allows for the liquid's ability to flow. Despite being able to move about, molecules in a liquid are still confined within the sample.

The relationship between intermolecular forces and molecular kinetic energies is vastly different in a gas. Molecules in a gas are so energetic that they easily overcome intermolecular attraction. Thus gas molecules spread about to evenly fill the volume of whatever container they are in.

So when you boil some water, what really happens? Adding heat to the water increases the kinetic energy of water molecules. At the boiling point, molecules have become energetic enough to overcome the intermolecular forces between H_2O molecules. This allows them to rearrange into a gas—characterized by relatively large amounts of space between molecules. When steam condenses into water, the opposite occurs. Molecules lose energy to the point that intermolecular forces become significant, bringing them close together and limiting their movement. Notice that changes of state involve intermolecular forces and not covalent bonds. As ice, water, or steam, H_2O molecules are still intact. What changes is the extent to which H_2O molecules can move about.

What's a Network Solid?

You may need to know about something called a "network solid." No, it has nothing to do with television. A **network solid** is a covalently bonded substance that does not consist of individual molecules. Instead it consists of atoms forming molecules which attract each other through intermolecular forces, atoms throughout the substance attract each other through covalent bonding. So in a sense the substance is one giant molecule. For this reason network solids are sometimes called macromolecular substances. Since covalent bonds are much stronger than intermolecular forces, network solids are extremely hard and difficult to melt. Diamond (pure carbon network) and quartz (SiO_2 network) are both network solids.

Yikes! Do I Need to Know about Hydrates?

Yeah. But they're nothing you can't handle. A **hydrate** (or hydrated salt) is an ionic substance in which water molecules bind to the ions in a fixed ratio. For example, in copper sulfate pentahydrate the ratio is given by the formula: $CuSO_4 \cdot 5H_2O$. Anytime you see "$\cdot H_2O$" in a formula, figure that it's a hydrate. You may need to determine the percent composition of water in the hydrate (called its "water of hydration"). Just remember to multiply the molecular weight of water (18 amu) by the coefficient that precedes H_2O in the formula. For a unit of $CuSO_4 \cdot 5H_2O$, the formula weight is approximately $64 + 32 + (4)(16) + 5(18) = 250$ amu. The percent water in the hydrate is about

$$\frac{90}{250} \times 100\% \text{ or } 36\%.$$

PHASE CHANGES

Every substance "knows" how to be a solid, liquid, or gas, each of which is called a "state" or a "phase." Whether a substance is in one phase or another depends on temperature and pressure. H_2O, for instance, turns from solid to liquid or from liquid to solid at 0°C and 1 atm. It turns from liquid to gas or gas to liquid at 100°C and 1 atm.

When a substance turns from solid to liquid, we say it "melts." When it moves in the reverse direction—from liquid to solid—we say it "freezes." So when we think of H_2O at 1 atm we say 0°C is the melting point, or freezing point: the temperature at which it melts and freezes. When a substance turns from liquid to gas it vaporizes, and when it goes the other way—from gas to liquid— it condenses. When we think of H_2O at 1 atm we say 100°C is the boiling point, which means, generally, the temperature at which it vaporizes or condenses.

You should also be aware of "sublimation." This occurs when a solid turns directly into a gas. Dry ice (solid carbon dioxide) does this when it is exposed to room temperature conditions.

THE PHASE CHANGE DIAGRAM

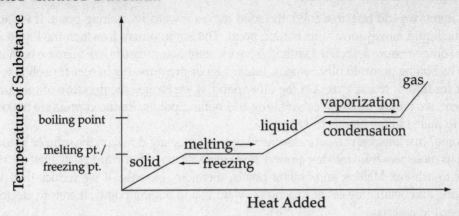

You might very well see one of these diagrams on the Chemistry Subject Test. Let's understand what it's telling us. This is the phase change diagram for some substance at some pressure. Starting from the lower left, we see that as heat is added to the substance, its temperature rises. Moving left to right, we reach the first plateau. That's the substance's freezing point/melting point. Notice that the curve (line) is flat for a little while as the substance passes its melting point. In other words, to move from a solid to liquid phase, we add heat—but for a while the substance doesn't change temperature. Without changing temperature, it absorbs the heat needed just to get from one phase to the next. The amount of heat that it takes a substance just to move from solid to liquid phase—just to pass through its melting point—is called the "heat of fusion." For H_2O at 1 atm, the heat of fusion is 80 cal/g, meaning that it takes 80 calories to get 1 gram of H_2O from 0 °C in the solid phase (ice) to 0 °C in the liquid phase (water).

After the substance melts, if we continue to add heat, it moves toward its boiling point. In order to get the liquid through its boiling point—to move from a liquid to gaseous phase—we add heat, and for a while the substance doesn't change temperature. It absorbs heat just to get from one phase to the next. The amount of heat it takes just to move the substance from the liquid to gaseous phase—just to get through its boiling point—is called the "heat of vaporization," or "heat of condensation." For H_2O at 1 atm, the heat of vaporization is 540 cal/g, meaning that it takes 540 calories to get 1 gram of H_2O from 100 °C in the liquid phase (water) to 100 °C in the gaseous phase (steam).

Look again at the phase change diagram. This time start at the right and move to the left. Here's what the diagram tells you:

1. you start with a gas.

2. you remove heat until the gas reaches its condensation point.

3. you continue to remove heat equal to the heat of condensation, and then without a change in temperature, the substance turns from gas to liquid.

4. you continue to remove heat and reach the substance's freezing point.

5. you continue to remove heat, equal to the substance's heat of fusion, and then without a change in temperature, the substance turns from liquid to solid.

6. you continue to remove heat and the solid becomes colder.

PHASE CHANGE AND PRESSURE

We know that if we add heat to a solid, the solid moves toward its melting point. If we add heat to a liquid, the liquid moves toward its boiling point. The environment in which the liquid or solid is sitting has some pressure associated with it. If we increase that pressure, we increase both its melting point and its boiling point. In other words, under higher pressure, it's harder for solids to melt and it's harder for liquids to vaporize. On the other hand, if we reduce the pressure of the surrounding environment, we reduce a substance's melting and boiling points. Reduced pressure makes it easier for solids to melt and for liquids to vaporize.

How come? Just imagine pressure as something that's pushing down on the solid or liquid, tending to prevent its molecules from moving around. If we increase that downward push, melting and boiling are harder to achieve. Melting and boiling points, therefore, increase. If we reduce that downward push, melting and boiling are easier to achieve. Melting and boiling points, therefore, decrease.

Learn to associate:

Increased pressure with: <u>higher</u> melting and boiling points

Decreased pressure with: <u>lower</u> melting and boiling points

A very important exception is ice (water) which displays the opposite relationship.

ANOTHER TYPE OF PHASE DIAGRAM

We mentioned that whether a particular substance is a solid, liquid, or gas depends on its pressure and temperature. The relationship between pressure, temperature, and phase can be neatly shown in the following type of phase diagram:

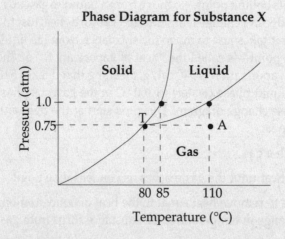

Phase Diagram for Substance X

Each region—solid, liquid, and gas—represents the phase that will exist for substance X at a given set of pressures and temperatures. For example, at a pressure of 0.75 atm and 110 °C (point A), substance X is a gas. The normal freezing point (freezing point at 1 atm) for substance X is 85 °C and the normal boiling point (at 1 atm) is 110 °C. Any point on the phase diagram that lies on a line means that the substance can exist in both phases at that particular pressure and temperature. For instance, substance X can be a solid or a liquid at 1 atm and 85 °C. Point T is a special combination of pressure and temperature called the **triple point**. At this particular pressure and temperature combination a substance can exist as a solid, liquid, or a gas. For substance X the triple point is at 0.75 atm and 80 °C.

In general, when a substance is at relatively low pressure and high temperature it exists as a gas. When it is at relatively high pressure and low temperature, it is a solid. The liquid phase dominates at moderate pressures and temperatures. Keeping these relationships in mind can help you to predict how a change in pressure or temperature will affect the phase of a substance. For instance, if substance X at 0.75 atm and 110 °C (point A) is put under increasing pressure and its temperature is maintained, what phase change will eventually occur? Look at the phase diagram for substance X. Follow the dotted line up from point A (in the direction of increasing pressure). You'll see that beyond 1.0 atm (at 110 °C) substance X will become a liquid. So an increase in pressure at constant temperature causes substance X to condense.

Phase Changes without Melting Points and Boiling Points: Vapor Pressure

When a solid reaches its melting point and absorbs its heat of fusion, all of its molecules have enough kinetic energy to become liquid. When a liquid reaches its boiling point and absorbs its heat of vaporization, all of its molecules have enough kinetic energy to become gaseous.

—But—

even if a solid is well below its melting point, a small number of its molecules always get hold of enough kinetic energy to become liquid. So when you have a block of ice stored in a freezer a little bit of it is always melting to form liquid. Then the molecules of that liquid immediately lose some kinetic energy, and the liquid becomes solid again. But right away, a few other molecules gain enough kinetic energy for a few seconds to become liquid. They, too, become solid again after a few seconds. But a few other molecules take their place, becoming liquid, and then solid again. In other words, every solid is always melting—on the molecular level—and the molecules that melt are always refreezing.

The same goes for liquids. Even if it's well below the boiling point, a few molecules of liquid are always grabbing hold of enough kinetic energy for a second or two to escape into the gaseous phase. This is called **evaporation**. If they're in a closed system (like a pot with a lid on it) they quickly lose some kinetic energy and "fall back" into the liquid phase only to be replaced continuously by a couple of other molecules that manage to escape. They, too, fall back into the liquid phase to be replaced by other molecules that manage to escape for a few seconds. So a sample of liquid below its boiling point is always evaporating—a little bit—and then condensing again (if the liquid is enclosed).

When liquids below their boiling point are evaporating—a tiny little bit all of the time—this creates a **vapor pressure**. All liquids in a closed system at all temperatures exert some vapor pressure, which means they're evaporating, always—a little bit—and then falling back again into the liquid state.

Now, what if the liquid is *not* in a closed system, but is out in the open environment? Here's what happens. A little bit evaporates and is blown away. Then a little more evaporates and is blown or drifts away. Ultimately the whole sample evaporates, and it's gone. If you put a pot of water outside at a temperature of 10 °C, it will eventually evaporate, although it will take some time. At any one moment, most of the molecules don't have enough kinetic energy to escape as gas. But a few of them do. As these few evaporate and blow away, a few more somehow gain enough kinetic energy to evaporate. They, too, are blown away. This keeps happening until the entire sample disappears.

If, instead of leaving the water outside on a cold day we put it on the stove and brought it to its boiling point, all of the molecules would have enough kinetic energy to escape as gas and the whole sample would quickly vaporize.

While we're talking about all of this, let's look at the word "volatile." For some liquids, molecules need less kinetic energy to become a gas. If you leave a bucket of gasoline and a bucket of water outside on a cold day—a temperature well below the boiling point of either substance—both will eventually evaporate. But the gasoline will evaporate much faster than will the water. That's because the intermolecular forces that attract gasoline molecules to each other are weaker than the hydrogen bonds that attract water molecules. Thus gasoline molecules need less kinetic energy than do water molecules to overcome the intermolecular forces that hold them in the liquid state. Because gasoline evaporates more readily than water, we can say that its *vapor pressure is higher* and *it is more volatile* than water.

Learn to associate:

Vapor pressure with:	molecules of liquid escaping into gas phase even though temperature is below boiling point
More volatile with:	liquid that has higher vapor pressure; evaporates <u>more</u> readily when temperature is below boiling point (compared to a less volatile liquid)
Less volatile with:	liquid that has lower vapor pressure; evaporates <u>less</u> readily when temperature is below boiling point

ENERGY AND PHASE CHANGES

As we saw from the phase change diagram, a substance has to absorb heat to turn from solid to liquid to gas. It has to lose heat to turn from gas to liquid to solid. Heat, as you remember, is a form of energy. So, when we think of phases and energy we remember that among the three phases for a particular substance, solid is lowest in potential energy and gas is highest in potential energy. We say "potential energy" because that is the form of energy that depends on the arrangement of particles (which is different in the solid, liquid, and gaseous states).

IF THE UNIVERSE LIKES LOW ENERGY, HOW COME IT'S WILLING TO LET SOLIDS MELT AND TO LET LIQUIDS VAPORIZE? THE ANSWER IS: *ENTROPY*

When ice melts and turns into water, its entropy increases. How do we know that? Well, just think of the fact that ice is solid—it stays put—it's very orderly. Water can run, flow, and spill all over the place. It's not so orderly. And steam? It runs all over the whole room if you let it: fogs up the windows, gets the walls wet—very disorderly.

Under some conditions, the increase in entropy (which the universe likes) is enough to overcome the increase in energy (which it dislikes) and make the phase change from solid to liquid or liquid to gas spontaneous. What are these conditions? Well, if we are considering melting, we need a temperature above the melting point for the phase change to be spontaneous. Better to put ice in an oven than in a freezer if we want it to melt. For boiling to be spontaneous, we need a temperature above the boiling point. No surprise there.

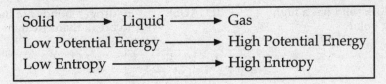

Learn to associate:

Melting point/freezing point with:	solid to liquid/liquid to solid heat of fusion
Boiling point with:	liquid to gas/gas to liquid heat of vaporization/heat of condensation
Solid to liquid to gas with:	addition of heat lower potential energy to higher potential energy lower entropy to higher entropy
Gas to liquid to solid with:	removal of heat higher potential energy to lower potential energy higher entropy to lower entropy

Take time to review what we've discussed since the last set of Subject Test-type questions and then give this set a shot:

QUESTION TYPE A

(A) $N_2O_4(g) + heat \rightarrow 2NO_2(g)$
(B) $I_2(s) \rightarrow I_2(g)$
(C) $CHCl_3(\ell) \rightarrow CHCl_3(g)$
(D) $Br_2(s) \rightarrow Br_2(\ell)$
(E) $O_2(g) \rightarrow O_2(\ell)$

12. At constant pressure, requires a decrease in heat to occur

13. Is an example of sublimation   B

14. Produces a decrease in system entropy   E

15. Enthalpy change for the process can equal heat of fusion for the process   A

QUESTION TYPE B

	I		II
111.	A network solid has a high melting point	BECAUSE	hydrogen bonds are more difficult to break than covalent bonds.

	I	II	CE
111	Ⓣ Ⓕ	Ⓣ Ⓕ	◯

	I		II
112.	A pot of water will boil above 100°C at high elevations	BECAUSE	the average kinetic energy of molecules must increase as the pressure on them increases.

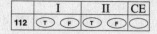

	I	II	CE
112	Ⓣ Ⓕ	Ⓣ Ⓕ	◯

QUESTION TYPE C

52. A 10 gram sample of which substance is held to-gether by hydrogen bonding?

    (A) H_2
    (B) NH_3
    (C) C_3H_8
    (D) CaH_2
    (E) HBr

60. A substance possessing a characteristically low vapor pressure can be expected to have

    (A) extremely weak intermolecular forces
    (B) a relatively small heat of vaporization
    (C) a relatively high boiling point
    (D) a relatively high rate of evaporation
    (E) a significantly high percentage of molecules having high kinetic energy

ANSWER TIME

Question 12: Think back to the first phase change diagram. Which way did processes go that required a removal of heat? From right to left. Which process is clearly doing that here? In choice E a gas is being condensed into a liquid. Gas to liquid is a right-to-left change on the phase change diagram. So E is the answer.

Question 13: Recall that sublimation is the direct conversion of a solid into a gas. That's what is happening in B. So B is correct.

Question 14: A decrease in entropy means an increase in order. There is an increase in order (and restriction in molecular motion) as you change from a gas to a liquid to a solid. Which choice involves a change like this? Choice E does. So E is right.

Question 15: Heat of fusion is associated with the process of melting or freezing. Do any choices involve one of these? Yep. In choice D solid bromine melts into liquid bromine. If this change took place solely at the melting point, then the heat of fusion of bromine (multiplied by the mass of bromine) would equal the enthalpy change for the process. This makes D the answer.

Question 111: You know what to do with this question-type by now. Is statement I true or false? It's true. What about statement II? It's false. Hydrogen bonds are stronger than most intermolecular forces but far weaker than covalent or ionic bonds.

Question 112: As you go up into higher elevations the atmosphere thins and, as a result, exerts less pressure. As the pressure over substances decreases, so do their boiling points. Since water boils at 100°C at sea-level pressure (1 atm), it will boil below 100°C at higher elevations. So statement I is false. Statement II is also false. Average kinetic energy is a measure of temperature, not pressure. So even if the pressure on a sample increases, if its temperature remains constant, so will its average kinetic energy.

Question 52: In a substance that has hydrogen bonding, a hydrogen atom (H) will be bonded to either N, O, or F in that substance's molecule. This partial positive end will become attracted to the partial negative end of a nearby molecule, creating a hydrogen bond. So which choice has hydrogen bonded to N, O, or F? B does. So B is right.

Question 60: A substance with a low vapor pressure doesn't evaporate readily because it possesses relatively strong intermolecular attractions. So eliminate A and D. What would be the result of strong intermolecular forces? Recall that these must be overcome for a substance to boil. If they are strong, boiling will occur only at relatively high temperatures. So C is correct.

9

Solutions

This short chapter summarizes what you'll need to know regarding solutions on the Subject Test.

SOLUTIONS

Think about dissolving table salt (NaCl) in a glass of water. Because the water dissolves the salt, it's called the **solvent.** Because the salt is dissolved in the water, it's called the **solute**. Salt water is an **aqueous** solution. All that means is that the solution is water–based. A solute need not be solid. And solvents do not have to be liquids. In fact solutes and solvents can be solids, liquids, or gases. But our focus is on the Subject Test. Since it concentrates on solids (and occasionally gases) dissolved in water, that is what we will focus on.

MEASURING CONCENTRATIONS

The most commonly used unit for concentration is called **molarity**. Its symbol is M. It gives the number of moles of solute dissolved per liter of solution (volume).

$$\text{molarity } (M) = \frac{\text{number of moles solute}}{\text{number of liters solution}}$$

Molality is the number of moles of solute dissolved per kilogram of solvent (mass). Its symbol is m.

$$\text{molality } (m) = \frac{\text{number of moles solute}}{\text{number of kilograms solvent}}$$

Associate:

Molarity with:	moles of dissolved solute per <u>liter</u> of <u>solution</u>
Molality with:	moles of dissolved solute per <u>kilogram</u> of <u>solvent</u>

MORE ABOUT SOLUTIONS: SOLUBILITY AND SATURATION

Suppose you take a glass of water and start adding table salt to it. The table salt dissolves. Suppose you keep adding table salt to it like there's no tomorrow. After a while, the water says "no more," and the table salt doesn't dissolve. It just sits in the bottom of the glass. At that point we say the water is **saturated** with table salt: It's had enough and won't take any more. If we want to talk about the table salt instead of the water, we say the table salt has reached the limit of its **solubility** in water. Table salt is soluble in water only up to a certain limit—and you've reached it.

The temperature of the solvent affects solubility. Generally a solid solute is *more* soluble in a liquid solvent at *higher* temperatures, and *less* soluble at *lower* temperatures. If we take our glass of water and heat it, some of the undissolved table salt will dissolve. The increased temperature increases the table salt's water solubility.

Associate:

Higher temperature with:	increased solubility of solids in water
Lower temperature with:	decreased solubility of solids in water

Substances that are held together by ionic bonds are generally soluble in water. Table salt (NaCl) is but one example.

Other solutes are completely insoluble. For instance, try dissolving a glob of butter in a glass of water. It won't dissolve, ever, even if you heat it. This illustrates a general principle, that polar solutes dissolve in polar solvents, and nonpolar solutes dissolve in nonpolar solvents. Just remember, "like dissolves like." Since water molecules are polar, they can dissolve other polar molecules and ionic compounds.

The solubility of gases in water is quite different from that of solids. Think about a bottle of soda: carbon dioxide gas is dissolved in water (along with some flavoring and other additives). Once the bottle has been opened, should you store it where it's warm or cold to prevent it from going "flat" (losing too much CO_2)? You should store it where it's cold, of course. The CO_2 gas is more soluble in water at lower temperatures. This is typical of the solubility of gases in water. One more thing about the solubility of gases in water: The more pressure you put a gas under, the more it will dissolve in water. Again consider soda, bottled under pressure. Once you open the bottle, the pressure over the soda decreases and CO_2 starts to come out of solution.

Associate:

High temperature and
low pressure with: decreased solubility of gases in water

Low temperature and
high pressure with: increased solubility of gases in water

A LITTLE SOMETHING MORE ABOUT IONIC SOLUTES:
DISSOCIATION AND ELECTROLYTES

When an ionic substance (like NaCl, KCl, $CaBr_2$, or $CuSO_4$) dissolves in water, its bonds break up. Ions are then free to run around in the water. For instance, when KCl dissolves in water, K^+ ions and Cl^- ions are running around loose. We say that the ions have dissociated, meaning they've stopped hanging around together.

When ionic compounds dissociate like that, there's always an equal number of positive and negative charges running around. The solution as a whole is electrically neutral. One mole of NaCl will dissociate into 1 mole of Na^+ ions and 1 mole of Cl^- ions. One mole of $CaBr_2$ will dissociate into 2 moles of Br^- ions and 1 mole of Ca^{2+} ions. The solution has equal amounts of positive and negative charge running around in it, and it's neutral.

Even though the solution is neutral, the charged particles—the ions—are running around loose in the solution, which means that the solution will conduct electricity. When we think about the fact that an ionic solution will conduct electricity, we stop calling it an ionic solution and call it an "electrolytic solution." And instead of ions, we call them electrolytes. When running around in a solution of water, sodium ions, chloride ions, potassium ions, and bromide ions are all called electrolytes. The solution is an electrolytic solution, and it conducts electricity.

Associate:

Ions in solution with: electrolytes
                                electrolytic solutions
                                electrical conduction

ONE LAST THING ABOUT SOLUTIONS:
BOILING POINT ELEVATION AND FREEZING POINT DEPRESSION

When a solute is dissolved in a liquid solvent, it raises the solvent's boiling point, lowers its freezing point, and lowers its vapor pressure. By how much? The change in boiling point (ΔT_b) or freezing point (ΔT_f) is always equal to some constant (k) times the number of moles of *dissolved particles* of solute per kilogram of solvent.

$$\Delta T = km$$

The value of constant k changes for different solvents but, for all liquid solvents, notice that *the extent of boiling point elevation or freezing point depression is directly proportional to the molality of the solution*. It's also directly proportional to the number of dissolved particles produced by each unit of solute. Suppose, therefore, we dissolve 1 mole of sucrose (table sugar) in 1 kilogram of water. Sucrose does dissolve in water, but it's not an ionic substance, so it doesn't dissociate into ions/electrolytes. The molality of the solution, therefore, is 1. There will be some elevation of boiling point and depression of freezing point.

Now suppose we take the same amount of water and add 1 mole of KCl. KCl is an ionic substance. It does dissociate when it dissolves. Each unit of KCl produces two dissolved particles: 1 K^+ ion and 1 Cl^- ion. *The boiling point elevation and freezing point depression will be twice as great as they were in the case of sucrose.*

Again, what's the reason? Boiling point elevation and freezing point depression are directly proportional to the number of particles dissolved in a solution, but independent of the type of particle (i.e., sucrose and KCl equally affect melting point and freezing point at the same molality.) Sucrose doesn't ionize and KCl does. When 1 mole of sucrose is dissolved in water, it yields 1 mole of dissolved particles. When 1 mole of KCl is dissolved in water, it yields 2 moles of dissolved particles. If the sucrose elevated the water's boiling point by 0.5°C, the KCl would raise it by 1°C. If the sucrose depressed the water's freezing point by 2°C, the KCl would depress it by 4°C. Remember the relationship of proportionality we've just described.

There are many practical applications of boiling point elevation and freezing point depression. Adding table salt to a pot of boiling water raises the water's boiling point. So when you cook food in the water it will cook faster, since the water will be hotter when it boils. Spreading calcium chloride onto roadways during snow storms makes it harder for ice to form on them (since the freezing point of water is made lower).

Associate:

Boiling point elevation and freezing point depression with:	proportional to number of particles dissolved in solution

Review what we've said about solutions, and try this question set:

QUESTION TYPE A

(A) Nitrogen dioxide, $NO_2(g)$
(B) Iodine, $I_2(s)$
(C) glucose, $C_6H_{12}O_6(s)$
(D) naphthalene, $C_{10}H_8(s)$
(E) calcium oxide, $CaO(s)$

9. Yields an electrolytic solution upon dissolution in water

10. Water solubility increases as temperature is decreased

11. Produces the greatest boiling point elevation per mole dissolved into 1 L of water

QUESTION TYPE B

Directions: Each question below consists of two statements, I in the left-hand column and II in the right-hand column. For each question, determine whether statement I is true or false and whether statement II is true or false and fill in the corresponding T or F ovals on your answer sheet. Fill in oval CE only if statement II is a correct explanation of statement I.

	I		**II**

106. Aqueous solutions with ionic solutes conduct electricity

BECAUSE

a liquid solvent becomes saturated when the solute reaches the limit of its solubility.

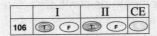

107. Freezing point depression caused by a 2-molal aqueous solution of nonionic solute is equal to one half the freezing point depression caused by a 2-molal aqueous solution of NaCl

BECAUSE

the constant associated with freezing point depression does not vary with the nature of the solvent.

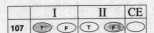

QUESTION TYPE C

27. Which of the following will most likely increase the solubility of NaCl in water?

   (A) Reducing the temperature of the water
   (B) Raising the temperature of the water
   (C) Reducing the molality of the solution
   (D) Raising the molality of the solution
   (E) Raising the molarity of the solution

34. Which of the following would most likely give a sample of water the capacity to conduct electricity?

   (A) Reducing the temperature of the water
   (B) Raising the temperature of the water
   (C) Removing all electrolytes from the water
   (D) Dissolving a nonionic substance in the water
   (E) Dissolving $CaCl_2$ in the water

DONE? LET'S CHECK THE ANSWERS

Question 9: When ionic solutes dissolve in water they produce electrolytic solutions. Are there any ionic solutes among the choices? Look for a metal and nonmetal in the same substance. Calcium oxide is ionic. So E is correct.

Question 10: Think gas solutes in water when you are told that solubility increases as temperature decreases. Any gases out there? Yes, one—NO_2. The answer is A.

Question 11: Remember that boiling point elevation is proportional to the moles of dissolved particles. Choices A through D are substances composed solely of nonmetals. They are molecular compounds. In general, molecular compounds don't dissociate (acids, which we'll look at later, are an important exception) so 1 mole of the substances in A through D gives 1 mole of dissolved particles. Calcium oxide is different. As it dissolves, CaO dissociates into Ca^{2+} and O^{2-} ions. Thus 1 mole of CaO yields 2 moles of dissolved particles. So CaO is the solute that will most raise water's boiling point. The answer is E.

Question 106: We're into type B, divide and conquer. Look at the first statement by itself. Is it true? Yes. You associate "ions dissolved in solution" with the idea of conducting electricity.

The second statement is true. When a solvent has "had enough" solute, it's saturated—the solute has reached the limit of its solubility. Let's see whether the whole sentence makes sense. "Aqueous solutions with ionic solutes conduct electricity because a liquid solvent becomes saturated when the solute reaches the limit of its solubility." The sentence is nonsense.

Question 107: Again, we use divide and conquer. Is the first statement true or false? It's tricky but true. For each mole of original solute, a nonionic solute produces only <u>one</u> mole of particles in solution. One mole of NaCl, on the other hand, dissociates into <u>two</u> moles of particles. So, the number of particles floating around in the NaCl solution will be twice that associated with the nonionic solution. The freezing point depression for the nonionic solution will be one half what it is for the NaCl solution.

What about the second statement? It's false. The freezing point depression constant does vary with the solvent. Since the first statement is true and the second is false, and we're finished.

Question 27: You've learned to associate increased temperature with increased solubility of solids in water. The question is simple, and B is right.

Question 34: The question is about water that conducts electricity. Think electrolyte, and associate that word with "ions in solution." Which of the answer choices says ions will be running around in solution? E does. Ca is a metal and Cl is a nonmetal, which tells you that $CaCl_2$ is most likely an ionic substance. That's why E is right.

10

Kinetics and Equilibrium

Kinetics deals with how fast reactants are converted into products. Equilibrium involves the extent to which reactants are converted into products. As we will show you, these are two fundamentally different concerns.

KINETICS

The speed with which reactants are converted into products is called the **reaction rate**. Remember that chemical reactions involve breaking old bonds (in the reactants) and making new bonds (to form products). For bond breaking and bond making to occur, reactant molecules (or atoms or ions) must collide with sufficient energy and proper orientation. Why are energy and orientation important? Well, reactant molecules need to collide with enough kinetic energy to break their bonds. Proper orientation of reactant molecules is needed to allow new bonds to form. Consider the gas phase reaction:

$$H_2(g) + I_2(g) \rightarrow 2HI(g)$$

Notice that if an H_2 and I_2 molecule collide with enough kinetic energy and in the orientation shown below, hydrogen and iodine atoms are in an ideal position to form new H–I bonds:

First: Reactant molecules H_2 and I_2 speed toward each other with sufficient energy.

$$
\begin{array}{cc}
H & I \\
| \rightarrow \leftarrow | \\
H & I
\end{array}
$$

Next: The collision causes H–H and I–I bonds to begin breaking. Since the reactant molecules were properly aligned, new H–I bonds also start to form

$$
\begin{array}{ccc}
H & \cdots\cdots & I \\
\vdots & & \vdots \\
\vdots & & \vdots \\
H & \cdots\cdots & I
\end{array}
$$

The above species is an extremely unstable, high-energy arrangement of atoms called an **activated complex** or **transition state.** Reactants must form an activated complex before products can be made.

Finally: H–H and I–I bonds are completely broken and H–I bonds are formed. The chemical reaction has produced hydrogen iodide:

$$
\begin{array}{c}
H–I \\
H–I
\end{array}
$$

Although the preceding was a somewhat simplified account of what actually happens during a chemical reaction, the ideas of molecular collisions, bond breaking and making, and the activated complex are very real.

FACTORS THAT AFFECT REACTION RATE

The Subject Test writers will expect you to be familiar with several key factors that influence the rate of a reaction. All of these factors impact the reaction rate by affecting the rate of molecular collisions, the energy per molecular collision, or both.

1. Concentration of Reactants: Reactant molecules must collide to have any hope of forming products. If the rate at which reactant molecules collide is increased, then the reaction rate will also increase. One way to increase the rate of reactant collisions is to increase the amount of reactant per volume, or in other words, to increase the concentration of reactants. For example, wood burns much faster in a pure (100%) oxygen environment than in air (which is only about 20% oxygen by mass). An increase in the concentration of the reactant oxygen causes an increase in the rate of combustion. When we speak of increasing (or decreasing) the concentration of reactants, we are referring only to reactants that are gaseous or in solution. These types of reactants can have their concentrations changed. For instance, a gas can be compressed into a smaller volume (increasing the concentration of gas molecules per volume). Since the molecules in a pure solid or liquid are relatively close together, solids and liquids cannot be significantly compressed. Thus, the concentration of pure solids and liquids is essentially constant. We'll also make use of this when we discuss equilibrium a little later. For now realize that if one or more reactants is gaseous or in solution, the reaction rate can be increased by increasing the concentration of those reactants. Obviously a decrease in reactant concentration will produce a decrease in reaction rate. If we have gas phase reactants, increasing their pressure will also increase their concentration, thereby accelerating the reaction rate.

2. Surface Area of Reactants: The more surface area reactants expose to each other, the greater the number of reactant molecular collisions and hence, the faster the reaction rate. For instance, a log that is chopped up into smaller pieces will burn faster. Only solids and liquids can have their surface area changed. We can increase the surface area of a solid by breaking it up or grinding it into a powder. A liquid's surface area can be increased by spraying it out as a mist of fine droplets.

3. Temperature: The factor that has the most profound effect on reaction rate is temperature. This is because a temperature change affects both rate of reactant collisions and the energy involved in each collision. Remember that temperature is a measure of the average kinetic energy of molecules. As the temperature of reactants is increased, their molecules move around faster. This results in more frequent and energetic collisions, so it is more likely that a given collision will have sufficient energy to break bonds. To continue with our example, wood will burn faster in a warm house than outside on a cold winter night. A good rule of thumb says that for every 10°C increase in temperature, the reaction rate doubles.

4. Nature of Reactants: Bond breaking is part of the reaction process. So it makes sense that reactant molecules that have weaker bonds will react faster than reactant molecules held together by strong bonds. Reactions between dissolved ions tend to be rapid, since bond breaking has already occurred with the dissolution of the ion-supplying substance.

5. Catalysts: A **catalyst** increases the rate of a chemical reaction without being consumed by it. Enzymes are an example of catalysts. They enable many biological reactions to occur fast enough to sustain life as we know it. How do catalysts accelerate reaction rates? Before we get to that let's first consider the energy changes that occur in a reaction.

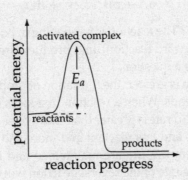

This figure is sometimes referred to as a potential energy diagram. Notice that the potential energy of the activated complex is greater than that of the reactants. The difference between the two is called the **activation energy** (symbolized as E_a). The activation energy is the minimum energy that must be supplied by colliding reactant molecules to produce the activated complex. It is an energy barrier that must be overcome by reactant molecules if they are to form products. Reactant molecules acquire the necessary activation energy by absorbing heat from the surroundings.

The size of the activation energy barrier indicates how difficult it is for reactant molecules to have collisions that will lead to product formation. A relatively small barrier, indicating a low activation energy, means that reactant collisions need less energy to produce an activated complex. Thus, a greater percentage of reactant collisions are likely to lead to product formation. This would result in a relatively high rate of reaction.

Now let's return to the question: **How do catalysts work?** Catalysts increase the reaction rate by enabling the reaction to proceed through a different series of steps that has a lower activation energy than the uncatalyzed reaction does. So a catalyst reduces the minimum energy requirement that a reactant molecular collision needs to form an activated complex (and later to form a product). This leads to a greater percentage of product-forming collisions and thus an increased rate of reaction. Since a catalyst is not consumed by the process, it is able to work its activation energy-reducing magic over and over throughout a sample of reactants.

Associate:

Catalyst with:	reduced activation energy; present at beginning and end of reaction (not consumed)

REVERSIBLE REACTIONS AND CHEMICAL EQUILIBRIUM: THE TWO-WAY STREET

We've been talking about chemical reactions as if they're one-way streets—from reactants to products:

$$aA + bB \rightarrow cC + dD$$

Lots of reactions are what we call "reversible." As products are formed, some of them go through the reverse reaction (read from right to left) and re-form the reactants. When we think about reversible reactions, we write an equation that looks like this:

$$aA + bB \rightleftharpoons cC + dD$$

What do the two arrows mean? The reaction is happening in both directions. Reactants are getting together to form products (the forward reaction), and products are getting together to form reactants (the reverse reaction). That raises a question:

When this is happening, which is greater: the formation of products or the formation of reactants?

Here's the answer: It all depends. When a reaction first kicks off, there's lots of reactant around and very little product. The forward rate is greater than the reverse rate. After a while, as the products start getting together, there's less and less reactant and more and more product.

Ultimately, if pressure and temperature are maintained and the system is closed (meaning no species are allowed to escape), the rate of the reverse reaction will be equal to the rate of the forward reaction. In other words, reactants are being made as rapidly as products are being made. When that happens, we say that the reaction is in equilibrium. To sound fancier we sometimes say, "dynamic equilibrium." When a reaction is in **dynamic equilibrium**, the forward and reverse reaction rates are equal. That means the concentrations of products and reactants are constant: They don't change.

But here's what equilibrium definitely does not mean: It does not mean that the concentrations of products and reactants are equal. It just means that whatever the concentrations of products and reactants may be, they're not changing once the reaction reaches equilibrium.

If we want to know about the relative concentrations of products and reactants for a reaction at equilibrium, we think about two things: (1) the reaction's equilibrium constant, or K_{eq}, and (2) the reaction's equilibrium expression.

For the reaction, aA + bB $\leftrightharpoons$ cC + dD, the equilibrium expression is:

$$K_{eq} = \frac{[C]^c [D]^d}{[A]^a [B]^b}$$

(Note: The symbol [ ] means concentration of, so [A] means concentration of A.)

Keep in mind that the concentrations referred to in an equilibrium expression are those of species *at equilibrium*. Notice that coefficients in the balanced equation become exponents in the equilibrium expression. And one more thing about writing equilibrium expressions: only include those species whose concentrations can be varied. So only species that are gaseous or in solution belong in an equilibrium expression.

Thus given the reaction:

$$BF_3(g) + 3H_2O(\ell) \leftrightharpoons 3HF(aq) + H_3BO_3(aq),$$

(Note: The notation "(aq)" indicates that a species is dissolved in water.)

we get the equilibrium expression:

$$K_{eq} = \frac{[HF]^3 [H_3BO_3]}{[BF_3]}$$

Take a close look at the above equilibrium expression. Notice that the equilibrium constant, K_{eq}, is roughly proportional to product concentrations over reactant concentrations or $\frac{[products]}{[reactants]}$.

What's the significance of that ratio? Suppose in a particular reaction almost all of the reactants are converted into products. Additionally let's say that for this reaction products do not reform reactants to any great extent. Well, this would be an example of a reaction that *does* behave much like a one-way street. How would the K_{eq} of the reaction reflect such behavior? In this situation, product concentrations would be much greater than reactant concentrations at equilibrium. As a result K_{eq}, which is roughly a ratio of product concentrations to reactant concentrations, will be a relatively large number (at least greater than 100).

If, instead, we have a reaction in which reactants form relatively little product, then K_{eq} will be relatively small (at least smaller than $\frac{1}{100}$ or 1×10^{-2}). If product and reactant concentrations at equilibrium are somewhat close, then K_{eq} will be close to 1 (not particularly large or small). So the size of the equilibrium constant, K_{eq}, can give us a good idea about the extent to which reactants form products in a particular reaction.

So, when you think about any reversible reaction, associate:

Equilibrium/
dynamic equilibrium with: constant (not equal)
                                        concentrations of products
                                        and reactants

Equilibrium constant with:

equilibrium concentration of products (all multiplied together) over equilibrium concentration of reactants

Equilibrium constant/ greater than one with:

<u>forward</u> reaction is favored (equilibrium concentration of products exceeds equilibrium concentration of reactants)

Equilibrium constant/ less than one with:

<u>reverse</u> reaction is favored (equilibrium concentration of reactants exceeds equilibrium concentration of products)

AND NOW WE TALK ABOUT A SIMPLE THING CALLED LE CHATELIER'S PRINCIPLE

Look at this equilibrium:

$$A + B \rightleftharpoons C + D$$

On the left side of the equilibrium equation we find A and B. On the right side, we find C and D. A and B act together to produce C and D; meanwhile, C and D act together to produce A and B. If we add more A to the reaction system, we're going to get *more* C and D at equilibrium.

$$\overset{A}{\searrow} A + B \rightleftharpoons \uparrow C + \uparrow D$$

If we add more B to the reaction we're also going to get more C and D at equilibrium.

$$\overset{B}{\searrow} A + B \rightleftharpoons \uparrow C + \uparrow D$$

Adding more A *and* B, of course, will also increase the production of C and D. When we increase the production of C and D, we are "driving the equilibrium to the right."

$$\overset{A}{\underset{B}{\searrow}} A + B \rightleftharpoons \uparrow\uparrow C + \uparrow\uparrow D$$

Adding more C or more D to the system has an analogous but opposite effect.

$$\uparrow\uparrow A + \uparrow\uparrow B \rightleftharpoons C + D \overset{C}{\underset{D}{\swarrow}}$$

Think about it this way. When you add more A to the system, you're making things kind of crowded on the left side of the equation. In order to relieve the crowding, the system decides to move over to the right. Similarly, if you add more C or D to the system, you're making things kind of crowded on the right. The system adjusts by moving to the left.

When we increase the concentration of one species on the left side of an equation, what happens to the concentration of the *other* species on the left side of the equation?

It goes down. When we add more A to the system, there will be more collisions between A particles and B particles. Since we did not add any B to the system, the increased collisions among A and B particles and the increased production of C and D will tend to reduce the concentration of B at equilibrium.

In other words, adding more A to the system crowds things on the left. In order to relieve themselves of the crowding some A particles and B particles form more C and D.

The overall concentration of A at equilibrium does *not* go down. The crowding began because we added A. It's true that some of the newly added A particles will get together with B and produce more C and D. But not all of the added A will do that. After the equilibrium has shifted there will be more A particles than there were before we added any more A. There will be fewer B particles than there were before we began, and there will, of course, be more C and D particles.

To give you an idea of what we mean by "driving or shifting equilibrium to the right," consider this example:

Suppose for the reaction, $2A(g) + B(g) \rightleftharpoons C(g)$, equilibrium concentrations at a particular temperature are [A] = 2 M, [B] = 6 M, and [C] = 8 M.

When we plug these into the equilibrium expression $K_{eq} = \dfrac{[C]}{[A]^2[B]}$ we get $K_{eq} = \dfrac{[8]}{[2]^2[6]} = \dfrac{1}{3}$.

Now by Le Chatelier's principle if we add more A into the system at equilibrium we shift equilibrium to the right. So what does that mean? It means that once equilibrium is re-established the concentration of C will be greater than 8 M and the concentration of B will be less than 6 M. Of course the concentration of A will also be greater than before. But as long as we maintain the original temperature, K_{eq} will stay the same. So when the new equilibrium concentrations are plugged back into the equilibrium expression it still must equal $\dfrac{1}{3}$. For instance, the new equilibrium concentrations could be [A] = 3 M, [B] = 4 M, and [C] = 12 M. Notice how the equilibrium concentrations have changed. That's what we mean by equilibrium shifting to the right. A shift to the left involves the same type of thing, with reactant concentrations increasing and product concentrations decreasing (in general).

WHAT HAPPENS IF WE TAKE SOME A, B, C, OR D AWAY FROM THE SYSTEM?

If we take something away from the system we alleviate the crowding on the side where that species is present. The results are exactly opposite in all respects to those that arise when we add a species.

Apply the same logic when heat is involved

Consider this equilibrium equation:

$$H + I + Heat \rightleftharpoons J + K$$

The reaction consumes heat when it moves to the right, and it evolves heat when it moves to the left. When you think in equilibrium terms just imagine that heat is, in a sense, one of the species on the left side of this equation.

Now, what happens if we increase the temperature? That is, what happens if we add heat to the system? We produce crowding on the left, and we drive the equilibrium to the right. <u>What happens if we decrease the system's temperature? We alleviate crowding on the left and drive the equilibrium *to* the left.</u>

Among all the ways to shift equilibrium there is one thing special about a temperature change: it is the only stress that causes an equilibrium shift *and* changes the value of K_{eq} for a given reaction. The others, such as concentration change, do not alter K_{eq}.

So to summarize, Le Chatelier's principle basically says: If, in a chemical equilibrium, some stress is imposed, the equilibrium will shift in a direction that relieves the stress. When he says "stress," he means the thing we call crowding. When you think about reversible reactions, you should think of Le Chatelier's principle, which means you should think about the crowding principle.

Associate:

$\qquad$ *Le Chatelier's principle* with: $\qquad$ the crowding principle

PRESSURE CHANGES CAN ALSO STRESS OUT A REACTION

If one or more species are gaseous, then changing the system's pressure can affect equilibrium. Consider the important ammonia-producing reaction that is at the heart of what is known as the Haber Process:

$$N_2(g) + 3H_2(g) \leftrightharpoons 2NH_3(g)$$

If the above reaction at equilibrium is stressed by reducing its volume (thereby increasing its pressure) then the reaction will relieve this stress by trying to better fit into this smaller volume. It does so by shifting equilibrium in the direction that produces fewer moles of gas. So the above reaction will shift equilibrium to the right. If the reaction system was stressed by increasing its volume (which decreases its pressure) then the system would shift equilibrium to the left. A reaction involving equal moles of gaseous reactants and products does not have its equilibrium shifted by a volume (or pressure) change.

HEY, WHAT EFFECT DO CATALYSTS HAVE ON EQUILIBRIUM?

Absolutely none. Catalysts change reaction rates, but they do not affect equilibrium. So a catalyst can help you achieve equilibrium faster, but it won't give you more or less product at equilibrium. This emphasizes what we said at the start of this chapter: kinetics and equilibrium address quite different aspects of a chemical reaction.

THE CROWDING PRINCIPLE WORKS FOR ALL KINDS OF PROCESSES

The principle of equilibrium does not apply only to chemical reactions. It applies to any system in which one thing(s) is (are) transforming, reversibly, into another—like a phase change, for instance. Remember vapor pressure? Suppose water is in a sealed container. The temperature is not above water's boiling point, but some molecules gather enough kinetic energy to escape from the liquid and become gas. Then they lose their kinetic energy—they cool down and fall back into the container as water. Other liquid molecules gain enough kinetic energy to escape into the gas phase, and the process goes on and on. Some liquid is being converted to gas, and some gas is being converted to liquid. The process is in equilibrium.

$$H_2O(\ell) + Heat \leftrightharpoons H_2O(g)$$

What happens if we add heat? The equilibrium shifts to the right. We get a new equilibrium with more water vapor and less water. What happens, on the other hand, if we reduce the temperature? The equilibrium shifts to the left. What happens if we somehow draw water vapor away from the system (reducing the concentration of gaseous water)? The equilibrium shifts to the right.

Whenever the Subject Test presents you with a reversible chemical process, whether it's truly a reaction or not, apply the crowding principle and you can't miss.

K_{sp}—A Special Kind of Equilibrium Constant

Some combinations of cation and anion form ionic solids that have very low water solubilities. We call these virtually insoluble ionic solids **precipitates**. Even the most insoluble ionic precipitate dissolves ever so slightly into ions in water. If pressure and temperature are maintained for a precipitate in water, an equilibrium will occur between the precipitate and its dissolved ions. For instance, consider the equilibrium that is set up between the precipitate lead chloride ($PbCl_2$) and its dissolved ions:

$$PbCl_2(s) \rightleftharpoons Pb^{2+}(aq) + 2Cl^-(aq)$$

The equilibrium expression for the above equilibrium is

$$K_{sys} = [Pb^{2+}][Cl^-]^2$$

When we consider the equilibrium between a so-called insoluble ionic solid and its dissolved ions, we call the equilibrium constant a solubility product constant and symbolize it as K_{sp}. As you might expect, since the forward reaction is so insignificant for these precipitates, K_{sp} values are typically very small. For $PbCl_2$ at 25°C, $K_{sp} = 1.6 \times 10^{-5}$ (or 0.000016). The smaller K_{sp} is for a given ionic solid, the more insoluble it is.

Review everything we've said about kinetics, reversible reactions, and equilibrium. Then answer these Subject Test-type questions.

Question Type A

(A) $Ca^{2+}(aq) + CO_3^{2-}(aq) \rightleftharpoons CaCO_3(s)$
(B) $N_2(g) + 2O_2(g) \rightleftharpoons 2NO_2(g)$
(C) $4NH_3(g) + 5O_2(g) \rightleftharpoons 4NO(g) + 6H_2O(g)$
(D) $H_2(g) + I_2(g) \rightleftharpoons 2HI(g)$
(E) $Na_2O_2(s) + H_2O(\ell) \rightleftharpoons NaOH(aq) + H_2O_2(aq)$

18. Reaction rate can be increased by increasing the surface area of reactants   E

19. Increasing system pressure by decreasing reaction volume shifts equilibrium to the right   B

20. Impossible to increase rate of reverse reaction by increasing the concentration of reactant(s)   E

QUESTION TYPE B

Directions: Each question below consists of two statements, I in the left-hand column and II in the right-hand column. For each question, determine whether statement I is true or false <u>and</u> whether statement II is true or false and fill in the corresponding T or F ovals on your answer sheet. <u>Fill in oval CE only if statement II is a correct explanation of statement I.</u>

<table>
<tr><td align="center">I</td><td></td><td align="center">II</td></tr>
</table>

109. For any chemical reaction in dynamic equilibrium, increasing the concentration of one product will decrease the concentration of all reactants

BECAUSE

a dynamic equilibrium will shift in a direction that tends to relieve a stress imposed on it.

110. When a reversible chemical reaction reaches equilibrium, concentrations of products and reactants are always equal

BECAUSE

on the right side of any equilibrium expression, numerator and denominator are always equal.

111. Increasing the concentration of a gaseous reactant typically increases the reaction rate

BECAUSE

the reaction rate is increased as the energy per molecular collision increases.

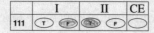

QUESTION TYPE C

(1) $N_2(g) + 3H_2(g) \rightleftharpoons 2NH_3(g)$, K_{eq} (472°C) = 0.105

(2) $H_2(g) + I_2(g) \rightleftharpoons 2HI(g)$, K_{eq} (448°C) = 50

53. In comparing the two reactions above, performed at the indicated temperatures, which of the following is true?

(A) Reaction 1 is favored in the forward direction and reaction 2 is favored in the reverse direction.

(B) Reaction 1 is favored in the reverse direction and reaction 2 is favored in the forward direction.

(C) Both reactions 1 and 2 are favored in the forward direction.

(D) Both reactions 1 and 2 are favored in the reverse direction.

(E) Neither reaction favors either the forward or reverse direction.

$$2SO_3(g) \rightleftharpoons 2SO_2(g) + O_2(g)$$

56. If the reaction given above is at equilibrium, the result of a sudden increase in the concentration of O_2 will result in

    (A) increased concentration of SO_2 and decreased concentration of SO_3

    (B) increased concentration of SO_2 and increased concentration of SO_3

    (C) decreased concentration of SO_2 and increased concentration of SO_3

    (D) decreased concentration of SO_2 and decreased concentration of SO_3

    (E) no change in concentration of any product or reactant

58. All of the following are true regarding the activated complex EXCEPT:

    (A) It represents the highest energy state achieved during the course of a reaction.

    (B) It is not consumed during the course of a reaction. → catalyst

    (C) It is very unstable.

    (D) It is formed before reactant bonds are completely broken.

    (E) It is formed before product bonds are completely formed.

ANSWER TIME

Question 18: What kinds of species can have their surface area increased? Solids and liquids. Which reaction has solid or liquid reactants? E does. It's the answer.

Question 19: When a system's volume is decreased, it tries to compensate by making itself "smaller." This means shifting equilibrium in the direction that produces fewer moles of gas. Eliminate A and E. Neither has a gaseous species, so pressure changes do not affect equilibrium. Of the other three choices, which has fewer moles of gas on the right than on the left? B does (3 on the left, 2 on the right). So the answer is B.

Question 20: We're asked about reverse reactions, so read choices A to E from right to left. Recall that gaseous and aqueous species can have their concentration increased. Choices B, C, D, and E have either a gaseous or aqueous species on the right side (these would be the reactants of the *reverse* reaction). That leaves A, which has a single solid reactant for its reverse reaction. The concentration of pure solids cannot be changed, so A is right.

Question 109: We're into type B, so we divide and conquer! Assess the first statement by itself. True or false? If you increase the concentration of a product, things get crowded on the right and start moving the equilibrium to the left. We see an increase, not a decrease, in the concentration of reactants. The statement is false.

And what about the second statement? It basically states Le Chatelier's principle—the crowding principle. It's true. The first statement is false and the second is true.

Question 110: Divide and conquer. Ask yourself if the first statement is true or false—and don't be tricked! At equilibrium, rates of forward and reverse reactions are equal, but concentrations of products and reactants usually are not. The assertion refers to concentrations, not rates, and it's false.

Let's look at the second statement. What is the "right side of any equilibrium expression?" An equilibrium expression, remember, is:

$$K_{eq} = \frac{[\text{Products}]}{[\text{Reactants}]}$$

What's on the right side? The fraction whose numerator talks about product concentrations and whose denominator talks about reactant concentrations. As we know, those are not usually equal at equilibrium. So, the second statement and the first statement are false.

Question 111: As concentrations of reactants increase, so do molecular collisions. This produces a higher reaction rate. So statement I is true.

How about statement II? It's also true. As collisions become more energetic, they are more likely to lead to product formation.

Now put the sentences together. Does it make sense? It sounds good, but don't fall into the temptation trap. Only a temperature change, not a concentration change, can change the energy of molecular collisions. So don't fill in CE.

Question 53: Remember what we said about the size of K_{eq}.
Associate:

An equilibrium constant *greater than one* with:	a reaction that favors the forward direction
An equilibrium constant *less than one* with:	a reaction that favors the reverse direction

The constant is less than 1 for the first reaction and greater than 1 for the second. That means the first reaction favors the reverse direction and the second favors the forward direction. B is right.

Question 56: Think crowding (Le Chatelier's principle), and look at what's happened here. A reaction is in equilibrium and then someone increases the concentration of the product O_2. Things crowd up on the right. The concentration of the other product, SO_2, goes down, and the concentration of reactant(s) goes up. So the concentration of SO_2 decreases, the concentration of SO_3 increases, and C is right.

Question 58: Don't fall into the temptation trap. You've probably heard the phrase "not consumed by the reaction" in connection with kinetics. But it has to do with a catalyst, not an activated complex. An activated complex is quickly broken down into the products of a reaction. So B is the answer. Review what we said earlier about the activated complex, and you'll see that A, C, D, and E are all accurate.

Acids and Bases

To do well on the Subject Test, you'll need to know a few things about acids and bases: What they are, how they behave in water, and how they react with each other. So let's get started.

ACIDS AND BASES

THE IONIZATION OF WATER

Whenever you have a container of pure water, some of it is ionized. How does a water molecule ionize? For the Subject Test, imagine that it dissociates into hydrogen ions (H^+) and hydroxide ions (OH^-). Think of it like this:

$$H_2O(l) \rightarrow H^+(aq) + OH^-(aq)$$

Incidentally, lots of people don't say "hydrogen ion." They say "proton" instead. After all, a positive hydrogen ion is a proton. A hydrogen atom consists of a proton and an electron and nothing else. If the atom loses its electron, it's just a proton. Proton and hydrogen ion mean the same thing.

Actually, the ionization of water is a reversible reaction, and it comes to equilibrium.

$$H_2O(l) \rightleftharpoons H^+(aq) + OH^-(aq)$$

As we just said, when you have a container of water at a given temperature, it's at equilibrium. Now, does the equilibrium favor the forward reaction (meaning the H^+ and OH^- concentrations are relatively high), or the reverse reaction (meaning the H^+ and OH^- concentrations are relatively low)? The answer is that it favors the reverse reaction—by a lot. It favors the reverse reaction to the extent that the concentration of H^+ is equal to 1.0×10^{-7} moles/L (also written as 10^{-7} moles/L) at 25°C. (That's 0.0000001 moles/L, right?) And the concentration of OH^- in any sample of pure water is equal to the same thing: 1.0×10^{-7} moles/L at 25°C.

Now, get this. When we think about the hydrogen ion concentration of any sample of water, whether it's pure water or not, we say "pH." pH is related to hydrogen ion concentration by the equation:

$$pH = -\log[H^+]$$

If we express $[H^+]$ in scientific notation such that $[H^+] = 1 \times 10^x$, then pH = $-x$. So if $[H^+] = 1.0 \times 10^{-7}$ (as for pure water), then pH = 7. And by the way, pH of 7 is a neutral pH: Pure water is neutral.

If the hydrogen ion (proton) concentration of the water was increased from 10^{-7} moles/L (that's 0.0000001 moles/L) to 10^{-3} moles/L (that's 0.001 moles/L), we'd *decrease* the pH from 7 to 3. Lower pH means greater hydrogen ion (proton) concentration. Higher pH means lower hydrogen ion concentration. If we decrease the water's proton concentration from 10^{-7} moles/L (that's 0.0000001 moles/L) to 10^{-11} moles/L (that's 0.00000000001 moles/L), we'd increase the pH from 7 to 11.

Associate:

pH *of* 7 with: hydrogen ion concentration of 10^{-7} moles/L
                                         neutral pH; pH of pure water

Lower pH with: higher hydrogen ion concentration

Higher pH with: lower hydrogen ion concentration

Why is the hydrogen ion concentration of pure water 1.0×10^{-7} moles/L (which means its pH is 7), and the OH^- concentration of pure water also 1.0×10^{-7} moles/L? Because the dissociation of one water molecule yields one H^+ ion and one OH^- ion. In pure water, the H^+ concentration is equal to the OH^- concentration, and each, as it happens, is equal to 1.0×10^{-7} moles/L at 25°C.

WATER'S ION PRODUCT

Let's consider the ionization of water again:

$$H_2O\ (l) \rightleftharpoons H^+(aq) + OH^-(aq)$$

The equilibrium expression for this reaction would be $K = [H^+][OH^-]$. At 25°C (the temperature at which the Subject Test writers would ask you about acids and bases), $[H^+] = [OH^-] = 1.0 \times 10^{-7}$ M. So $K = (1.0 \times 10^{-7}\text{ M})(1.0 \times 10^{-7}\text{ M}) = 1.0 \times 10^{-14}$. The equilibrium constant for the ionization of water is so important that it is given the special name "ion product of water" and the special notation K_w. At 25°C, $K_w = 1.0 \times 10^{-14}$.

Now this is important: When we say that water's ion product is 1.0×10^{-14} at 25°C, we mean that we always obtain that number when we multiply the H^+ concentration by the OH^- concentration, even if we're not dealing with pure water. So K_w for aqueous solutions at 25°C is also 1.0×10^{-14}.

Suppose we start with pure water at 25 °C and then add some H^+ ions. Think back to Le Chatelier's (crowding) principle. Imagine what's going to happen to H^+ and OH^- concentrations at our new equilibrium.

$$H_2O(l) \rightleftharpoons H^+(aq) + OH^-(aq)$$

The concentration of H^+ goes up, and the concentration of OH^- goes down, right? Imagine that we measure the H^+ concentration and we find out that it's now equal to 10^{-4} (0.0001) moles/L, which means we've reduced the pH from 7 to 4. If we want to know the OH^- concentration, we don't have to bother measuring it. We know automatically that the OH^- concentration is 10^{-10} moles/L. Why? Because *in any aqueous solution, the H^+ concentration multiplied by the OH^- concentration always, always, always equals 10^{-14} at 25 °C.*

$$(10^{-4})\,(10^x) = 10^{-14}$$
$$x = -10$$

From Le Chatelier's principle, we knew that increasing the H^+ concentration would reduce the OH^- concentration. But once we knew that we'd increased the H^+ concentration to 10^{-4} moles/L, water's ion product told us exactly what the new OH^- concentration would be.

Imagine that we start with pure water at 25 °C. Then, we <u>decrease</u> its hydrogen ion concentration from 10^{-7} moles/L to 10^{-9} moles/L (from 0.0000001 moles/L to 0.000000001 moles/L), which means we're automatically increasing its pH from 7 to 9. We know automatically that the OH^- concentration $= 10^{-5}$ moles/L. That's because of water's ion product: In any aqueous solution, the H^+ concentration multiplied by the OH^- concentration always equals 10^{-14} at 25 °C.

$$(10^{-9})\,(10^x) = 10^{-14}$$
$$x = -5$$

Special solutions called **buffers** do not experience dramatic changes to their pH upon the addition of an acid or basic substance.

NOW WE CAN ASK: WHAT'S AN ACID?

There are several different ways to define acids (and bases). A chemist named Arrhenius came up with one of the earliest definitions of acids and bases; Arrhenius said that an acid is any substance that, when added to pure water, <u>produces hydrogen ions</u>. Thus, the resultant aqueous solution has a pH less than 7.

Acids are special compounds that ionize when they're added to water. For instance, hydrogen chloride gas is a molecular substance that, when bubbled into water, becomes hydrochloric acid. Hydrochloric acid ionizes like this:

$$HCl(aq) \rightarrow H^+(aq) + Cl^-(aq)$$

Although hydrochloric acid ionizes completely, this is certainly not true of all acids. But more on that later. Now let's consider those properties that acids have in common:

1. Acids are electrolytes, meaning that their water solutions conduct electricity. An acid that ionizes completely in water, like $HCl(aq)$, is a strong electrolyte.

2. Acids react with many metals to produce hydrogen gas. For example, consider the reaction of nitric acid (HNO_3) and zinc metal:

$$2HNO_3(aq) + Zn(s) \rightarrow Zn^{2+}(aq) + H_2(g) + 2NO_3^-(aq)$$

3. **Indicators** are substances that turn different colors depending on the pH of the environment they're in. Litmus is an important indicator. In an acid, litmus is red.

4. Acids taste sour. Vinegar (acetic acid) and lemon juice (citric acid) are two good examples.

5. Nonmetal oxides dissolve in water to produce acids. For instance, the reaction between sulfur trioxide and water generates sulfuric acid (H_2SO_4):

$$SO_3(g) + H_2O(l) \rightarrow H_2SO_4(aq)$$

Now: What's a Base?

According to Arrhenius a base is anything that, when added to pure water, produces hydroxide ions. As a result, basic aqueous solutions will have a pH greater than 7.

Many bases are ionic compounds. One example is sodium hydroxide (NaOH). When solid sodium hydroxide is dissolved in water, NaOH dissociates into Na^+ and OH^- ions:

$$NaOH(aq) \rightarrow Na^+(aq) + OH^-(aq)$$

Bases that are ionic hydroxides such as NaOH dissociate completely in water. Alkali and alkaline earth elements combine with hydroxide ions to form some of the most common bases, including NaOH, KOH, $Ca(OH)_2$, and $Ba(OH)_2$. Not all bases are ionic hydroxides. For instance, ammonia gas (NH_3) is a molecular substance that, when bubbled into water, produces OH^- ions, so NH_3 is also a base. These are the properties that bases share:

1. Bases are electrolytes. The water solutions of some bases (such as ionic hydroxides) can conduct electricity better than those of others (such as NH_3).

2. Litmus is blue in a base.

3. Bases feel slippery. A common recipe for making soap includes sodium hydroxide.

4. Bases taste bitter. Just take our word for it.

5. Metal oxides dissolve in water to form bases. An example is the reaction between potassium oxide and water, which produces potassium hydroxide (KOH):

$$K_2O(s) + H_2O(l) \rightarrow 2KOH(aq)$$

Other Ways to Think about Acids and Bases

Besides the Arrhenius view of what acids and bases are, there are two other popular ways of defining acids and bases: Bronsted-Lowry acid-base theory and Lewis acid-base theory. According to the Bronsted-Lowry theory, an acid is a proton (H^+) donor and a base is proton acceptor. Let's see how this works by considering the reaction between hydrochloric acid and water:

$$HCl(aq) + H_2O(l) \rightarrow H_3O^+(aq) + Cl^-(aq)$$

The products of this reaction are the hydronium ion (H_3O^+) and chloride ion (Cl^-). How did they form? Check out the reactants. HCl acts as an acid by donating a proton (H^+) to H_2O. By donating a proton, HCl becomes Cl^-, and by receiving a proton, H_2O becomes H_3O^+. If one substance donates a proton, another must be there to accept it. So the proton donor HCl is a Bronsted-Lowry acid, and the proton acceptor H_2O is a Bronsted-Lowry base.

What happens if we mix an aqueous ammonia solution and water?

$$NH_3(aq) + H_2O(l) \rightleftharpoons NH_4^+(aq) + OH^-(aq)$$

To generate the products NH_4^+ and OH^-, H_2O donates an H^+ ion to NH_3. That makes H_2O an acid and NH_3 a base. Hold on! Wasn't H_2O considered a base in the previous reaction? Yep. In the Bronsted-Lowry (and Lewis) ways of looking at acids and bases, it is possible for a substance to act sometimes as an acid and sometimes as a base. We refer to such substances, like H_2O, as **amphoteric** or **amphiprotic**. It's just a fancy way of saying the substance can be an acid or a base. When trying to determine if a substance is amphoteric, check out its formula and see if it can give and accept an H^+ ion.

Let's stay on the reaction of aqueous ammonia and water for a little longer. Look at the products NH_4^+ and OH^-. How can they react to reform NH_3 and H_2O? Notice that if NH_4^+ donates a H^+ ion to OH^-, we'll get NH_3 and H_2O. So, for the reverse reaction, NH_4^+ acts as an acid and OH^- acts as a base. We refer to the acid and base of the reverse reaction as a **conjugate acid** and **conjugate base**. Labelling all four substances gives

$$NH_3(aq) + H_2O(l) \rightleftharpoons NH_4^+(aq) + OH^-(aq)$$

$$\text{base} \qquad\qquad \text{acid} \qquad\qquad \text{conjugate acid} \quad \text{conjugate base}$$

The acid (H_2O) and conjugate base (OH^-), and base (NH_3) and conjugate acid (NH_4^+) are both referred to as conjugate acid-base pairs. Notice that the two members of any conjugate acid-base pair differ by one H^+ ion.

Lewis acid-base theory focuses on the exchange of electron pairs rather than protons to classify species as an acid or base. We can see how this applies in the reaction of NH_3 and H_2O:

The hydrogen ion (H^+) that water donates to NH_3 needs an electron pair to fill its valence energy shell. NH_3 has a lone pair, which is available to be shared by the H^+ ion. Since the H^+ ion that came from H_2O accepts (shares) this lone pair, H_2O is considered to be an electron pair acceptor. In Lewis acid-base theory an electron pair acceptor is an acid. Electron pair donors are bases. That's what NH_3 is. It is donating (sharing) its lone pair to the H^+ ion. So, according to Lewis theory, H_2O is an acid and NH_3 is a base. This is consistent with the Bronsted-Lowry classifications.

So remember to associate:

Bronsted-Lowry acid with: proton donor

Bronsted-Lowry base with: proton acceptor

Lewis acid with: electron pair acceptor

Lewis base with: electron pair donor

ACIDS AND BASES CAN BE STRONG OR WEAK

We mentioned earlier that hydrochloric acid ionizes completely. Any acid that ionizes completely is considered strong. There are six common strong acids:

1. hydrobromic acid, HBr(aq)

2. hydrochloric acid, HCl(aq)

3. hydroiodic acid, HI(aq)

4. nitric acid, HNO$_3$(aq)

5. perchloric acid, HClO$_4$(aq)

6. sulfuric acid, H$_2$SO$_4$(aq)

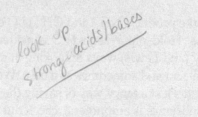

What do we mean when we say an acid ionizes completely? We mean that no acid molecules exist in water. Let's consider nitric acid:

$$HNO_3(aq) \rightleftharpoons H^+(aq) + NO_3^-(aq)$$

Since no HNO$_3$ molecules exist at equilibrium, the reverse reaction is essentially insignificant compared to the forward reaction. The equilibrium expression for the process is

$$K_{eq} = \frac{[H^+][NO_3^-]}{[HNO_3]}$$

Since [HNO$_3$] is approximately 0, the denominator is very small. That makes K very large ($>>$100). The equilibrium associated with the ionization of an acid is so important that we refer to this type of equilibrium constant as K_a, or the acid ionization constant. When K_a is very large, as for nitric acid or any strong acid, it indicates that only the forward reaction is significant. Thus, we can write the equation for the ionization of a strong acid with a single arrow:

$$HNO_3(aq) \rightarrow H^+(aq) + NO_3^-(aq)$$

This means that if we have a 0.1 M solution of HNO$_3$(aq), what we really have is a 0.1 M concentration of H$^+$(aq) ions and a 0.1 M concentration of NO$_3^-$(aq) ions. If [H$^+$] is 0.1 M (or 1×10^{-1} M), then the HNO$_3$(aq) solution has a pH of 1. Most acids only ionize slightly in water; this makes them weak. Consider the ionization of the common weak acid acetic acid [HC$_2$H$_3$O$_2$(aq)]:

$$HC_2H_3O_2(aq) \rightleftharpoons H^+(aq) + C_2H_3O_2^-(aq)$$

The acid ionization constant for acetic acid is $K_a = 1.8 \times 10^{-5}$ or 0.000018 at 25°C. This small K_a is typical of weak acids. It means that the reverse reaction is more significant than the forward reaction. At equilibrium, we can expect a much higher concentration of HC$_2$H$_3$O$_2$ molecules than H$^+$ or C$_2$H$_3$O$_2^-$ ions.

So how do you determine if an acid is strong or weak? Check out its K_a. If it's large ($>>$100), it's a strong acid. If it's small ($<<$100), it's weak. And the smaller K_a is, the weaker the acid is.

Bases can also be strong or weak. A strong base ionizes completely in water into some cation and OH$^-$. The alkali hydroxides (LiOH, NaOH, etc.) and heavy alkaline earth hydroxides [Ca(OH)$_2$, Sr(OH)$_2$, and Ba(OH)$_2$] make up the common strong bases. Calcium hydroxide is an example:

$$Ca(OH)_2(aq) \rightarrow Ca^{2+}(aq) + 2OH^-(aq)$$

Many bases are weak. The most important weak base on the Subject Test is NH_3. Recall what we get when NH_3 and H_2O react:

$$NH_3(aq) + H_2O(l) \rightleftharpoons NH_4^+(aq) + OH^-(aq)$$

The equilibrium constant for the reaction, K_b (for base ionization constant), is predictably small. This means that at equilibrium, the concentration of dissolved NH_3 molecules is much higher than the concentration of NH_4^+ or OH^- ions. So the meaning of K_b for bases is analogous to that of K_a for acids.

And one other thing: Strong acids and bases are strong electrolytes, which means they are excellent conductors of electricity. Weak acids and bases dissociate into relatively few ions, making them weak electrolytes and hence, poor conductors of electricity.

ADDING ACIDS AND BASES TOGETHER: TITRATION

Generally, when you add an acid to an aqueous base or a base to an aqueous acid you get a salt plus water. A **salt** is simply any ionic compound whose cation is not H^+ and whose anion is not OH^-. NaCl, KBr, and $CaCl_2$ are all salts. The reaction of an acid and base to form a salt and water is called a **neutralization reaction**.

Let's look at a couple of acid-base neutralization reactions:

$$HCl + NaOH \rightarrow NaCl + H_2O$$
$$\text{(a salt)}$$

$$H_2CO_3 + 2KOH \rightarrow K_2CO_3 + 2H_2O$$
$$\text{(a salt)}$$

$$H_2SO_4 + Ba(OH)_2 \rightarrow BaSO_4 + 2H_2O$$
$$\text{(a salt)}$$

Associate:

Acid + base with: water plus salt

When it comes to adding acids to bases or bases to acids, the test writers like to ask about acid-base "titration." Suppose you take beaker number 1 with an aqueous solution at pH 5 and beaker number 2 with an aqueous solution at pH of 9. Suppose you then start pouring solution from beaker number 2 into beaker number 1.

Two things will happen: (1) in beaker number 1, you'll start making more water and a salt, and (2) also in beaker number 1, the pH will start to increase because the base from beaker number 2 will neutralize the hydrogen ion concentration of the acid in beaker number 1. You'll start moving the pH in beaker number 1 upward from 5.

If you put in exactly enough of the base so that all of the acid has reacted to make salt and water, you've "titrated the acid with a base." The resulting solution will have a pH between 5 and 9. (Possibly, but not necessarily, 7.) The point in the titration at which enough base has been added to react with exactly all the acid is called the equivalence point.

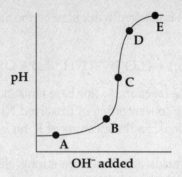

The equivalence point is the point when enough base has been added to neutralize all the acid that was initially present in the solution. This point is in the middle of the steep part of a titration curve. In this case, when a strong acid is titrated by a strong base, the pH at the equivalence point will be 7 and the solution will be neutral.

If, on the other hand, you did the experiment the other way around, and began by pouring acid from beaker number 1 into beaker number 2 you'd be adding acid to base. You'd make the same salt, and the acid from beaker number 1 would neutralize the pH in beaker number 2. If you added just enough acid so that all of the base reacted to produce salt and water, the resulting solution would have a pH between 5 and 9.

The pH of the resulting solution would depend on the strengths of the acid and base in the neutralization reaction. If a strong acid is exactly neutralized by a strong base, or vice versa, the resulting solution will have a pH of 7. If a strong acid is exactly neutralized by a weak base, the resulting solution will have a pH less than 7. If a weak acid is exactly neutralized by a strong base, the resulting solution will have a pH greater than 7.

TITRATION ON THE SUBJECT TEST

For the Subject Test, think of acid-base titration as a process in which you add acid to base (or base to acid) in order to combine equal amounts (moles) of acid and base.

Here's a typical Subject Test question:

> What volume of a 0.1 M solution of NaOH must be added in order to neutralize 1 L of 0.05 M HCl?

In order to neutralize an acidic solution, you've got to figure out how many moles of H^+ are running around and then add an equal number of OH^- ions. It's simple arithmetic. In 1 L of a 0.05 M solution of HCl, you've got 0.05 moles of H^+ running around (remember, a strong acid ionizes completely). In order to neutralize that solution you've got to add 0.05 moles of OH^-. You're working with NaOH that's 0.1 M. There's 0.1 M of OH^- in every liter of the solution. We only want to add 0.05 moles of OH^-, so we've got to add 0.5 L of the NaOH solution. If we add 0.5 L of the NaOH solution we'll be adding $(0.5)(0.1) = 0.05$ moles of OH^- ion—just what we want.

The test writers might turn this around and ask you to do the same kind of arithmetic in a different way:

> A beaker contains 3 L of an aqueous KOH solution of unknown concentration. If the solution is fully titrated by 0.3 L of a 0.02 M solution of H_2SO_4, what is the concentration of the KOH solution?

This time we don't know the concentration of the KOH solution. But we do know the volume and the concentration of the solution that neutralizes it. The thinking doesn't change: If some acid neutralized some base, then the number of H^+ ions in the acid is equal to the number of OH^- ions in the base.

Each molecule of H_2SO_4 dissociates to yield two H^+ ions. In 0.3 L of a 0.02 M solution of H_2SO_4 there are $(0.3)(0.02)(2) = 0.012$ moles of H^+ ions. Figure out what concentration of a 3 L KOH solution would provide 0.012 moles of OH^- ions.

$$3(x) = 0.012$$
$$x = 0.004$$

The KOH solution is 0.004 M.

Incidentally, the test writers will want you to know how we add acid to base or base to acid. We use a "buret." A buret is a little device that lets us drop small amounts of liquid into a container. That way we keep track of exactly how much we've added.

Review this section on acids and bases, and then try these Subject Test-type questions.

QUESTION TYPE A

     (A) HBr (*aq*)
     (B) NH_3 (*aq*)
     (C) H_2O (*l*)
     (D) HF (*aq*)
     (E) H_2CO_3 (*aq*)

17. A strip of litmus paper will appear blue in it   B

18. At 25°C, it has a pH > 7   B

19. Is essentially a non-electrolyte   C

20. Its aqueous ionization goes virtually to   D
     completion

QUESTION TYPE B

<u>Directions:</u> Each question below consists of two statements, I in the left-hand column and II in the right-hand column. For each question, determine whether statement I is true or false <u>and</u> whether statement II is true or false and fill in the corresponding T or F ovals on your answer sheet. <u>Fill in oval CE only if statement II is a correct explanation of statement I.</u>

I   II

110. If an acid is added to water   BECAUSE   the product of hydroxide ions and
      with original pH of 7, the   protons is equal to 1.0×10^{-14} in
      concentration of hydroxide   all aqueous solutions at 25°C.
      ions will increase

	I	II	CE
110	T Ⓕ	Ⓣ F	

111. An aqueous solution of HI is   BECAUSE   HI (*aq*) can accept an H^+ ion from
      considered to be a Bronsted-   another species.
      Lowry base

	I	II	CE
111	T Ⓕ	Ⓣ F	

QUESTION TYPE C

50. $HNO_3 (aq) + OH^- (aq) \rightleftharpoons H_2O (l) + NO_3^-$

In the reaction above, which species is the conjugate acid?

(A) $HNO_3 (aq)$
(B) $OH^- (aq)$
(C) $H_2O (l)$
(D) $NO_3^- (aq)$
(E) There is no conjugate acid in the above reaction.

53. A titration experiment is conducted in which 15 ml of a 0.015 M $Ba(OH)_2$ solution is added to 30 ml of an HCl solution of unknown concentration and titration is complete. What is the approximate concentration of the HCl solution?

(A) 0.015 M
(B) 0.03 M
(C) 1.5 M
(D) 2.5 M
(E) 3.0 M

55. Which is true regarding an aqueous solution of H_3PO_4 at 25 °C ?

(A) It has a very large acid ionization constant.
(B) It has a bitter taste.
(C) The concentration of $[OH^-] > 1.0 \times 10^{-7}$ M.
(D) It is a weak electrolyte.
(E) It can be formed by the reaction of a metal oxide and water.

WANT TO SEE SOME ANSWERS?

Question 17: Litmus is an indicator that is blue in a base. Since NH_3 is the only consistent base among the choices, the answer is B.

Question 18: At 25 °C, a pH greater than 7 indicates a basic solution. So B is right.

Question 19: A non-electrolyte does not break down into charge-carrying ions in water. Soluble ionic compounds, strong acids, and strong bases make strong electrolytes. So eliminate A (a strong acid). Weak acids and bases ionize to a slight extent, and, therefore, are weak electrolytes. So eliminate B (weak base), and D and E (both weak acids). What's left? Water. But doesn't water ionize to a slight extent? Yes, but check out how slight. K_w (equilibrium constant for the ionization of water) at 25 °C is 1.0×10^{-14}. That's so small that we can consider water to be a very, very weak electrolyte. So weak that it is essentially a non-electrolyte. So C is correct.

Question 20: The same species that make strong electrolytes (soluble ionics, strong acids, and strong bases) have an ionization reaction that essentially goes to completion. Are any of these species among the choices? Yes. HBr is a strong acid. It completely ionizes into H^+ and Br^- ions in water. So A is right.

Question 110: We're into type B: divide and conquer! Look at statement I by itself and decide if it's true or false. It's false. If you add an acid to neutral water you <u>in</u>crease the hydrogen ion concentration and <u>de</u>crease the hydroxide ion concentration.

Is the second statement true or false? It's true. The statement is accurately telling us about water's ion product. So, statement I is false and statement II is true.

Question 111: Remember the six common strong acids? HI is one of them. So statement I is false.

What about the second statement? Because HI is a strong acid it will donate, not accept, H^+ ions. So both statements are false.

Question 50: Conjugate acids and bases appear on the right side of the equation. So eliminate A and B. A conjugate acid donates an H^+ ion. Is either H_2O or NO_3^- doing that? Yep. H_2O donates an H^+ ion to NO_3^- to reform the reactants, HNO_3 and OH^-. So H_2O is the conjugate acid here and the answer is C.

Question 53: We're dealing with titration. We have to figure out concentration for one of the solutions.

We know that if we fully titrate an acid we need equal amounts of H^+ and OH^- ions. It's simple arithmetic. There are two moles of OH^- ion for each mole of $Ba(OH)_2$, and we're dealing with 0.015 L of a 0.015 M solution. So:

$$(2)(0.015)(0.015) = 0.00045 \text{ moles } OH^-$$

We need 0.00045 moles of H^+ ion, too. We're dealing with 0.03 L of an HCl solution, and there's only 1 mole of H^+ ion per mole of HCl. So:

$$(1)(0.03)(x) = 0.00045 \text{ moles } OH^-$$

$$x = 0.015 \text{ M}$$

What does all that mean? It means A is right.

Question 55: H_3PO_4 looks like the formula of an acid, and it is—phosphoric acid. Choices B, C, and E are properties of bases, so eliminate them. Now, is H_3PO_4 on our list of strong acids? No. So it must be a weak acid. Would a weak acid have a large K_a? No. So eliminate A. A weak acid is a weak electrolyte. So D is right.

12

Redox and Electrochemistry

Aside from the acid-base reaction, the other type of reaction you'll need to be comfortable with for the Subject Test is the oxidation-reduction or "redox" reaction. Electrochemistry involves using redox reactions to generate electricity and vice versa.

OXIDATION AND REDUCTION

When an atom gets involved in a bond, chemists like to think the atom has been "oxidized" or "reduced." But, what do these terms mean? Well, any chemistry teacher will tell you: An atom that loses electrons is oxidized; an atom that gains electrons is reduced. Then they'll tell you to recite "LEO says

GER." That's supposed to make you remember: Lose Electrons Oxidized and Gain Electrons Reduced. For the Subject Test, you should remember that sentence, and you should associate:

Reduction with: gaining electrons

Oxidation with: losing electrons

We know that the only kind of reaction in which one atom truly loses an electron and another truly gains one, is one that results in an ionic bond. But, as a way of keeping track of all the electrons, chemists assign each term in a compound either a positive or a negative charge based upon the relative electronegativities of the atoms. For example, take HF. We already talked about polar covalent bonds and we know that H-F has one, and that F gets more than its half of the shared electrons. Even though this isn't an ionic bond, chemists will assign a "formal charge" as a way of bookkeeping the electrons. For HF, the H gets a +1 charge and the F gets a –1 charge. These charges are called oxidation numbers and are always whole numbers. Even though the real, partial charges might be +0.271 for H and –0.271 for F, we go ahead and assign a whole charge to simplify the math.

Some important points to remember about oxidation states:

- The atoms in any compound can be assigned oxidation states. Just remember that the charges given to the atoms are "formal charges" that reflect their different electronegativities. Assigning oxidation states doesn't mean that the compounds are ionic.

- For a compound, the total number of electrons given up by atoms is the same as the number gained. So the oxidation states should add up to zero for a neutral compound.

OXIDATION STATES AND OXIDATION NUMBERS

Because we imagine that, for any compound, each atom has been oxidized or reduced, we assign atoms something called an "oxidation state." The oxidation state is positive if we're imagining that the atom has lost electrons and negative if we're imagining that it has gained electrons.

If, for instance, we imagine that some atom has gained two electrons, its oxidation state is –2. If we imagine that it's lost one electron, its oxidation state is +1. Since total reduction has to equal total oxidation, for all compounds the sum of all oxidation numbers, positive and negative, is always zero. Keep in mind that we only assign oxidation states to atoms when they aren't in their elemental forms. For example, each atom of H_2, O_2, Cl_2, N_2, Na, or Fe has an oxidation state of zero. In all other compounds, such as H_2CO_3, CaO, or N_2O, the atoms can be assigned an oxidation number that is not zero.

OXIDATION AND REDUCTION ON THE CHEMISTRY SUBJECT TEST

Now, here's what might happen to you on the Subject Test. The writers will show you some compound or other and then ask you to calculate the oxidation states of its atoms. You'll always be able to answer these questions by remembering a few simple rules.

For some elements, oxidation state is almost always the same, no matter what compound they're sitting in. For other elements, oxidation state varies depending on the compound in which we find them. For the Subject Test, remember:

1. When oxygen gets itself involved in a compound, its oxidation state is usually –2 (meaning it has been "reduced"). An important exception is oxygen in a "peroxide" such as hydrogen peroxide (H_2O_2). In a peroxide, oxygen has an oxidation state of –1.

2. When an alkali metal (Li, Na, etc.) gets itself involved in a compound, its oxidation state is always +1 (meaning it's been "oxidized").

3. When an alkaline earth metal (Be, Mg, etc.) gets itself involved in a compound, its oxidation state is +2.

4. When a halogen (F, Cl, etc.) gets itself involved in a compound, its oxidation state is often –1. The oxidation state of fluorine in a compound is always –1.

5. When hydrogen is combined with a nonmetal its oxidation state is +1. When hydrogen is combined with a metal its oxidation state is –1.

6. Again, in any compound, the sum of all oxidation states is zero.

Remember those six simple rules, and you'll be able to answer the Subject Test's oxidation state questions.

Figure out the oxidation state for nitrogen in the compound nitrogen monoxide (NO).

♦ Oxygen's oxidation number is –2, and there's one oxygen atom in the molecule. So oxygen contributes a total reduction of –2.

♦ Since the total reduction (gain of electrons) must equal the total oxidation (loss of electrons), nitrogen must have an oxidation state of +2 (which means it has been oxidized, having lost two electrons).

So, we're imagining that the oxygen atom has gained 2 electrons and the nitrogen atom has lost 2 electrons.

Try another one. Here's iron(III) carbonate, $Fe_2(CO_3)_3$. Figure out carbon's oxidation number.

If Fe's subscript is 2 and CO_3's is 3, that means the charge on Fe must be +3 and on CO_3 must be –2. The oxidation state of an ion is equal to its charge. So the oxidation state of Fe is +3. The total oxidation state of CO_3 is –2. The oxidation state of oxygen is –2. Since there are three oxygen atoms in CO_3 the total contribution by oxygen is –6. This means carbon's oxidation state must be +4 so that CO_3's total oxidation state is $(+4) + 3(-2) = -2$.

Now let's consider how these oxidation states add to give the total oxidation state of $Fe_2(CO_3)_3$.

♦ Oxygen contributes total reduction of $(3)(3)(-2) = -18$.

♦ Carbon contributes total oxidation of $3(+4) = +12$.

♦ Iron contributes total oxidation of $2(+3) = +6$.

Thus the oxidation state of $Fe_2(CO_3)_3$ is $(-18) + (+12) + (+6) = 0$. This is just what we would expect. We're imagining that each iron atom has lost 3 electrons, each oxygen atom has gained 2 electrons, and each carbon atom has lost 4 electrons. The losses equal the gains—total oxidation equals total reduction—and all is well.

REDOX REACTIONS

In an **oxidation reduction** or **redox** reaction, as reactants form products, one or more atoms are reduced while one or more atoms are oxidized. Why does redox occur? Well, the oxidation state for most elements depends on the compound they're in. So if an element is in some compound or molecule as a reactant, and in a different compound or molecule as a product, its oxidation state may change. In other words, the element's situation on the left side of the equation can give it a different oxidation state than its situation on the right side of the equation. Always remember that if reduction happened in a reaction, then oxidation must also take place. If one species gains electrons, another must have lost electrons.

If we want to represent just the reduction or just the oxidation that happens in a redox reaction we write something called a **half-reaction**.

Look at this reaction:

$$Fe + 2HCl \rightarrow FeCl_2 + H_2$$

On the left side of the equation, iron's oxidation state is 0 and hydrogen's is +1. On the right side of the equation, iron's oxidation state is +2 and hydrogen's is 0. To a Subject Test-type chemist who thinks about oxidation and reduction, iron has been oxidized (each atom has gone from an oxidation state of 0 to +2, so each has lost two electrons), and hydrogen has been reduced (each atom has gone from an oxidation state of +1 to 0, so each has gained one electron). Note that, in reduction, what gets reduced is the oxidation state of the species in going from reactants to products.

Next, the Subject Test chemist writes two half-reactions, one describing the oxidation of iron and the other describing the reduction of hydrogen. Here they are:

◆ **Oxidation:** $Fe \rightarrow Fe^{+2} + 2 e^-$
  meaning one iron atom loses 2 electrons and takes on an oxidation state of +2.

◆ **Reduction:** $2H^+ + 2e^- \rightarrow H_2$
  meaning that two hydrogen atoms each gain 1 electron to yield two hydrogen atoms with an oxidation state of 0.

Notice that if we take the two half-reactions together, oxidation equals reduction: In the oxidation half-reaction, iron loses 2 electrons. In the reduction half-reaction, two hydrogen atoms each gain 1 electron; the total electron gain is 2.

That's how these redox half-reactions work on the Subject Test. Let's try to write the half-reactions for this:

$$4NH_3 + 5O_2 \rightarrow 4NO + 6H_2O$$

◆ Hydrogen's oxidation state doesn't change (it's +1 on both sides).

◆ Oxygen's oxidation state changes from 0 to –2. That means nitrogen's oxidation state must change in order to balance the reduction of oxygen.

◆ What is the change in nitrogen's oxidation state? On the left side of the equation, its oxidation state is –3 (to balance the total +3 oxidation state of the three hydrogen atoms to which each is bonded). On the right side of the equation, its oxidation state is +2 (to balance the –2 oxidation of the oxygen atom to which each is bonded). So, its oxidation state changes from –3 to +2. In other words, nitrogen is oxidized.

Here's the half-reaction that tells us what's happening to it:

◆ **Oxidation:** $4N^{-3} \rightarrow 4N^{+2} + 20e^-$
  meaning that one nitrogen atom loses 5 electrons.

In order to keep the books straight, reduction has to balance oxidation. The nitrogen atoms lost a total of 20 electrons. Some other atoms have to gain a total of 20 electrons. What gains electrons and gets reduced? Oxygen does. It changes its oxidation state from 0 on the left to –2 on the right, and here's the half-reaction that tells us about it:

- **Reduction:** $5O_2 + 20e^- \rightarrow 10\ O^{-2}$

(Of the 10 oxygen atoms with a –2 oxidation state on the right side, 4 are in NO and 6 are in H_2O.) The nitrogen atoms lose a total of 20 electrons, and the oxygen atoms gain a total of 20 electrons. That's how redox reactions work.

Many important reactions are redox reactions. In a **combustion** reaction, a compound containing carbon and hydrogen (and possibly other elements) reacts with molecular oxygen, O_2, to produce CO_2 and H_2O. Look closely at the combustion of acetylene (C_2H_2) and you'll see it's a redox reaction:

$$2C_2^{-1}H_2^{+1} + 5O_2^0 \rightarrow 4\ C^{+4}O_2^{-2} + 2\ H_2^{+1}O^{-2}$$

Notice that carbon is oxidized and oxygen is reduced. The rusting of iron is also a redox reaction. Here's a simplified expression of the rusting process:

$$4Fe^0 + 3O_2^0 \rightarrow 2\ Fe_2^{+3}O_3^{-2}$$

Iron is oxidized and oxygen is reduced. The result is that iron is converted into the reddish-brown iron (II) oxide, commonly called "rust."

OXIDIZING AND REDUCING AGENTS

There are two other terms that should be familiar to you: **oxidizing agent** (or oxidant) and **reducing agent** (or reductant). An oxidizing agent causes another species to be oxidized. An oxidizing agent does this by undergoing reduction. A reducing agent causes some other substance to be reduced. A reducing agent is, itself, oxidized. Consider the two redox reactions we examined earlier:

(1) $Fe + 2HCl \rightarrow FeCl_2 + H_2$

(2) $4\ NH_3 + 5O_2 \rightarrow 4NO + 6\ H_2O$

In the first reaction, Fe (which is oxidized) is the reducing agent and HCl (which contains the species being reduced, H) is the oxidizing agent.

In the second reaction, NH_3 (which contains the species being oxidized, N) is the reducing agent and O_2 (which is reduced) is the oxidizing agent. Note that oxygen (O_2) is an excellent oxidizing agent. Fluorine (F_2) is also a powerful oxidizing agent. The active metals make strong reducing agents.

ELECTROCHEMISTRY

Electrochemistry studies how a spontaneous redox reaction can generate electricity and how electricity can cause a non-spontaneous redox reaction to happen.

ELECTROCHEMICAL CELLS

An **electrochemical cell** (sometimes called a **Voltaic** or **Galvanic Cell**) is a device used to produce an electric current from a spontaneous redox reaction. A battery is made up of one or more electrochemical cells. How do we know that a redox reaction is spontaneous? We must consider something called the **standard electrode potential** for both the oxidation and reduction half-reactions. ("Standard" just means any solutions are 1 M and any gases are at 1 atm.) The standard electrode potential (symbolized by E^0) measures, in volts, the electric potential difference (which is like potential energy) of a given half-reaction relative to the half-reaction:

$$2H^+(aq) + 2e^- \rightarrow H_2(g)$$

If we're measuring E^0_{ox} (oxidation potential), it is relative to the above reduction. If we're measuring E^0_{red} (reduction potential), it is relative to the reverse of the above reaction. To determine if a redox reaction is spontaneous, simply add E^0_{ox} for the oxidation half-reaction and E^0_{red} for the reduction half-reaction. The sum of E^0_{ox} and E^0_{red} is E^0_{cell}, which is the electric potential difference for the overall redox reaction. If E^0_{cell} is greater than 0, then the redox reaction is spontaneous. One other thing about E^0_{ox} and E^0_{red} values: even if a half-reaction is multiplied by some coefficient, never, ever multiply E^0_{ox} by that coefficient. Never multiply E^0 values by anything! The Subject Test writers will supply you with any E^0 values you'll need. Consider the following redox reaction:

$$Cu^{2+}(aq) + Zn(s) \rightarrow Cu(s) + Zn^{2+}(aq)$$

with these half-reactions and E^0 values:

♦ **Oxidation:** $Zn(s) \rightarrow Zn^{2+}(aq) + 2e^-$; $E^0_{ox} = 0.76$ V

♦ **Reduction:** $Cu^{2+}(aq) + 2e^- \rightarrow Cu(s)$; $E^0_{red} = 0.34$ V

For the above reaction, E^0_{cell} is 0.76 V + 0.34 V = 1.10 V. Since $E^0_{cell} > 0$, this redox reaction is spontaneous. This means we can turn the energy that this reaction releases into electrical energy. But how?

If we simply drop some zinc metal into an aqueous solution of Cu^{2+} ion [say, a water solution of $Cu(NO_3)_2$], the spontaneous redox reaction will happen. Electrons will leave the zinc metal as it is oxidized and be captured by the Cu^{2+} ion which will be reduced. All of this will happen, yet we will get no electrical energy out of the reaction. Why not? Because the electrons will immediately go from the zinc atoms to the Cu^{2+} ions. Electrical energy involves the flow of electrons. So if we want electrical energy out of this reaction we must force the electrons that leave zinc to flow through a wire in order to reach Cu^{2+}. This is precisely what the electrochemical cell makes electrons do. The electrochemical cell has the oxidation and reduction half-reactions occur in separate vessels. Each vessel contains an aqueous solution of the ions participating (as reactants or products) in the reaction. We can use $Zn(NO_3)_2(aq)$ and $Cu(NO_3)_2(aq)$ for aqueous solutions in the redox reaction under consideration. A strip of metal called an "electrode" is placed in each solution. Each electrode is made out of a metal that also participates in the reaction. The electrode in the vessel where **oxidation** occurs is called the **anode**. The **cathode** is the electrode in the vessel in which **reduction** takes place. In our electrochemical cell, the anode is a strip of zinc metal and the cathode is a strip of copper metal.

Just remember: **AN OX** and **RED CAT**

The anode and cathode are connected by an electricity-conducting wire. As electrons are freed by the oxidation process at the anode, they travel through the wire to the cathode where they participate in reduction. This flow of electrons is electrical energy, and it has been generated by the spontaneous redox reaction. This is what an electrochemical cell will look like for the reaction between Zn and Cu^{2+}:

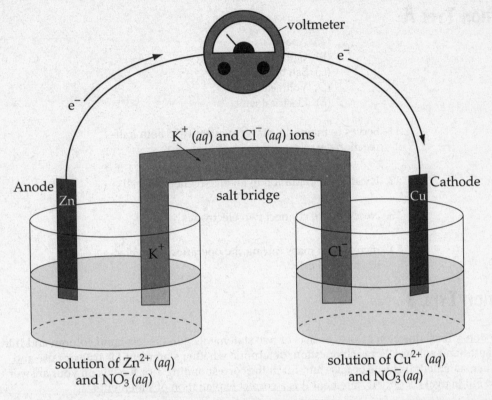

As electrons leave the vessel where oxidation is occurring, a net positive charge accumulates. A net negative charge grows in the reduction vessel where the electrons are going. If something did not neutralize these charge build-ups, the redox reaction would be short-lived since electrons are not going to readily flow from a region of positive charge to a region of negative charge. So, what neutralizes any excess charge build-up? The **salt bridge** does. The salt bridge contains a cation and an anion that don't participate in the redox reaction. As positive charge accumulates in the oxidation vessel, anions flow into it from the salt bridge. Cations leave the salt bridge to flow into the reduction vessel to neutralize any negative charge build-up. In our electrochemical cell we can fill the salt bridge with an aqueous solution of potassium chloride (KCl). K^+ ions flow into the reduction vessel, and Cl^- ions flow into the oxidation vessel.

We can connect a **voltmeter** to the wire to measure the voltage (electric potential) of the electrochemical cell. The actual electric potential is theoretically equal to E^0_{cell}. However, electrical resistance in the wire always causes the actual electric potential to be less than E^0_{cell}. As an electrochemical cell runs, its voltage decreases. When the voltage becomes 0 the spontaneous redox reaction has attained equilibrium and the electrochemical cell is "dead."

ELECTROLYSIS

Electrolysis is the process by which electrical energy is put into a nonspontaneous redox reaction to force it to occur. So during electrolysis, electrical energy is converted into chemical energy. Electrolysis is an important way to separate ionic compounds into their constituent elements. For example, running electricity through a sample of molten NaCl can produce sodium metal (Na) and chlorine gas (Cl_2).

Electroplating is a type of electrolysis in which one metal is deposited on another. For instance, a coating of silver can be electroplated onto a cheaper metal to make quality silverware.

Review what we've said about oxidation-reduction and electrochemistry, and try the following Subject Test-type questions.

QUESTION TYPE A

(A) Anode
(B) Cathode
(C) Salt bridge
(D) Voltmeter
(E) Electrical wire

11. Serves to maintain charge neutrality in both half-reaction vessels

12. Location of oxidation in an electrochemical cell

13. Necessary to connect two electrodes

14. Increases in mass during the operation of an electrochemical cell

QUESTION TYPE B

Directions: Each question below consists of two statements, I in the left-hand column and II in the right-hand column. For each question, determine whether statement I is true or false and whether statement II is true or false and fill in the corresponding T or F ovals on your answer sheet. Fill in oval CE only if statement II is a correct explanation of statement I.

I		II

104. Any reaction in which one atom is oxidized requires that another atom be reduced

BECAUSE

if one species donates electrons another must acquire them.

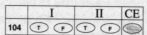

105. Electrolysis requires the input of electrical energy

BECAUSE

a redox reaction that has a positive overall E^0 is nonspontaneous.

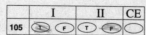

QUESTION TYPE C

32. $2Na + ...Cl_2 \rightarrow ... 2NaCl$

Which of the following is true of the reaction given by the equation above?

(A) Chlorine is oxidized
(B) Sodium is oxidized

(C) Sodium is the oxidizing agent
(D) Both sodium and chlorine are oxidized
(E) Neither sodium nor chlorine is oxidized nor reduced

35. The oxidation state of manganese (Mn) in the compound potassium permanganate ($KMnO_4$) is

(A) +7
(B) +4
(C) 0
(D) –4
(E) –7

54.
$$2Al + 6HCl \rightarrow 2AlCl_3 + 3H_2$$

If 2 moles of Al and 6 moles of HCl react according to the above equation, then how many moles of electrons are transferred during the redox reaction?

(A) 1
(B) 2
(C) 3
(D) 5
(E) 6

TIME FOR SOME ANSWERS

Question 11: Remember the parts of an electrochemical cell and what they do. A salt bridge neutralizes any charge build-up in the half-reaction vessels. So C is the answer.

Question 12: Did you recall AN OX and RED CAT? If so, then you know that oxidation occurs at the anode. Pick A.

Question 13: You may be tempted to pick C. However, a salt bridge really doesn't physically connect the anode to the cathode. An electrical wire (whether or not a voltmeter is also attached) connects the electrodes. So E is right.

Question 14: Think about what happens during the operation of an electrochemical cell. The anode is oxidized into an aqueous cation. That causes the anode to decrease in mass as the redox reaction progresses. The opposite happens at the cathode. An aqueous ion acquires electrons to form more of the metal that composes the cathode. So the cathode gets more massive as the reaction happens. The answer is B.

Question 104: We're into type B. Divide and conquer. Look at the first statement and evaluate it on its own. Is it true? Yes. Wherever there's oxidation there has to be reduction. So, the first statement is true.

Look at the second statement by itself. Is it true? Yes. If one species gives up electrons, it has to give them up to something. Some other species must gain electrons. See whether the whole sentence makes sense.

"Any reaction in which one atom is oxidized requires that another atom be reduced because if one species donates electrons another must acquire them."

Sensible? Absolutely. Oxidation means losing electrons, and reduction means gaining electrons. Oxidation must accompany reduction because if electrons are lost from one place, they must be gained by another. The second statement explains the first. Fill in oval CE.

Question 105: Divide and conquer. Evaluate the first statement on its own. Does electrolysis require the input of electricity? It sure does. So statement I is true.

What about the second statement? A spontaneous redox reaction has positive overall E^0_{cell}, so statement II is false.

Question 32: Do some simple oxidation/reduction arithmetic. Sodium starts with an oxidation state of 0, because it's not in a compound. When Cl is in a compound, its oxidation state is usually –1. In NaCl, Cl has an oxidation state of –1 and Na has an oxidation state of +1. The oxidation state of Na was 0 and is now +1; Na has lost electrons—it has been oxidized. That's why B is right.

Question 35: Again, some simple oxidation/reduction arithmetic is needed. Oxygen's oxidation state here is –2. Since there are 4 oxygen atoms in the formula, oxygen contributes total oxidation of $(-2)(4) = -8$. Potassium's oxidation state is +1. The oxidation state of the overall compound is 0. So $1 + (-8) + X = 0$. $X = +7$. That's why A is right.

Question 54: Let's begin by applying the rules for assigning oxidation states to the given reaction:

$$2Al^0 + 6H^{+1}Cl^{-1} \rightarrow 2\ Al^{+3}Cl_3^{-1} + 3H_2^0$$

Notice that each mole of Al that is oxidized to Al^{+3} loses 3 moles of electrons. So 2 moles of Al lose 6 moles of electrons during oxidation. The 6 moles of electrons that are given up by Al are acquired by H^+ ions to form H_2. So E is right.

13

Organic Chemistry

Organic chemistry is the study of carbon compounds; carbon compounds are especially important because all living things on Earth are based on carbon. Each carbon atom can form up to four bonds, the type of bonding present in organic compounds is almost always covalent, with little polarity. Here are some properties of organic compounds that you should know.

- ◆ Organic compounds are much more soluble in non-polar solvents than in polar solvents. Remember, like dissolves like, so since carbon compounds are generally non-polar, they will be soluble in non-polar solvents. That means that organic substances are not very soluble in water, which is a highly polar solvent.

◆ Organic compounds don't dissociate in solution. Since there is no ionic bonding in organic compounds, they will not dissociate into ions. That means that organic solutions are poor conductors of electricity and organic compounds do not behave as electrolytes in solution.

There are an infinite variety of organic molecules. Sometimes, two organic molecules may have the same chemical makeup with identical constituent elements but with these elements placed in a different geometrical arrangement. This happens fairly often and the two compounds can have completely different chemical properties. Compounds like this are called isomers.

HYDROCARBONS

The simplest organic compounds are hydrocarbons, which contain only carbon and hydrogen. Hydrocarbons can be grouped into three categories: Alkanes, which contain only single carbon-carbon bonds; alkenes, which contain a carbon-carbon double bond; and alkynes, which contain a carbon-carbon triple bond.

ALKANES

Alkanes are hydrocarbons that contain only single bonds. They are also known as saturated hydrocarbons because each carbon atom is bonded to as many other atoms as possible.

Alkane (C_nH_{2n+2})	Formula
Methane	CH_4
Ethane	C_2H_6
Propane	C_3H_8
Butane	C_4H_{10}
Pentane	C_5H_{12}

You can see that the prefixes indicate the number of carbons in the hydrocarbon chain.

Ethane   Propane

ALKENES

Alkenes are hydrocarbons that contain double bonds. They are examples of unsaturated hydrocarbons because the double bond can be broken and each of the two carbons can use the freed electrons to bond with another atom.

Alkene (C_nH_{2n})	Formula
Ethylene	C_2H_4
Propene	C_3H_6
Butene	C_4H_8
Pentene	C_5H_{10}

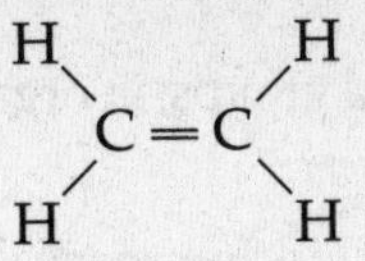

Ethylene 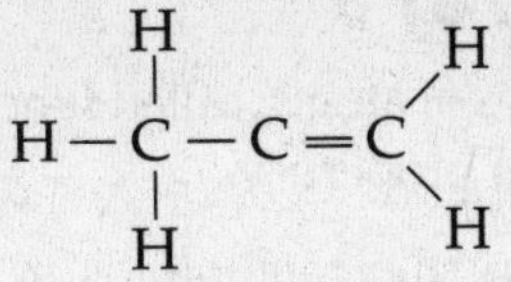   Propene

ALKYNES

Alkynes are hydrocarbons that contain triple bonds. They are also examples of unsaturated hydro-carbons.

Alkyne (C_nH_{2n-2})	Formula
Ethyne	C_2H_2
Propyne	C_3H_4
Butyne	C_4H_6
Pentyne	C_5H_8

Ethyne 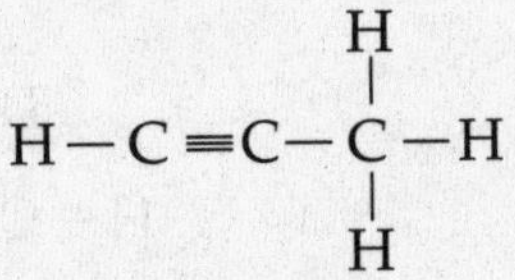   Propyne

HYDROCARBON RINGS

Many hydrocarbons form rings instead of chains. One of most important classes of these compounds is the aromatic hydrocarbons, the simplest of which is benzene, C_6H_6.

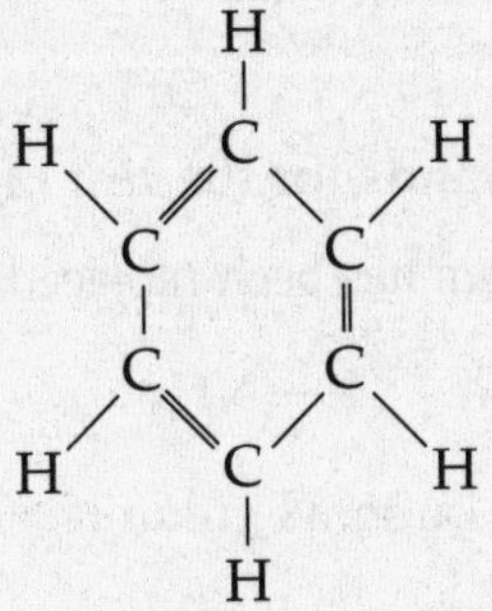

Benzene

FUNCTIONAL GROUPS

The presence of certain groups of atoms, called functional groups, in organic compounds can give the compounds specific chemical properties.

Alcohols — Alcohols are organic compounds in which a hydrogen has been replaced with a hydroxyl group (OH). The hydroxyl group makes an alcohols polar, with the result that alcohols are more soluble in water than most other organic compounds.

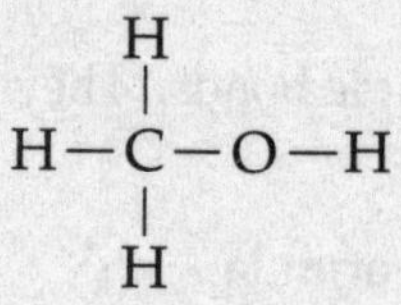

$$
\begin{array}{c}
H \\
| \\
H-C-O-H \\
| \\
H
\end{array}
$$

Methanol

Halides — Halides are organic compounds in which one or more hydrogens have been replaced with a halide (F, Cl, Br, I).

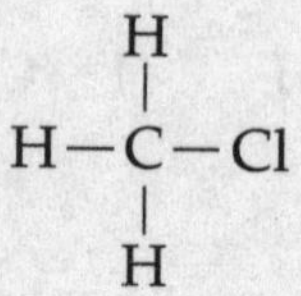

$$
\begin{array}{c}
H \\
| \\
H-C-Cl \\
| \\
H
\end{array}
$$

Organic Acids — Organic acids are organic compounds in which a hydrogen has been replaced with a carboxyl group (COOH).

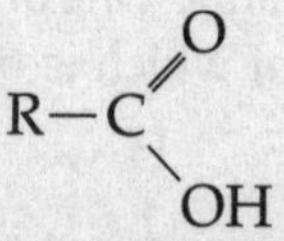

$$
\begin{array}{c}
\quad\quad\quad O \\
\quad\quad\quad \| \\
R-C \\
\quad\quad\quad \backslash \\
\quad\quad\quad OH
\end{array}
$$

The 'R' in the diagram stands for the rest of the hydrocarbon chain.

Amines — In an amine, a hydrogen atom has been replaced by an amino group (NH$_2$).

$$R-NH_2$$

Aldehydes — An aldehyde contains a carbonyl group (C=O) connected to at least one hydrogen atom.

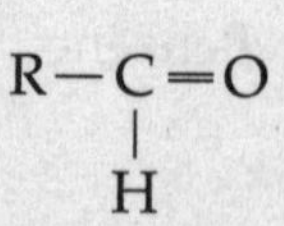

$$
\begin{array}{c}
R-C=O \\
| \\
H
\end{array}
$$

Ketones — A ketone is similar to an aldehyde in that it also contains a carbonyl group (C=O), but in a ketone the carbon in the carbonyl is not connected to any hydrogen atoms.

$$R_1 \diagdown C = O$$
$$R_2 \diagup$$

Ethers — In an ether, an oxygen atom serves as a link in a hydrocarbon chain.

$$R_1 - O - R_2$$

Esters — In an ester, an ester group (COO) serves as a link in a hydrocarbon chain.

$$\overset{\displaystyle O}{\underset{\displaystyle \|}{R_1 - C - O - R_2}}$$

ORGANIC REACTIONS

You should be familiar with a handful of organic reactions in which the organic substances described above are created or combined.

Addition — In an addition reaction, a carbon-carbon double bond is converted into a single bond, freeing each of the two carbons to bond with another element. In the same way, a triple bond can be converted into a double bond in an addition reaction.

Substitution — In a substitution, one atom or group in a compound is replaced with another atom or group. Chemically, this very rarely happens (i.e. direct replacement of H).

Polymerization — In polymerization, two smaller compounds, called monomers, are joined to form a much larger third compound. In condensation polymerization, two monomers are joined in a reaction that produces water.

Cracking — In cracking, a larger compound is broken down into smaller compounds.

Oxidation — An organic compound can react with oxygen at high temperatures to form carbon dioxide and water. This reaction should be familiar to you as combustion, or burning.

$$CH_4 + 2O_2 \rightarrow CO_2 + 2H_2O$$

Esterification — In esterification, an organic acid reacts with an alcohol to produce an ester and water.

Fermentation — In fermentation, an organic compound reacts in the absence of oxygen to produce an alcohol and carbon dioxide. Wine is produced through fermentation.

You're Ready

If you've gone through this whole book, answered our questions, and read our explanations all along the way, you're going to raise your Subject Test score. Go on to the next chapter. Take our simulated Chemistry Subject Tests. If you like, you might also take the Chemistry Subject Tests the College Board has released.

Will there be some questions you can't answer? Of course. But that's okay. Use our elimination strategies and guess from among the choices that remain, and there will be so many questions that you *can* answer, you won't be bothered by the few that you have to guess at. We've taught you the chemistry you need to beat the Subject Test because, right now, your Subject Test score is the only thing we care about.

So great job sticking with us. Go to it, and good luck!

14
Laboratory

SAFETY RULES

❗ Safety goggles should always be worn in the laboratory.

❗ Always work with good ventilation; many common chemicals are toxic.

❗ Take extra care when working with an open flame.

❗ When diluting an acid, always add the acid to the water. This is to avoid the spattering of hot solution.

❗ When heating substances, do it slowly. When you heat things too quickly, they can spatter, burn, or explode.

ACCURACY

◎ When titrating, rinse the buret with the solution to be used in the titration instead of with water. If you rinse the buret with water, you might dilute the solution, which will cause the volume added from the buret to be too large.

◎ Allow hot objects to return to room temperature before weighing. Hot objects on a scale create convection currents which may make the object seem lighter than it is.

◎ Don't weigh reagents directly on a scale. Use a glass or porcelain container to prevent corrosion of the balance pan.

◎ Don't contaminate your chemicals. Never insert another piece of equipment into a bottle containing a chemical. Instead you should always pour the chemical into another clean container. Also, don't let the inside of the stopper for a bottle containing a chemical touch another surface.

◎ When mixing chemicals, stir slowly to ensure even distribution.

◎ Be conscious of significant figures when you record your results. The number of significant figures that you use should indicate the accuracy of your results.

SIGNIFICANT FIGURES

When you do calculations based on measurements that you take in the lab, your answers can only be as precise as the measurements that you took. The way to make sure all your calculations reflect the precision of your measurements is to be aware of significant figures (or significant digits). The more significant figures in the numbers you use, the more precise your answer will be. The number of significant figures you use will be determined by the precision of your measuring device.

The rules for recognizing and calculating with significant figures are given below.

1. Non-zero digits and zeros between non zero digits are significant.

362	3 significant figures
4.609	4 significant figures
103.06	5 significant figures

2. Zeros to the left of the first non-zero digit in a number are not significant.

0.004	1 significant figure
0.0802	3 significant figures

3. Zeros at the end of a number to the right of the decimal point are significant.

67.000	5 significant figures
0.030	2 significant figures
2.0	2 significant figures

4. Zeros at the end of a number greater than 1 are not significant, unless their significance is indicated by the presence of a decimal point.

2,600	2 significant figures
2,600.	4 significant figures
50	1 significant figure
50.	2 significant figures

5. The coefficients of a balanced equation and numbers obtained by counting objects are infinitely significant. So if a balanced equation calls for 3 moles of carbon, we can think of it as $3.0\bar{0}$ moles of carbon.

When multiplying and dividing, the result should have the same number of significant figures as the number in the calculation with the smallest number of significant figures.

$$0.352 \times 0.90876 = 0.320$$
$$864 \times 12 = 1.0 \times 10^4$$
$$7.0 \div 0.567 = 12$$

When adding and subtracting, the result should have the same number of decimal places as the number in the calculation with the smallest number of decimal places.

$$26 + 45.88 + 0.09534 = 72.$$
$$780 + 35 + 4 = 820$$

Remember: The result of a calculation can not be more accurate than the least accurate number in the calculation.

LAB PROCEDURES

METHODS OF SEPARATION

Filtration — In filtration, solids are separated from liquids when the mixture is passed through a filter. Typically, porous paper is used as the filter. To find the amount of solid that is filtered out of a mixture, the filter paper containing the solid is allowed to dry and is then weighed. The initial weight of the clean dry filter is is then subtracted from the weight of the dried filter paper and solid.

Distillation — In distillation, the differences in the boiling points of liquids can be used to separate them. The temperature of the mixture is raised to a temperature that is greater than the boiling point of the more volatile substance and lower than the boiling point of the less volatile substance. The more volatile substance will vaporize, leaving the less volatile substance as a liquid.

Chromatography — In chromatography, substances are separated by the differences in the degree to which they are adsorbed onto a surface. The substances are passed over the adsorbing surface and the ones that stick to the surface with greater attraction will move slower than the substances that are less attracted to the surface. This difference in speeds is what separates the substances. The name 'chromatography' came about because the process is used to separate pigments.

TITRATION

Titration is one the the most important laboratory procedures. In titration, a acid-base neutralization reaction is used to find the concentration of an unknown acid or base. It takes exactly one mole of hydroxide ions (base) to neutralize one mole of hydrogen ions (acid), so the concentration of an unknown acid solution can be found by finding out how much of a known basic solution is required to neutralize a sample of given volume. The most important formula in titration experiments is derived from the definition of molarity:

$$Molarity = moles/Liters$$
$$moles = (Molarity)(Liters)$$

The moment when exactly enough base has been added to the sample to neutralize the acid present is called the equivalence point. In the lab, an indicator is used to tell when the equivalence point has been reached. In indicator is a substance that is one color in acid solution and a different color in basic solution. Two popular indicators are phenolphthalein, which is clear in acidic solution and pink in basic solution; and litmus, which is pink in acidic solution and blue in basic solution.

IDENTIFYING CHEMICALS

Precipitation — Unknown ions in solution can be identified by precipitation. If you know which salts are soluble and which are insoluble, you can use process of elimination to identify unknown ions in solution. For instance, nearly all salts containing chlorine are soluble, but silver chloride is not. So if you put chloride ions into a solution and you get a precipitate, that probably means that silver ions were present in the solution.

Conduction — You can tell whether a solution contains ions or not by checking to see if the solution conducts electricity. Ionic solutes conduct electricity in solution, non—ionic solutes do not.

Flame Tests — Certain chemicals burn with distinctly colored flames. This is especially true of the alkali metals and the alkaline earth metals.

Colored Solutions — The color of a solution will sometimes indicate which chemicals are present. For instance, the colors of solutions containing transition metals will vary depending on the element present.

LABORATORY EQUIPMENT

The pictures below show some standard chemistry lab equipment.

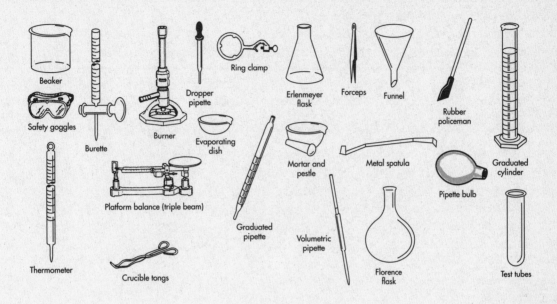

Beaker

Safety goggles

Burette

Dropper pipette

Burner

Evaporating dish

Ring clamp

Erlenmeyer flask

Forceps

Funnel

Rubber policeman

Graduated cylinder

Thermometer

Platform balance (triple beam)

Crucible tongs

Graduated pipette

Mortar and pestle

Metal spatula

Pipette bulb

Volumetric pipette

Florence flask

Test tubes

15

The Princeton Review SAT II: Chemistry Subject Test I

CHEMISTRY
SUBJECT TEST I

You are about to take the first of The Princeton Review's two simulated SAT II: Chemistry Subject Tests.

After answering questions 1–23, which constitute part A, you'll be directed to answer questions 101–116, which constitute part B. Then begin again at question 24. Questions 24–69 constitute Part C.

When you're ready to score yourself, refer to the scoring instructions and answer key on pages 164 and 165. Full explanations regarding the correct answers to all questions start on page 187.

Material in the following table may be useful in answering the questions in this examination.

PERIODIC CHART OF THE ELEMENTS

1 **H** 1.0																	2 **He** 4.0
3 **Li** 6.9	4 **Be** 9.0											5 **B** 10.8	6 **C** 12.0	7 **N** 14.0	8 **O** 16.0	9 **F** 19.0	10 **Ne** 20.2
11 **Na** 23.0	12 **Mg** 24.3											13 **Al** 27.0	14 **Si** 28.1	15 **P** 31.0	16 **S** 32.1	17 **Cl** 35.5	18 **Ar** 39.9
19 **K** 39.1	20 **Ca** 40.1	21 **Sc** 45.0	22 **Ti** 47.9	23 **V** 50.9	24 **Cr** 52.0	25 **Mn** 54.9	26 **Fe** 55.8	27 **Co** 58.9	28 **Ni** 58.7	29 **Cu** 63.5	30 **Zn** 65.4	31 **Ga** 69.7	32 **Ge** 72.6	33 **As** 74.9	34 **Se** 79.0	35 **Br** 79.9	36 **Kr** 83.8
37 **Rb** 85.5	38 **Sr** 87.6	39 **Y** 88.9	40 **Zr** 91.2	41 **Nb** 92.9	42 **Mo** 95.9	43 **Tc** (98)	44 **Ru** 101.1	45 **Rh** 102.9	46 **Pd** 106.4	47 **Ag** 107.9	48 **Cd** 112.4	49 **In** 114.8	50 **Sn** 118.7	51 **Sb** 121.8	52 **Te** 127.6	53 **I** 126.9	54 **Xe** 131.3
55 **Cs** 132.9	56 **Ba** 137.3	57 ***La** 138.9	72 **Hf** 178.5	73 **Ta** 180.9	74 **W** 183.9	75 **Re** 186.2	76 **Os** 190.2	77 **Ir** 192.2	78 **Pt** 195.1	79 **Au** 197.0	80 **Hg** 200.6	81 **Tl** 204.4	82 **Pb** 207.2	83 **Bi** 209.0	84 **Po** (209)	85 **At** (210)	86 **Rn** (222)
87 **Fr** (223)	88 **Ra** 226.0	89 †**Ac** 227.0															

*Lanthanum Series

58 **Ce** 140.1	59 **Pr** 140.9	60 **Nd** 144.2	61 **Pm** (145)	62 **Sm** 150.4	63 **Eu** 152.0	64 **Gd** 157.3	65 **Tb** 158.9	66 **Dy** 162.5	67 **Ho** 164.9	68 **Er** 167.3	69 **Tm** 168.9	70 **Yb** 173.0	71 **Lu** 175.0

†Actinium Series

90 **Th** 232.0	91 **Pa** 231.0	92 **U** 238.0	93 **Np** 237.0	94 **Pu** (244)	95 **Am** (243)	96 **Cm** (247)	97 **Bk** (247)	98 **Cf** (251)	99 **Es** (252)	100 **Fm** (258)	101 **Md** (258)	102 **No** (259)	103 **Lr** (260)

CHEMISTRY TEST I

Note: For all questions involving solutions and/or chemical equations, assume that the system is in water unless otherwise stated.

Part A

Directions: Each set of lettered choices below refers to the numbered statements or formulas immediately following it. Select the one lettered choice that best fits each statement or formula, and then fill in the corresponding oval on the answer sheet. A choice may be used once, more than once, or not at all in each set.

Questions 1–4

    (A) Thermometer
    (B) Conductivity tester
    (C) Salt bridge
    (D) Buret
    (E) Graduated cylinder

1. May be used in combination with a calorimeter to compare the specific heats of two substances

2. Is used to measure the volume of a solid by water displacement

3. Useful for adding small quantities of acid into a base

4. Completes the circuit of an electrochemical cell

Questions 5–9

    (A) Alkali metals
    (B) Alkaline earth metals
    (C) Noble gases
    (D) Halogens
    (E) Transition metals

5. The most unreactive family of elements

6. Form negative ions in an ionic bond

7. Consist of atoms that have valence electrons in a d subshell

8. Exist as diatomic molecules at room temperature

9. Members possess the lowest first ionization energy in their respective period

GO ON TO THE NEXT PAGE

Questions 10–13

(A) $Ag^+ + Br^- \rightarrow AgBr$

(B) $^{14}_{6}C \rightarrow {}^{14}_{7}N + {}^{0}_{-1}e$

(C) $^{234}_{92}U \rightarrow {}^{230}_{90}Th + {}^{4}_{2}He$

(D) $^{30}_{15}P \rightarrow {}^{30}_{14}Si + {}^{0}_{1}e$

(E) $2HgO \rightarrow 2Hg + O_2$

10. Represents the decomposition of a compound into its constituent elements

11. Represents alpha decay

12. Represents an oxidation-reduction reaction

13. Causes the neutron-to-proton ratio in a nucleus to be lowered

Questions 14–16

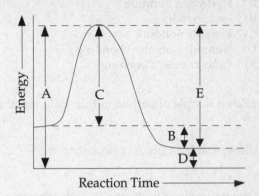

14. Is the activation energy of the reverse reaction

15. Is the enthalpy change of the forward reaction

16. Represents energy of the activated complex

GO ON TO THE NEXT PAGE

CHEMISTRY I—*Continued*

Questions 17–20

(A) Hydrogen bonding
(B) Ionic bonding
(C) Metallic bonding
(D) Nonpolar covalent bonding
(E) Polar covalent bonding

17. Holds a sample of barium iodide, BaI_2, together

18. Allows solids to conduct electricity

19. Attracts atoms of hydrogen to each other in a H_2 molecule

20. Responsible for relatively low vapor pressure of water

Questions 21–23

(A) Iron(III) chloride, $FeCl_3(s)$
(B) Iodine, $I_2(s)$
(C) Sodium hydroxide, $NaOH(s)$
(D) Sucrose, $C_{12}H_{22}O_{11}(s)$
(E) Graphite, $C(s)$

21. Gives off a purplish vapor as it sublimes

22. Can conduct electricity in the solid state

23. Its dissolution in water is highly exothermic

GO ON TO THE NEXT PAGE

CHEMISTRY I—*Continued*

Part B

Directions: Each question below consists of two statements, I in the left-hand column and II in the right-hand column. For each question, determine whether statement I is true or false and whether statement II is true or false and fill in the corresponding T or F ovals on your answer sheet. Fill in oval CE only if statement II is a correct explanation of statement I.

EXAMPLES:

	I		II
EX 1.	H_2SO_4 is a strong acid	BECAUSE	H_2SO_4 contains sulfur.
EX 2.	An atom of oxygen is electrically neutral	BECAUSE	an oxygen atom contains an equal number of protons and electrons.

SAMPLE ANSWERS

	I	II	CE
EX 1	● F	● F	
EX 2	● F	● F	●

	I		II

	I		**II**
101.	Carbon is a nonmetal	BECAUSE	carbon atoms can bond with each other.
102.	Two isotopes of the same element have the same mass number	BECAUSE	isotopes have the same number of protons.
103.	The density of a sample of water is doubled by doubling its mass	BECAUSE	compared to a gas, the molecules in a liquid are relatively far apart.
104.	Sodium and cesium exhibit similar chemical properties	BECAUSE	their atoms have the same number of valence electrons.
105.	An endothermic reaction can be spontaneous	BECAUSE	both enthalpy and entropy changes affect the value of a reaction's Gibbs free energy change.
106.	The $4s$ orbital fills before the $3d$ orbitals	BECAUSE	subshells fill in the order from lower to higher energy.
107.	Calcium acts as a reducing agent when it reacts with bromine	BECAUSE	mass is conserved in a chemical reaction.
108.	If an acid is added to pure water, it increases the water's pH	BECAUSE	adding an acid to water raises the hydrogen ion concentration in the water.

GO ON TO THE NEXT PAGE ➡

I		**II**
109. Covalent bonds must be broken for a liquid to boil	BECAUSE	heat must be released for a liquid to change into a gas.
110. Alpha particles can be detected using a Geiger counter	BECAUSE	all radioactive elements are highly chemically reactive.
111. As ice absorbs heat and begins to melt, its temperature remains constant	BECAUSE	the absorbed heat is consumed by the breaking of intermolecular interactions.
112. When a solute is added to pure water, the vapor pressure of the water will decrease	BECAUSE	all solutes dissociate into positive and negative ions.
113. The rate of a reaction is accelerated by increasing temperature	BECAUSE	a large equilibrium constant favors the formation of product.
114. Hydrofluoric acid, HF(aq), is a weaker electrolyte than hydrochloric acid, HCl(aq)	BECAUSE	fluorine has a lower electronegativity than chlorine.
115. A nonpolar molecule can have polar bonds	BECAUSE	polar bonds can be symmetrically arranged in a molecule so that there are no net poles.
116. The electrolysis of potassium iodide, KI, produces electrical energy	BECAUSE	electrons flow from the anode to the cathode.

RETURN TO THE SECTION OF YOUR ANSWER SHEET YOU STARTED FOR CHEMISTRY AND ANSWER QUESTIONS 24–69.

GO ON TO THE NEXT PAGE

Part C

Directions: Each of the questions or incomplete statements below is followed by five suggested answers or completions. Select the one that is best in each case and then fill in the corresponding oval on the answer sheet.

24. What is the number of protons and neutrons in an atom with mass number 89 and atomic number 39?

    (A) 50 protons and 50 neutrons
    (B) 50 protons and 39 neutrons
    (C) 39 protons and 89 neutrons
    (D) 39 protons and 50 neutrons
    (E) 39 protons and 39 neutrons

25. $$...C_4H_{10}(g) + ...O_2(g) \rightarrow ...CO_2(g) + ...H_2O(l)$$

    When the above equation is balanced using the lowest whole-number terms, the coefficient of CO_2 is

    (A) 2
    (B) 4
    (C) 8
    (D) 10
    (E) 13

26. Which of the following is closest in mass to a proton?

    (A) alpha particle
    (B) positron
    (C) neutron
    (D) electron
    (E) hydrogen molecule

27. What is the approximate percentage composition by mass of the element oxygen in the compound $HClO_4$?

    (A) 16%
    (B) 32%
    (C) 50%
    (D) 64%
    (E) 75%

28. If two atoms that differ in electronegativity combine by chemical reaction and share electrons, the bond that joins them will be

    (A) metallic
    (B) ionic
    (C) a hydrogen bond
    (D) nonpolar covalent
    (E) polar covalent

29. When the temperature of a 20-gram sample of water is increased from 10 °C to 30 °C, the heat transferred to the water is

    (A) 600 calories
    (B) 400 calories
    (C) 200 calories
    (D) 30 calories
    (E) 20 calories

30. What is the oxidation state of chromium, Cr, in the compound potassium dichromate, $K_2Cr_2O_7$?

    (A) +1
    (B) +2
    (C) +3
    (D) +6
    (E) +12

31. An aqueous solution with pH 5 at 25 °C has a hydroxide ion (OH^-) concentration of

    (A) 1×10^{-11} molar
    (B) 1×10^{-9} molar
    (C) 1×10^{-7} molar
    (D) 1×10^{-5} molar
    (E) 1×10^{-3} molar

GO ON TO THE NEXT PAGE

32.
$$2H_2O(g) \rightarrow 2H_2(g) + O_2(g)$$

The volume of water vapor required to produce 44.8 liters of oxygen by the above reaction is

(A) 11.2 liters
(B) 22.4 liters
(C) 44.8 liters
(D) 89.6 liters
(E) 100.0 liters

33. When 190 grams of $MgCl_2$ are dissolved in water and the resulting solution is 500 ml in volume, what is the molar concentration of $MgCl_2$ in the solution?

(A) 2.0 M
(B) 4.0 M
(C) 8.0 M
(D) 12.0 M
(E) 16.0 M

34. When a fixed amount of gas has its Kelvin temperature doubled and its pressure doubled, the new volume of the gas is

(A) four times greater than its original volume
(B) twice its original volume
(C) unchanged
(D) one half its original volume
(E) one fourth its original volume

35. In 12.4 hours, a 100 gram sample of an element decays so that its mass is 25 grams. What is the approximate half-life of this radioactive substance?

(A) 1.6 hours
(B) 3.1 hours
(C) 6.2 hours
(D) 24.8 hours
(E) 49.6 hours

36. In the equation $Q \rightarrow {}_{2}^{4}He + {}_{85}^{216}At$, the species represented by Q is

(A) ${}_{87}^{220}Fr$

(B) ${}_{83}^{212}Bi$

(C) ${}_{87}^{220}At$

(D) ${}_{83}^{212}Fr$

(E) ${}_{85}^{216}Bi$

37. A compound with a molecular weight of 56 amu has an empirical formula of CH_2. What is its molecular formula?

(A) C_2H_2
(B) C_2H_4
(C) C_4H_8
(D) C_4H_{10}
(E) C_6H_{12}

38. The change in heat energy for a reaction is best expressed as a change in

(A) enthalpy
(B) absolute temperature
(C) specific heat
(D) entropy
(E) kinetic energy

39. $\ldots NF_3(g) + \ldots H_2O(g) \rightarrow \ldots HF(g) + \ldots NO(g) + \ldots NO_2(g)$

When the equation for the reaction above is balanced, how many moles of NF_3 would be required to react completely with 6 moles of H_2O ?

(A) 0.5 mole
(B) 1 mole
(C) 2 moles
(D) 3 moles
(E) 4 moles

40. Which characteristic is associated with bases?

(A) React with metal to produce hydrogen gas
(B) Donate an unshared electron pair
(C) Always contain the hydroxide ion in its structure
(D) Taste sour
(E) Formed by the reaction of a nonmetal oxide and water

GO ON TO THE NEXT PAGE

41. An element has the following properties: shiny, brittle, poor electrical conductivity, and high melting point. This element can be best classified as a(n)

    (A) alkali metal
    (B) halogen
    (C) metalloid
    (D) transition metal
    (E) noble gas

42. Which of the following forward processes produces a decrease in entropy?

    I. $H_2O(g) \rightarrow H_2O(l)$
    II. $Fe^{2+}(aq) + S^{2-}(aq) \rightarrow FeS(s)$
    III. $2SO_3(g) \rightleftharpoons 2SO_2(g) + O_2(g)$

    (A) I only
    (B) III only
    (C) I and II only
    (D) II and III only
    (E) I, II, and III

43. Which of the following will raise the boiling point of a sample of water?

    (A) Heat the water
    (B) Mix gasoline into the water
    (C) Bring the water sample to a higher altitude
    (D) Place the water sample on a magnetic stirrer
    (E) Dissolve table sugar into the water

44. Elements H and J lie in the same period. If the atoms of H are smaller than the atoms of J, then compared to atoms of J, atoms of H are most likely to

    (A) exist in a greater number of isotopes
    (B) exist in a lesser number of isotopes
    (C) exist in a greater number of oxidation states
    (D) have a greater positive charge in their nuclei
    (E) have a lesser positive charge in their nuclei

45. $$\ldots Al(s) + \ldots O_2(g) \rightarrow \ldots Al_2O_3(s)$$

    When the equation representing the reaction shown above is completed and balanced and all coefficients are reduced to lowest whole-number terms, the coefficient of $O_2(g)$ is

    (A) 1
    (B) 2
    (C) 3
    (D) 4
    (E) 6

46. Which of the following solids has a brilliant blue color?

    (A) $Ca(OH)_2$
    (B) KCl
    (C) $NaBr$
    (D) Fe_2O_3
    (E) $CuSO_4$

47. Twenty-five percent of element X exists as ^{210}X and 75% of it exists as ^{214}X. What is the atomic weight of element X in amu?

    (A) 85
    (B) 211
    (C) 212
    (D) 213
    (E) 214

48. A 600 ml container holds 2 moles of $O_2(g)$, 3 moles of $H_2(g)$, and 1 mole of $He(g)$. Total pressure within the container is 760 torr. What is the partial pressure of O_2?

    (A) 127 torr
    (B) 253 torr
    (C) 380 torr
    (D) 507 torr
    (E) 760 torr

GO ON TO THE NEXT PAGE

49.
$$Fe(OH)_3(s) \rightleftharpoons Fe^{3+}(aq) + 3OH^-(aq)$$

The ionic solid $Fe(OH)_3$ is added to water and dissociates into its component ions, as shown above. The solubility product expression for the saturated solution is

(A) $K_{sp} = [Fe^{3+}][OH^-]$
(B) $K_{sp} = [Fe^{3+}][3OH^-]$
(C) $K_{sp} = [Fe^{3+}][3OH^-]^3$
(D) $K_{sp} = [Fe^{3+}][OH^-]^3$
(E) $K_{sp} = \dfrac{[Fe^{3+}][OH^-]^3}{[Fe(OH)_3]}$

50. Which of the following electron configurations represents an atom of magnesium in an excited state?

(A) $1s^2 2s^2 2p^6$
(B) $1s^2 2s^2 2p^6 3s^2$
(C) $1s^2 2s^2 2p^5 3s^2 3p^2$
(D) $1s^2 2s^2 2p^6 3s^1 3p^1$
(E) $1s^2 2s^2 2p^6 3s^1 3p^2$

51. All of the following when added to water will produce an electrolytic solution EXCEPT

(A) $N_2(g)$
(B) $HCl(g)$
(C) $KOH(s)$
(D) $NaI(s)$
(E) $CaCl_2(s)$

52. $NH_3(aq) + H_2CO_3(aq) \rightleftharpoons NH_4^+(aq) + HCO_3^-(aq)$

In the reaction represented above, NH_4^+ acts as a(n)

(A) indicator
(B) hydrate
(C) acid
(D) base
(E) salt

53. Which species has the ground state electron configuration $1s^2 2s^2 2p^6 3s^2 3p^6$?

(A) Sulfide ion, S^{2-}
(B) Bromide ion, Br^-
(C) Neon atom, Ne
(D) Chromium ion, Cr^{3+}
(E) Potassium atom, K

54. Which of the following species is amphoteric?

(A) Na_3PO_4
(B) HSO_4^-
(C) KOH
(D) HNO_3
(E) $C_2O_4^{2-}$

55. An ideal gas has a volume of 10 liters at 20 °C and a pressure of 750 mmHg. Which of the following expressions is needed to determine the volume of the same amount of gas at STP ?

(A) $10 \times \dfrac{750}{760} \times \dfrac{0}{20}$ L

(B) $10 \times \dfrac{750}{760} \times \dfrac{293}{273}$ L

(C) $10 \times \dfrac{760}{750} \times \dfrac{0}{20}$ L

(D) $10 \times \dfrac{760}{750} \times \dfrac{273}{293}$ L

(E) $10 \times \dfrac{750}{760} \times \dfrac{273}{293}$ L

GO ON TO THE NEXT PAGE

Questions 56–57 pertain to the phase diagram for substance Z below:

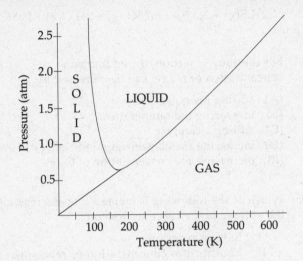

56. Substance Z is at 0.5 atm and 200 K. If the pressure on substance Z is steadily increased and its temperature is kept constant, what phase change will eventually occur?

   (A) Condensation
   (B) Freezing
   (C) Melting
   (D) Sublimation
   (E) Vaporization

57. The normal boiling point of substance Z is closest to

   (A) 100 K
   (B) 200 K
   (C) 300 K
   (D) 400 K
   (E) 500 K

58. The shape of a PCl_3 molecule is described as

   (A) bent
   (B) trigonal pyramidal
   (C) linear
   (D) trigonal planar
   (E) tetrahedral

59. What volume of 0.4 M $Ba(OH)_2$ *(aq)* is needed to exactly neutralize 100 milliliters of 0.2 M HBr*(aq)* ?

   (A) 25 ml
   (B) 50 ml
   (C) 100 ml
   (D) 200 ml
   (E) 400 ml

60. Which of the following is true regarding the aqueous dissociation of HCN, $K_a = 4.9 \times 10^{-10}$ at 25 °C ?

   I. At equilibrium, $[H^+] = [CN^-]$
   II. At equilibrium, $[H^+] > [HCN]$
   III. HCN*(aq)* is a strong acid.

   (A) I only
   (B) II only
   (C) I and II only
   (D) II and III only
   (E) I, II, and III

61. Which of the following atoms has the largest second ionization energy?

   (A) Silicon, Si
   (B) Calcium, Ca
   (C) Chlorine, Cl
   (D) Iron, Fe
   (E) Sodium, Na

GO ON TO THE NEXT PAGE

Question 62 refers to the overall reaction and half-reactions with standard reduction potentials below:

$$2Fe^{2+} + Cl_2 \rightarrow 2Fe^{3+} + 2Cl^-$$

$$Fe^{3+} + e^- \rightarrow Fe^{2+} \; ; E°_{red} = 0.77 \text{ volts}$$

$$Cl_2 + 2e^- \rightarrow 2Cl^- \; ; E°_{red} = 1.36 \text{ volts}$$

62. The standard potential difference of an electrochemical cell using the overall reaction above is

    (A) 0.18 volts
    (B) 0.59 volts
    (C) 1.05 volts
    (D) 2.13 volts
    (E) 2.90 volts

63. The reaction of zinc metal, Zn, and hydrochloric acid, HCl, produces which of the following?

    I. $H_2(g)$
    II. $Cl_2(g)$
    III. $Zn^{2+}(aq)$

    (A) II only
    (B) III only
    (C) I and II only
    (D) I and III only
    (E) I, II, and III

Questions 64–65 refer to the following reaction:

$$2H_2S(g) + 3O_2(g) \leftrightharpoons 2SO_2(g) + 2H_2O(g) + heat$$

64. For the above reaction, the equilibrium concentration of $SO_2(g)$ can be increased by

    (A) adding neon gas
    (B) increasing the temperature
    (C) adding a catalyst
    (D) increasing the concentration of $H_2O(g)$
    (E) increasing the concentration of $O_2(g)$

65. Which of the following is increased by decreasing the volume of the reaction system?

    I. Rate of reaction
    II. Equilibrium concentration of reactants
    III. Value of K_{eq}

    (A) I only
    (B) III only
    (C) I and II only
    (D) II and III only
    (E) I, II, and III

GO ON TO THE NEXT PAGE

66. $$Fe_2O_3(s) + 3CO(g) \rightarrow 2Fe(s) + 3CO_2(g)$$

When 3.0 moles of Fe_2O_3 is allowed to completely react with 56 grams of CO according to the above equation, approximately how many moles of iron, Fe, are produced?

(A) 0.7
(B) 1.3
(C) 2.0
(D) 2.7
(E) 6.0

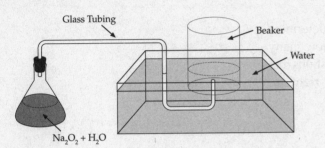

Glass Tubing — Beaker — Water

$Na_2O_2 + H_2O$

$$2Na_2O_2(s) + 2H_2O(l) \rightarrow 4NaOH(aq) + O_2(g)$$

67. Sodium peroxide, Na_2O_2, and water react in the flask at 25 °C according to the equation and in the apparatus above. If water levels are equal inside and outside the beaker, then the gas pressure inside the beaker is equal to the

(A) pressure of oxygen gas collected
(B) vapor pressure of water at 25 °C
(C) sum of pressure of oxygen gas collected and atmospheric pressure
(D) sum of vapor pressure of water at 25 °C and atmospheric pressure
(E) sum of pressure of oxygen gas collected and vapor pressure of water at 25 °C

68. Which of the following molecules has the strongest carbon-to-carbon bond?

(A) C_2H_2
(B) C_2H_4
(C) C_2H_6
(D) C_3H_8
(E) C_4H_{10}

69. $$N_2O_4(g) \rightleftharpoons 2NO_2(g)$$

The following concentration data were gathered for the above reaction at 5 minute intervals from the start of an experiment:

Time After Start of Experiment	$[N_2O_4]$	$[NO_2]$
0 min (start)	0.00 M	0.50 M
5 min	0.10 M	0.33 M
10 min	0.20 M	0.20 M
15 min	0.25 M	0.15 M
20 min	0.28 M	0.13 M
25 min	0.28 M	0.13 M

If the experiment was carried out in a closed system at constant temperature, then during which time interval (from the start of the experiment) did the reaction most likely achieve equilibrium?

(A) 0 min (start) to 5 min
(B) 5 min to 10 min
(C) 10 min to 15 min
(D) 15 min to 20 min
(E) 20 min to 25 min

STOP

IF YOU FINISH BEFORE TIME IS CALLED, YOU MAY CHECK YOUR WORK ON THIS TEST ONLY. DO NOT TURN TO ANY OTHER TEST IN THIS BOOK.

HOW TO SCORE THE PRINCETON REVIEW
CHEMISTRY SUBJECT TEST

When you take the real exam, the proctors will collect your test booklet and bubble sheet and send your answer sheet to New Jersey where a computer (yes, a big, old-fashioned one that has been around since the '60s) looks at the pattern of filled-in ovals on your answer sheet and gives you a score. We couldn't include even a small computer with this book, so we are providing this more primitive way of scoring your exam.

DETERMINING YOUR SCORE

STEP 1   Using the answer key on the next page, determine how many questions you got right and how many you got wrong on the test. Remember, questions that you do not answer don't count as either right answers or wrong answers.

STEP 2   List the number of right answers here.   (A) _____

STEP 3   List the number of wrong answers here. Now divide that number by 4. (Use a calculator if you're feeling particularly lazy.)

(B) _____ ÷ 4 = _____

STEP 4   Subtract the number of wrong answers divided by 4 from the number of correct answers. Round this score to the nearest whole number. This is your raw score.

(A) _____ – (B) _____ = _____

STEP 5   To determine your real score, take the number from Step 4 above and look it up in the left column of the Score Conversion Table on page 166; the corresponding score on the right is your score on the exam.

ANSWERS TO THE PRINCETON REVIEW
CHEMISTRY SUBJECT TEST I

Question Number	Correct Answer	Right	Wrong
1.	A	____	____
2.	E	____	____
3.	D	____	____
4.	C	____	____
5.	C	____	____
6.	D	____	____
7.	E	____	____
8.	D	____	____
9.	A	____	____
10.	E	____	____
11.	C	____	____
12.	E	____	____
13.	B	____	____
14.	E	____	____
15.	B	____	____
16.	A	____	____
17.	B	____	____
18.	C	____	____
19.	D	____	____
20.	A	____	____
21.	B	____	____
22.	E	____	____
23.	C	____	____
24.	D	____	____
25.	C	____	____
26.	C	____	____
27.	D	____	____
28.	E	____	____
29.	B	____	____
30.	D	____	____
31.	B	____	____
32.	D	____	____
33.	B	____	____
34.	C	____	____
35.	C	____	____
36.	A	____	____
37.	C	____	____
38.	A	____	____
39.	E	____	____
40.	B	____	____
41.	C	____	____
42.	C	____	____
43.	E	____	____
44.	D	____	____
45.	C	____	____

Question Number	Correct Answer	Right	Wrong
46.	E	____	____
47.	D	____	____
48.	B	____	____
49.	D	____	____
50.	D	____	____
51.	A	____	____
52.	C	____	____
53.	A	____	____
54.	B	____	____
55.	E	____	____
56.	A	____	____
57.	C	____	____
58.	B	____	____
59.	A	____	____
60.	A	____	____
61.	E	____	____
62.	B	____	____
63.	D	____	____
64.	E	____	____
65.	A	____	____
66.	B	____	____
67.	E	____	____
68.	A	____	____
69.	D	____	____

Question Number	Correct Answer
101.	T, T
102.	F, T
103.	F, F
104.	T, T, CE
105.	T, T, CE
106.	T, T, CE
107.	T, T
108.	F, T
109.	F, F
110.	T, F
111.	T, T, CE
112.	T, F
113.	T, T
114.	T, F
115.	T, T, CE
116.	F, T

THE PRINCETON REVIEW CHEMISTRY SUBJECT TEST
SCORE CONVERSION TABLE
Recentered scale as of April 1995

Raw Score	Scaled Score	Raw Score	Scaled Score	Raw Score	Scaled Score
85	800	45	620	5	390
84	800	44	620	4	390
83	800	43	610	3	380
82	800	42	610	2	380
81	800	41	600	1	370
80	800	40	590	0	370
79	800	39	590	−1	370
78	790	38	580	−2	360
77	780	37	580	−3	360
76	780	36	570	−4	350
75	780	35	560	−5	340
74	780	34	560	−6	340
73	780	33	550	−7	330
72	770	32	550	−8	330
71	770	31	540	−9	320
70	750	30	530	−10	310
69	750	29	530	−11	310
68	740	28	520	−12	300
67	740	27	520	−13	300
66	740	26	520	−14	290
65	730	25	510	−15	280
64	730	24	510	−16	280
63	710	23	500	−17	270
62	710	22	500	−18	270
61	710	21	490	−19	260
60	700	20	480	−20	250
59	700	19	480	−21	250
58	690	18	470		
57	690	17	470		
56	680	16	460		
55	680	15	450		
54	680	14	450		
53	670	13	440		
52	670	12	440		
51	660	11	430		
50	650	10	420		
49	650	9	420		
48	630	8	410		
47	630	7	410		
46	630	6	400		

16

Answers and Explanations

PART A

QUESTIONS 1–4

(A) Thermometer
(B) Conductivity tester
(C) Salt bridge
(D) Buret
(E) Graduated cylinder

1. May be used in combination with a calorimeter to
compare the specific heats of two substances

A is correct. *See pages 23–24.* When we talk of specific heat, we're talking about the amount of heat necessary to produce a change in temperature. The calorimeter is used to measure heat input or output and the thermometer, choice A, would be used in combination with it to ascertain the associated change in temperature.

2. Is used to measure the volume of a solid by water
displacement

E is correct. *See page 20.* A graduated cylinder can be used to help find the volume of an irregularly-shaped solid. How? Fill the graduated cylinder with water and read the water's volume. Next add the solid. The difference between the volume of the water and solid together and the volume of the water alone is the volume of the solid.

3. Useful for adding small quantities of acid into a
base

D is correct. *See page 120.* When an acid and base are being combined, think "titration." And when you consider titration remember that a buret is typically used to deliver small amounts of acid into a base and vice versa.

4. Completes the circuit of an electrochemical cell

C is correct. *See page 131.* Electrons travel from the anode to the cathode in an electrochemical cell. But what allows the redox reaction to go on by maintaining charge neutrality in each vessel? That's the function of a salt bridge. By doing so, the salt bridge completes the circuit of the electrochemical cell.

QUESTIONS 5–9

(A) Alkali metals
(B) Alkaline earth metals
(C) Noble gases
(D) Halogens
(E) Transition metals

5. The most unreactive family of elements

C is correct. *See page 55.* The atoms of noble gas elements have filled valence shells and, therefore, are extremely unreactive—more so than any other family.

6. Form negative ions in an ionic bond

D is correct. *See pages 65 and 70.* To form a negative ion, an atom needs to acquire electrons. This sounds like a nonmetal, not a metal. Eliminate A, B, and E. Noble gases are essentially inert, so that leaves the halogens. Halogens need one valence electron to complete their valence shell and will readily gain an electron and form an anion to do so.

7. Consist of atoms that have valence electrons in a *d*
   subshell

E is correct. *See page 65.* When the Subject Test writers start talking about the "*d*" subshell, think "transition metals."

8. Exist as diatomic molecules at room temperature

D is correct. *See pages 38 and 65.* Did you remember: **H**ave **N**o **F**ear **O**f **I**ce **C**old **B**ears? If so, you'd realize that some of the most common diatomic molecules are halogens—F_2, Cl_2, Br_2, and I_2.

9. Members possess the lowest first ionization
   energy in their respective period

A is correct. *See pages 64 and 66–67.* Ionization energy is needed to remove an electron from an atom. Which kind of elements tend to give up electrons? Metals, of course. Of the metals, alkali metals, having only one valence electron per atom, will lose one electron easiest. This allows an alkali metal atom to assume a stable noble gas electron configuration.

Questions 10–13

(A) $Ag^+ + Br^- \rightarrow AgBr$

(B) $^{14}_{6}C \rightarrow ^{14}_{7}N + ^{0}_{-1}e$

(C) $^{234}_{92}U \rightarrow ^{230}_{90}Th + ^{4}_{2}He$

(D) $^{30}_{15}P \rightarrow ^{30}_{14}Si + ^{0}_{1}e$

(E) $2HgO \rightarrow 2Hg + O_2$

10. Represents the decomposition of a compound
    into its constituent elements

E is correct. *See page 30.* Any problem you might have with this question is with words, not ideas. Don't let phrases like "constituent elements" throw you off course. The question asks you to identify a situation in which a compound is broken down into its elements. Mercury(II) oxide, HgO, is decomposed into the elements mercury, Hg, and oxygen, O_2, in choice E.

11. Represents alpha decay

C is correct. *See page 58.* When a radioactive atom undergoes alpha decay, it loses 2 protons and 2 neutrons. That means its atomic number decreases by 2 and its mass number decreases by 4. That's exactly what has happened here. Uranium (atomic number = 92, mass number = 234) has been converted to thorium (atomic number = 90, mass number = 230).

12. Represents an oxidation-reduction reaction

E is correct. *See pages 126–127.* The phrase "oxidation-reduction reaction," describes a reaction in which one atom loses electron(s) to another. The atom that loses electrons is oxidized, and the one that gains electrons is reduced. In HgO, the oxidation state of Hg is +2 and that of oxygen is –2. HgO is decomposed into the free elements Hg and O$_2$, each having an oxidation state of 0. So the oxidation state of Hg goes from +2 to 0; it has been reduced. Oxygen has been oxidized; its oxidation state has changed from –2 to 0. This is clearly a redox reaction.

13. Causes the neutron-to-proton ratio in a nucleus to be lowered

B is correct. *See page 58.* Check out choice B. In an atom of carbon-14 there are 8 neutrons to 6 protons, a ratio greater than 1. In nitrogen-14, the neutron-to-proton ratio is 7 to 7 or equivalent to 1. Choice B gives an example of beta decay. As you can see, beta decay causes the neutron-to-proton ratio to decrease.

QUESTIONS 14–16

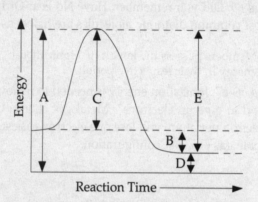

14. Is the activation energy of the reverse reaction

E is correct. *See pages 103–104.* The activation energy of forward and reverse reactions is always characterized by the "hump" that you see in pictures of this kind. It's the energy necessary to get the reaction going. The reactants of the reverse reaction have energy that is expressed by the flat portion of the curve to the right of the hump. In order for a reaction to occur, these reactants must gain an energy equal to that represented by the top of the hump. This energy that must be acquired is represented by E. Remember that catalysts reduce activation energy and let the reaction get going more quickly.

15. Is the enthalpy change of the forward reaction

B is correct. *See page 46.* When we talk about the enthalpy change of a reaction, we mean the amount of heat it absorbs or gives out. In this case we see that the reactants begin at one energy level (represented by the flat portion of the curve to the left of the hump) and that the products are associated with another (represented by the flat portion of the curve to the right of the hump). The difference represents enthalpy change of the reaction (which, in this case, is negative—the reaction liberates heat; it's exothermic).

16. Represents energy of the activated complex

A is correct. *See page 103.* Recall that the activated complex represents the highest energy state reactants achieve as they are transformed into new substances. So the energy of the activated complex is measured from the bottom of the diagram to the top of the activation energy barrier. This distance is represented by A.

QUESTIONS 17–20

(A) Hydrogen bonding
(B) Ionic bonding
(C) Metallic bonding
(D) Nonpolar covalent bonding
(E) Polar covalent bonding

17. Holds a sample of barium iodide, BaI_2, together

B is correct. *See page 70.* BaI_2 is composed of a metal (Ba) and nonmetal (I) bonded together. This is an ionic compound which is held together by—surprise—ionic bonding.

18. Allows solids to conduct electricity

C is correct. *See pages 70–72.* You may be tempted to go with "ionic bonding" here, but resist that impulse. The ions in an ionic solid are too restricted in their movement to conduct a charge. So B is incorrect. Now think: what solids conduct electricity? Why, metals of course. And why can copper wire be used to conduct electricity? Because the metallic bonds that hold a sample of copper together do so through the motion of many free electrons, which can conduct electricity as they move.

19. Attracts atoms of hydrogen to each other in a H_2 molecule

D is correct. *See page 71.* Don't be fooled by A. Hydrogen bonds occur *between* not *within* molecules. A hydrogen molecule consists of two nonmetal hydrogen atoms in a bond. Nonmetals bond covalently, and identical nonmetal atoms do so in nonpolar fashion. So D is right.

20. Responsible for relatively low vapor pressure of water

A is correct. *See pages 85 and 90.* Water's vapor pressure (its tendency to evaporate) is low compared to other similarly-sized molecules. What keeps molecules together in the liquid state? Intermolecular forces do. And the intermolecular force most prevalent in water is hydrogen bonding. Since hydrogen bonds are a relatively strong intermolecular force, water molecules are significantly attracted to each other and do not evaporate as readily as comparably-sized molecules.

QUESTIONS 21–23

(A) Iron (III) chloride, $FeCl_3(s)$
(B) Iodine, $I_2(s)$
(C) Sodium hydroxide, $NaOH(s)$
(D) Sucrose, $C_{12}H_{22}O_{11}(s)$
(E) Graphite, $C(s)$

21. Gives off a purplish vapor as it sublimes

B is correct. *See page 65.* You might be asking yourself: purplish vapor? How am I supposed to know that? Unfortunately there will be a few questions on the Subject Test that will see how familiar you are with the properties of certain substances. Hopefully your experiences in chemistry lab will carry you through. If not, don't panic. You'll only see a few of these types of questions. By the way, iodine is a grayish-purple solid that gives off a similarly colored vapor as it sublimes.

22. Can conduct electricity in the solid state

E is correct. *See pages 70 and 86.* If you don't know that graphite, a form of carbon, can conduct electricity, you can still get the answer by eliminating the other choices. A and C are ionic solids—they can conduct electricity in solution or in the molten state, but not as solids. Choices B and D (table sugar) are molecular solids. You wouldn't expect molecular solids to be particularly conductive. That leaves graphite, which happens to be a network solid.

23. Its dissolution in water is highly exothermic

C is correct. *See page 46.* If you've dissolved sodium hydroxide pellets in a beaker of water and felt the side of the beaker, you know that the process gives off heat.

PART B

    101. Carbon is a nonmetal   BECAUSE   carbon atoms can bond with each other.

T, T *See pages 65 and 76.* Use the divide and conquer strategy. Carbon is a nonmetal, so statement I is true. Do carbon atoms bond with each other? They sure do. Otherwise we wouldn't have oils, waxes, fossil fuels, diamonds, and literally thousands of different substances. Now, does the sentence make sense? No. Metal atoms can also bond with each other. So this ability is not unique to nonmetals. Fill in both "true" ovals, but not the CE oval.

    102. Two isotopes of the same   BECAUSE   isotopes have the same number of
           element have the same mass   protons.
           number

F, T *See pages 31–33.* Isotopes of the same element do not have the same mass number. But since they come from the same element, their atomic numbers are identical. So the first statement is false and the second is true.

    103. The density of a sample of   BECAUSE   compared to a gas, the molecules
           water is doubled by doubling   in a liquid are relatively far apart.
           its mass

F, F *See pages 20 and 85.* Divide and conquer. At a given temperature, the density of water stays the same whether we have 10 grams or 20 grams. So statement I is false. Statement II is also false. Molecules in the liquid (and solid) state are much closer than they are in the gaseous state.

    104. Sodium and cesium exhibit   BECAUSE   their atoms have the same number
           similar chemical properties   of valence electrons.

T, T, CE *See pages 64–65.* Sodium and cesium are both in the alkali metal family. As such, they have similar chemical properties. So statement I is true. Statement II is also true. Alkali metals such as sodium and cesium have one valence electron in their atoms. Do the two statements make sense when they are combined? Do sodium and cesium exhibit similar chemical properties because their atoms have the same number of valence electrons? That's what we've been saying. So fill in oval CE.

105. An endothermic reaction   BECAUSE   both enthalpy and entropy changes
     can be spontaneous   affect the value of a reaction's
                                                   Gibbs free energy change.

T, T, CE *See pages 46–47.* Divide and conquer. Can an endothermic reaction be spontaneous? Can it? Ever see an ice cube melt at room temperature? That's a spontaneous endothermic process. Thus, the first statement is true. What about the second statement? Remember that the change in Gibbs free energy, ΔG, depends on enthalpy change, ΔH, and entropy change, ΔS: $\Delta G = \Delta H - T\Delta S$. So statement II is also true. Does the second statement explain the first? Yes, it does. That ice cube melts at room temperature because the increase in entropy for the process overcomes the change to a higher energy state. Fill in the CE oval.

106. The 4s orbital fills before   BECAUSE   subshells fill in the order from lower
     the 3d orbitals   to higher energy.

T, T, CE *See pages 53–54.* The first statement is true. The 3d orbitals are of higher energy than the 4s orbital, so the 4s orbital fills first. Evaluate the second statement. It is true. Subshells do fill in order of lower to higher energy. Does the second statement explain the first? Yes, it does. The 4s orbital fills before the 3d orbitals because it is lower in energy. Fill in oval CE.

107. Calcium acts as a reducing   BECAUSE   mass is conserved in a chemical
     agent when it reacts with   reaction.
     bromine

T, T *See pages 43 and 129.* Divide and conquer. Here's what happens when calcium and bromine react: $Ca + Br_2 \rightarrow CaBr_2$. Bromine's oxidation state decreases from 0 to –1. So it is reduced. Calcium (which is oxidized) is responsible for reducing bromine. In other words, calcium acts as a reducing agent. Statement I is true. Look at Statement II. Is mass conserved in a chemical reaction? Yep. If it wasn't, there would be no need to balance equations. So both statements are true. Does statement II explain why statement I is true? No, it doesn't. Do not fill in oval CE.

108. If an acid is added to pure   BECAUSE   adding an acid to water raises the
     water, it increases the   hydrogen ion concentration in
     water's pH   water.

F, T *See pages 113–116.* Adding an acid to water increases the hydrogen ion concentration in the water, which means the water's pH is reduced. So the first statement is false, and the second is true.

109. Covalent bonds must be   BECAUSE   heat must be released for a liquid
     broken for a liquid to boil   to change into a gas.

F, F *See pages 86–87.* Boiling is about overcoming intermolecular forces in a liquid, not about breaking covalent bonds. When water boils, H_2O molecules still exist, only now they're arranged as steam. While we're considering boiling, take a look at statement II. You need to heat water to make it boil. So boiling absorbs, not releases, heat. Both statements are false.

110. Alpha particles can be   BECAUSE   all radioactive elements are highly
     detected using a Geiger   chemically reactive.
     counter

T, F *See pages 56 and 58.* Divide and conquer. A Geiger counter is used to detect radioactive particles, so statement I is true. Be careful with statement II. Radioactive elements have atoms with unstable nuclei. However, that has nothing to do with an atom's valence electrons. Radon (Rn) is a perfect example. The nuclei of radon atoms emit alpha particles. However, radon is a noble gas. Radon atoms have filled valence shells and thus are unreactive chemically. So statement II is false.

111. As ice absorbs heat and   BECAUSE   the absorbed heat is consumed by
     begins to melt, its temperature   the breaking of intermolecular
     remains constant   interactions.

T, T, CE *See pages 87 and 90–91.* The first statement is true. If the temperature of a substance didn't remain constant during melting there would be no such thing as a melting point. Instead, at a given pressure, a substance would melt over a range of temperatures. Statement II is also true. The heat being absorbed by the ice is being used to break intermolecular hydrogen bonds, so we don't see the temperature rise even though heat is being added. Does the second statement explain the first? Yes, it does. Since the average kinetic energy of molecules stays constant during a phase change (such as melting), temperature also remains constant. Fill in oval CE.

112. When a solute is added to   BECAUSE   all solutes dissociate into positive
     pure water, the vapor pressure   and negative ions.
     of the water will decrease

T, F *See page 98.* The first statement is true. Adding a solute to a solvent reduces its freezing point, raises its boiling point and reduces its vapor pressure. The second statement is false. Some, but not all, solutes dissociate into positive and negative ions.

113. The rate of a reaction is   BECAUSE   a large equilibrium constant favors
     accelerated by increasing   the formation of product.
     temperature

T, T *See pages 103 and 105.* Divide and conquer. Statement I is true. A reaction will occur faster if its temperature is raised. Check out the second statement. A large K_{eq} absolutely means that a reaction favors the forward reaction or, in other words, favors product formation. So both statements are true. Put them together. Does the second explain the first? No, it doesn't. The first deals with reaction rates (kinetics) and the second with equilibrium. These are different areas of chemistry. Don't fill in CE.

114. Hydrofluoric acid, HF(*aq*), is   BECAUSE   fluorine has a lower
     a weaker electrolyte than   electronegativity than chlorine.
     hydrochloric acid, HCl (*aq*)

T, F *See pages 67 and 118–119.* Hydrofluoric acid is not one of the six common strong acids. Thus it will partially ionize. The relatively few ions put in solution by the ionization of hydrofluoric acid make it a weak electrolyte. Hydrochloric acid is a strong acid, and it ionizes completely. So HCl(*aq*) is a strong electrolyte. Statement I is true. The second statement is false. Remember that electronegativity values decrease down a given column. So from fluorine to chlorine, electronegativity decreases.

115. A nonpolar molecule can   BECAUSE   polar bonds can be symmetrically
     have polar bonds   arranged in a molecule so that
                                                      there are no net poles.

T, T, CE *See pages 74–76.* The first statement is true. An example is the carbon tetrachloride molecule, CCl_4. It consists of four polar bonds. However, the bonds are arranged such that the overall molecule is nonpolar. If this sounds like it means the second statement is true, well it does. Since the second statement explains the first, we fill in the CE oval.

116. The electrolysis of potassium   BECAUSE   electrons flow from the anode to
     iodide, KI, produces electrical   the cathode.
     energy

F, T *See page 131.* Divide and conquer. Does electrolysis generate electricity? No, electrolysis uses electrical energy to force a chemical reaction to occur. So statement I is false. What about statement II? It's true. Electrons flow from the anode to the cathode in both electrochemical and electrolytic cells.

PART C

24. What is the number of protons and neutrons in an atom with mass number 89 and atomic number 39?

    (A) 50 protons and 50 neutrons
    (B) 50 protons and 39 neutrons
    (C) 39 protons and 89 neutrons
    (D) 39 protons and 50 neutrons
    (E) 39 protons and 39 neutrons

D is correct. *See pages 31–32.* The atomic number is the number of protons in the nucleus, and the mass number is the sum (number of protons) + (number of neutrons). If the atomic number is 39 and the mass number is 89, then the number of neutrons in the nucleus must be (89) − (39) = 50.

25. $...C_4H_{10}(g) +...O_2(g) \rightarrow ...CO_2(g) +...H_2O(l)$

    When the above equation is balanced using the lowest whole-number terms, the coefficient of CO_2 is

    (A) 2
    (B) 4
    (C) 8
    (D) 10
    (E) 13

C is correct. *See pages 43–44.* Use the "plug-in" balancing strategy. Since there are at least 4 carbon atoms on the left, the coefficient of CO_2 cannot be 2. So eliminate A. If the coefficient of carbon is 4, we must place a "1" in front of C_4H_{10} to keep carbons in balance. This will give 10 hydrogens on the left. If we put a "5" in front of H_2O on the right, we then have 13 oxygens on the right. The only way we can get 13 oxygens on the left is to place "$\frac{13}{2}$" in front of O_2 on the left. This puts all the elements in balance, but violates the rule of using only whole numbers. So B is wrong. However, if we multiply the coefficients we just determined by 2, we will maintain balance and have all whole numbers. So the balanced equation becomes:

$$2C_4H_{10}(g) + 13O_2(g) \rightarrow 8CO_2(g) + 10H_2O(l)$$

26. Which of the following is closest in mass to a proton?

    (A) alpha particle
    (B) positron
    (C) neutron
    (D) electron
    (E) hydrogen molecule

C is correct. *See page 31.* The mass of a proton is approximately 1 amu. This is very nearly the mass of a neutron. A positron and electron are much lighter than 1 amu. A hydrogen molecule weighs roughly twice as much as a proton, and an alpha particle weighs about four times as much.

27. What is the approximate percentage composition by mass of the element oxygen in the compound $HClO_4$?

    (A) 16%
    (B) 32%
    (C) 50%
    (D) 64%
    (E) 75%

D is correct. *See page 39.* Add up the mass of one mole of this substance. From the periodic table we know that

   ◆ 1 mole of hydrogen atoms has a mass of about 1 g.

   ◆ 1 mole of chlorine atoms has a mass of about 35 g.

   ◆ 4 moles of oxygen atoms have a mass of about 64 g.

The total gram-molecular weight of this substance, then, is 100 g. Oxygen's "contribution" is 64 g, which means the compound is 64% oxygen by mass.

28. If two atoms that differ in electronegativity combine by chemical reaction and share electrons, the bond that joins them will be

    (A) metallic
    (B) ionic
    (C) a hydrogen bond
    (D) nonpolar covalent
    (E) polar covalent

E is correct. *See page 71.* As soon as you hear of electron sharing, you know you're dealing with a covalent bond. Eliminate A, B, and C. The fact that the two atoms differ in electronegativity tells you that one has more attraction for the shared electrons than the other. The result? A polar covalent bond—the molecule has a negative and a positive pole.

29. When the temperature of a 20-gram sample of water is increased from 10°C to 30°C, the heat transferred to the water is

    (A) 600 calories
    (B) 400 calories
    (C) 200 calories
    (D) 30 calories
    (E) 20 calories

B is correct. *See pages 23–24.* Use $q = mc\Delta T$ to compute the amount of heat transfer. For water, the specific heat, c, is about 1 calorie/g-°C. So a 20g sample of water experiencing a 20°C increase in temperature has (20g) (1 calorie/g-°C)(20°C), or 400 calories of heat, transferred to it.

30. What is the oxidation state of chromium, Cr, in the compound potassium dichromate, $K_2Cr_2O_7$?

    (A) +1
    (B) +2
    (C) +3
    (D) +6
    (E) +12

D is correct. *See page 126.* Remember the oxidation state rules. An oxygen atom usually has a –2 state. Potassium atoms are always given a +1 state. In $K_2Cr_2O_7$, we have 2 potassium atoms and 7 oxygen atoms. So potassium atoms contribute 2(+1), or a state of +2. Oxygen atoms contribute 2 (–7), or –14. For $K_2Cr_2O_7$ to be neutral, each chromium atom must have a state of +6.

31. An aqueous solution with pH 5 at 25 °C has a hydroxide ion (OH⁻) concentration of

    (A) 1×10^{-11} molar
    (B) 1×10^{-9} molar
    (C) 1×10^{-7} molar
    (D) 1×10^{-5} molar
    (E) 1×10^{-3} molar

B is correct. *See pages 114–115.* If pH is 5, then [H⁺] is 1×10^{-5} moles/L. Water's "ion product" is 1×10^{-14} at 25°C, meaning that the product [H⁺] × [OH⁻] is 1×10^{-14}. So [OH⁻] = $1 \times 10^{-14} \div 1 \times 10^{-5}$ = 1×10^{-9} moles/L. So B is right.

32. $$2H_2O(g) \rightarrow 2H_2(g) + O_2(g)$$

The volume of water vapor required to produce 44.8 liters of oxygen by the above reaction is

    (A) 11.2 liters
    (B) 22.4 liters
    (C) 44.8 liters
    (D) 89.6 liters
    (E) 100.0 liters

D is correct. *See pages 44–45.* Based on the balanced equation, the ratio of water vapor consumed to oxygen produced is 2 moles H_2O to 1 mole O_2. The volume of gas will also be in this 2:1 ratio. So 89.6 liters of $H_2O(g)$ are required to produce 44.8 liters of $O_2(g)$.

33. When 190 grams of $MgCl_2$ are dissolved in water and the resulting solution is 500 ml in volume, what is the molar concentration of $MgCl_2$ in the solution?

    (A)   2.0 M
    (B)   4.0 M
    (C)   8.0 M
    (D) 12.0 M
    (E) 16.0 M

B is correct. *See pages 39–40 and 96.* Molarity refers to moles of solute per liter of solution. We know we've got 500 ml of solution, but we don't know how many moles of solute we've got. So let's first figure out the mass of 1 mole of $MgCl_2$. Looking at the periodic table, we find that 1 mole of Mg has a mass of 24.3 g. Two moles of Cl have a mass of about 71 g. For 1 mole of $MgCl_2$, therefore, mass = 95.3 g.

Now, we're dealing with 190 g of $MgCl_2$, which means $\frac{190}{95.3}$ = (about) 2 moles. But don't be duped and jump to choice A! We're looking for the solution's molarity. We have 2 moles of solute in 500 ml (0.5 L) of solution, which means that the molarity is 4 moles/L. That's why B is right.

34. When a fixed amount of gas has its Kelvin
temperature doubled and its pressure doubled,
the new volume of the gas is

(A) four times greater than its original volume
(B) twice its original volume
(C) unchanged
(D) one half its original volume
(E) one fourth its original volume

C is correct. *See pages 79–81.* We'll need the ideal gas equation: $PV = nRT$. What does this equation tell us? It means that volume is directly related to Kelvin temperature and inversely related to pressure. Doubling a gas's Kelvin temperature will double its volume if other variables are held constant. Doubling a gas's pressure will halve its volume if other variables are held constant. So the effect on volume of doubling pressure cancels out the effect of doubling Kelvin temperature. The net result is that the gas's volume will stay the same.

35. In 12.4 hours, a 100 gram sample of element X
decays so that its mass is 25 grams. What is the
approximate half-life of this radioactive substance?

(A) 1.6 hours
(B) 3.1 hours
(C) 6.2 hours
(D) 24.8 hours
(E) 49.6 hours

C is correct. *See page 58.* This is about radioactive decay. In one half-life, a 100 g sample has a mass of 50 g. In two half-lives it has a mass of 25 g. So we're talking about the expiration of 2 half-lives. If 2 half-lives = 12.4 hours, then one half-life = 6.2 hours.

36. In the equation Q $\rightarrow$ $^4_2$He + $^{216}_{85}$At, the species
represented by Q is

(A) $^{220}_{87}$Fr

(B) $^{212}_{83}$Bi

(C) $^{220}_{87}$At

(D) $^{212}_{83}$Fr

(E) $^{216}_{85}$Bi

A is correct. *See page 58.* We're looking at alpha decay, in which a radioactive atom loses 2 protons and 2 neutrons. The loss of 2 protons means the atomic number decreases by 2. Now it's 85, which means it *was* 87. The element with an atomic number of 87 is Fr (francium). The loss of 2 neutrons together with the loss of 2 protons means the mass number has decreased by (2) + (2) = 4. The mass number is now 216, which tells us that it *was* 220. Notice that choice C has the right numbers, but the element is wrong. Remember that the atomic number uniquely identifies an element, so an atomic number of 87 must be Francium no matter what the mass number. This also means that an element can have several different mass numbers, collectively called isotopes.

37. A compound with a molecular weight of 56 amu has an empirical formula of CH_2. What is its molecular formula?

(A) C_2H_2
(B) C_2H_4
(C) C_4H_8
(D) C_4H_{10}
(E) C_6H_{12}

C is correct. *See pages 37–39.* The empirical formula tells us that the ratio of carbon to hydrogen is 1:2. So we're looking first of all for an answer that reflects the same ratio. Only choices B, C, and E do that, so we can eliminate A and D. Now, among B, C, and E, we're looking for the one whose molecular weight is 56 amu. Look at the periodic table. Every carbon atom has an atomic weight of 12 amu, and every hydrogen atom has an atomic weight of 1 amu. Rather than pursue algebra, let's just try the three choices:

Choice B would give us a molecular weight of $(2 \times 12) + (4 \times 1) = 28$ amu.
Choice C would give us a molecular weight of $(4 \times 12) + (8 \times 1) = 56$ amu.
Choice E would give us a molecular weight of $(6 \times 12) + (12 \times 1) = 84$ amu.
So C is right.

38. The change in heat energy for a reaction is best expressed as a change in

(A) enthalpy
(B) absolute temperature
(C) specific heat
(D) entropy
(E) kinetic energy

A is correct. *See page 46.* Don't fall into the trap and pick B. Temperature differences can indicate the direction of heat flow. However, temperature is not a direct measure of heat energy. Instead, associate heat energy with enthalpy.

39. $...NF_3(g) + ...H_2O(g) \rightarrow ...HF(g) + ...NO(g) + ...NO_2(g)$

When the equation for the reaction above is balanced, how many moles of NF_3 would be required to react completely with 6 moles of H_2O ?

(A) 0.5 mole
(B) 1 mole
(C) 2 moles
(D) 3 moles
(E) 4 moles

E is correct. *See pages 43–45.* The easiest way to balance a Subject Test equation is by plugging in the answers. The question writer tells you that the coefficient in front of H_2O is 6, so you put it there. Now you see which of the answer choices, if placed in front of NF_3, would result in a balanced equation. If, for instance, we try choice B, we'd have one mole of N on the left which would give us 3 moles of F on the left. In order to have three moles of F on the right we'd have to put a 3 in front of the HF on the right. That means we'd have 3 moles of H on the right and 12 moles of H on the left. We'd be way out of balance.

Suppose we try option D and put a 3 in front of the NF_3 on the left? That gives us 9 moles of F on the left, which means we'd have to put a 9 in front of the HF on the right. That in turn would provide 9 moles of H on the right when we have 12 moles of H on the left. Once again, we're out of balance.

Now, let's try choice E. We put a 4 in front of NF_3 on the left. That gives us 12 F on the left, which means we must put a 12 in front of the HF on the right. That gives us a 12 H on the right, balanced by 12 H on the left. So E is clearly correct. The coefficients for both NO and NO_2 would be 2, which would balance both the nitrogens (N) and the oxygens (O).

40. Which characteristic is associated with bases?

(A) React with metal to produce hydrogen gas
(B) Donate an unshared electron pair
(C) Always contain the hydroxide ion in its structure
(D) Taste sour
(E) Formed by reacting a nonmetal oxide and water

B is correct. *See page 116.* Make sure you can distinguish between an acid and a base. A base can donate an unshared electron pair according to the Lewis definition. So B is right. Choices A, D, and E are characteristics of acids. And what about C? Not all bases contain the OH^- ion their structure—NH_3 is an example.

41. An element has the following properties: shiny, brittle, poor electrical conductivity, and high melting point. This element can be best classified as a(n)

(A) alkali metal
(B) halogen
(C) metalloid
(D) transition metal
(E) noble gas

C is correct. *See page 65.* What is being described has some metallic characteristics (shiny and high melting point) and some nonmetallic ones (brittle and poor electrical conductivity). In short it sounds like something that is between a metal and a non-metal. That's what a metalloid or semi-metal is. This is a general description of the metalloid silicon.

42. Which of the following forward processes produces a decrease in entropy?

   I. $H_2O(g) \rightarrow H_2O(l)$
   II. $Fe^{2+}(aq) + S^{2-}(aq) \rightarrow FeS(s)$
   III. $2SO_3(g) \rightleftharpoons 2SO_2(g) + O_2(g)$

(A) I only
(B) III only
(C) I and II only
(D) II and III only
(E) I, II, and III

C is correct. *See pages 45 and 90.* The freer molecules are to move in a particular state, the greater the entropy of that state. In equation I we go from a gas (very high entropy) to a liquid (more ordered, less entropy). That's a decrease in entropy. Equation II also involves an entropy decrease. Here ions go from being able to move throughout a solution to being restricted in the solid state. Equation III shows an entropy increase because we are increasing the moles of gas (2 on left, 3 on right). So I and II illustrate an entropy decrease. That's choice C.

43. Which of the following will raise the boiling point
of a sample of water?

(A) Heat the water
(B) Mix gasoline into the water
(C) Bring the water sample to a higher altitude
(D) Place the water sample on a magnetic stirrer
(E) Dissolve table sugar into the water

E is correct. *See page 98.* Choices A and D will not change water's boiling point. Remember that when we dissolve something, the resultant solution will have a higher boiling point (and lower freezing point) than does the pure solvent. Only E involves dissolving a solute into water. Sugar water will boil at a higher temperature than water under identical conditions. Why doesn't the addition of gasoline into the water have the same effect? Gasoline molecules are nonpolar and will not dissolve into polar water molecules. So water's boiling point won't be affected. As for C, doing so will decrease the boiling point of water. So E is the answer.

44. Elements H and J lie in the same period. If the
atoms of H are smaller than the atoms of J, then
compared to atoms of J, atoms of H are most
likely to

(A) exist in a greater number of isotopes
(B) exist in a lesser number of isotopes
(C) exist in a greater number of oxidation states
(D) have a greater positive charge in their nuclei
(E) have a lesser positive charge in their nuclei

D is correct. *See page 67.* The question concerns periodic table trends and, in particular, atomic radius. As we move from left to right across a period, atomic radius decreases. So, within a period, the higher the atomic number, the smaller the atomic radius.

This question is spiced just a bit with the camouflage trap. You might be thinking higher atomic number, and the correct answer is phrased as "greater positive charge in its nucleus." But keep the blinders off your brain. You know the answer—just remember that there's more than one way of expressing it.

45. $...Al(s) + ...O_2(g) \rightarrow ...Al_2O_3(s)$

When the equation representing the reaction
shown above is completed and balanced and all
coefficients are reduced to lowest whole-number
terms, the coefficient of $O_2(g)$ is

(A) 1
(B) 2
(C) 3
(D) 4
(E) 6

C is correct. *See pages 43 and 70.* Aluminum is a metal and oxygen is a nonmetal. They will react to form an ionic compound. Aluminum (in the IIIA group) forms a +3 ion. Oxygen (in the VI A group) forms a –2 ion. They will produce aluminum oxide, Al_2O_3. When the equation is balanced, we'll get:
$4Al(s) + 3O_2(g) \rightarrow 2Al_2O_3(s)$

46. Which of the following solids has a brilliant blue
color?

(A) $Ca(OH)_2$
(B) KCl
(C) NaBr
(D) Fe_2O_3
(E) $CuSO_4$

E is correct. *See page 65.* Many colored compounds contain a transition metal (an element from the *d* region of the periodic table). Choices A, B, and C are ionic solids that possess an active metal (an element from the *s* region). Such compounds appear white (for instance, NaCl or table salt). Choice D is rust, which is not blue. $CuSO_4$ contains the transition metal copper (Cu), and its crystals are bright blue.

47. Twenty-five percent of element X exists as ^{210}X
and 75% of it exists as ^{214}X. What is the atomic
weight of element X in amu ?

(A) 85
(B) 211
(C) 212
(D) 213
(E) 214

D is correct. *See pages 31–33.* Remember, the atomic weight is a weighted average of all the different isotopes an element exists in. If 50% of element X had a mass of 210 amu and 50% had a mass of 214 amu, the weighted average would be 212 amu. Notice that we are told element X exists as ^{214}X more than half of the time. So the answer must exceed 212. However, since element X also exists in an isotope with a mass less than 214, we expect that its atomic weight is less than 214 amu. Only D has a mass greater than 212 amu and less than 214 amu.

48. A 600 ml container holds 2 moles of $O_2(g)$, 3 moles
of $H_2(g)$, and 1 mole of He(*g*). Total pressure
within the container is 760 torr. What is the
partial pressure of O_2?

(A) 127 torr
(B) 253 torr
(C) 380 torr
(D) 507 torr
(E) 760 torr

B is correct. *See pages 81–82.* The container holds a total of 6 moles of gas. Oxygen (O_2) constitutes one-third of that content. If you know how to work partial pressure problems for the Subject Test, you know that oxygen's contribution to the total 760 torr of pressure is one-third. 760 torr ÷ 3 = approximately 253 torr.

49. $$Fe(OH)_3(s) \rightleftharpoons Fe^{3+}(aq) + 3OH^-(aq)$$

The ionic solid $Fe(OH)_3$ is added to water and dissociates into its component ions, as shown above. The solubility product expression for the saturated solution is

(A) $K_{sp} = [Fe^{3+}] [OH^-]$
(B) $K_{sp} = [Fe^{3+}] [3OH^-]$
(C) $K_{sp} = [Fe^{3+}] [3OH^-]^3$
(D) $K_{sp} = [Fe^{3+}] [OH^-]^3$
(E) $K_{sp} = \dfrac{[Fe^{3+}][OH^-]^3}{[Fe(OH)_3]}$

D is correct. *See page 109.* Since we're considering the dissolution of an ionic solid into water the type of equilibrium expression we need to consider is the solubility product expression. The solubility product constant, K_{sp}, will equal the product of aqueous ion concentrations raised to their coefficients. This is the relationship expressed in choice D.

50. Which of the following electron configurations represents an atom of magnesium in an excited state?

(A) $1s^22s^22p^6$
(B) $1s^22s^22p^63s^2$
(C) $1s^22s^22p^53s^23p^2$
(D) $1s^22s^22p^63s^13p^1$
(E) $1s^22s^22p^63s^13p^2$

D is correct. *See pages 53–54.* The normal electron configuration for magnesium would be $1s^22s^22p^63s^2$. Since we're talking about an "excited" magnesium atom, in which an electron has been pushed up into an energy state higher than normal, we're looking for a configuration that shows one electron in a higher state than it should be. The total number of electrons should still be equal to magnesium's atomic number, but the location of one electron should be "elevated."

Choice D is just what we're looking for. Total number of electrons? Twelve, just as it should be. But look at the last entry. Instead of $3s^2$, we see $3p^1$. The last electron has been elevated to the $3p$ subshell. The atom has been "excited."

51. All of the following when added to water will produce an electrolytic solution EXCEPT

(A) $N_2(g)$
(B) $HCl(g)$
(C) $KOH(s)$
(D) $NaI(s)$
(E) $CaCl_2(s)$

A is correct. *See pages 97 and 115–116.* To form an electrolytic solution, the solute must dissociate into ions. Adding $HCl(g)$ to water will produce hydrochloric acid, which ionizes into H^+ and Cl^- ions. Choices C, D, and E are all ionic solids, which will break into mobile ions upon dissolution in water. When $N_2(g)$ is dissolved into water, no ions are produced and the resultant solution is non-electrolytic.

52. $NH_3(aq) + H_2CO_3(aq) \rightleftharpoons NH_4^+(aq) + HCO_3^-(aq)$

In the reaction represented above, NH_4^+ acts as a(n)

(A) indicator
(B) hydrate
(C) acid
(D) base
(E) salt

C is correct. *See pages 116–117.* The double arrow indicates that the reaction is reversible. So NH_4^+ is a reactant of the reverse reaction. Notice that if NH_4^+ donates a proton to HCO_3^-, we will form NH_3 and H_2CO_3. Since NH_4^+ gives an H^+ ion (or proton) to another substance, it acts as an acid by the Bronsted-Lowry definitions.

53. Which species has the ground state electron configuration $1s^2\, 2s^2\, 2p^6\, 3s^2\, 3p^6$?

(A) Sulfide ion, S^{2-}
(B) Bromide ion, Br^-
(C) Neon atom, Ne
(D) Chromium ion, Cr^{3+}
(E) Potassium atom, K

A is correct. *See pages 53–54.* Add the superscripts to get the total number of electrons in the species: $2 + 2 + 6 + 2 + 6 = 18$. Which of the choices also has 18 electrons? A quick check of the periodic table shows that a sulfur atom has 16 electrons. Adding two more electrons gives the S^{2-} ion a total of 18 electrons. So A is right.

54. Which of the following species is amphoteric?

(A) Na_3PO_4
(B) HSO_4^-
(C) KOH
(D) HNO_3
(E) $C_2O_4^{2-}$

B is correct. *See page 117.* For a substance to be amphoteric it must be able to donate and receive an H^+ ion. Eliminate A and E—these species don't have an H^+ ion to donate. Choice C, KOH, is a strong base. We wouldn't expect it to ever act as an acid. Likewise, HNO_3 (choice D) is a strong acid that we would not expect to behave as a base. That leaves HSO_4^-. Notice that it can act as an acid and become a sulfate ion, SO_4^{2-}, or act as a base and become sulfuric acid, H_2SO_4. So B is right.

55. An ideal gas has a volume of 10 liters at 20°C and a pressure of 750 mmHg. Which of the following expressions is needed to determine the volume of the same amount of gas at STP?

(A) $10 \times \dfrac{750}{760} \times \dfrac{0}{20}$ L

(B) $10 \times \dfrac{750}{760} \times \dfrac{293}{273}$ L

(C) $10 \times \dfrac{760}{750} \times \dfrac{0}{20}$ L

(D) $10 \times \dfrac{760}{750} \times \dfrac{273}{293}$ L

(E) $10 \times \dfrac{750}{760} \times \dfrac{273}{293}$ L

E is correct. *See page 81.* The ideal gas equation is $PV = nRT$. When the amount of gas does not change, n becomes a constant like R. A little algebra gives us $\dfrac{PV}{T} = nR$. Since $\left(\dfrac{PV}{T}\right)$ is equal to a constant it will not change with time. Consider that we are dealing with two points in time. At first, the gas has a volume of 10 liters at 20°C or (293K) and 750 mmHg. So here, $\left(\dfrac{PV}{T}\right) = \dfrac{(750)(10)}{(293)}$. Later, the gas is under STP conditions, so $T = 273$ K and $P = 760$ mmHg. Now, $\left(\dfrac{PV}{T}\right) = \dfrac{(760)(V)}{(273)}$. If we set initial $\left(\dfrac{PV}{T}\right) = $ final $\left(\dfrac{PV}{T}\right)$, we get $\dfrac{(750)(10)}{(293)} = \dfrac{(760)(V)}{(273)}$. Applying some algebra and rearranging gives us $V = 10 \times \dfrac{750}{760} \times \dfrac{273}{293}$ L. This is choice E.

56. Substance Z is at 0.5 atm and 200 K. If the pressure on substance Z is steadily increased and its temperature is kept constant, what phase change will eventually occur?

(A) Condensation
(B) Freezing
(C) Melting
(D) Sublimation
(E) Vaporization

A is correct. *See pages 88–89.* Use the phase diagram. At 0.5 atm and 200K, substance Z is a gas. If we maintain this temperature and increase pressure, we can draw a vertical line from the point (0.5 atm, 200K). Eventually that vertical line will cross into the liquid region. This means that under steadily increasing pressure, substance Z (starting at 0.5 atm and 200K) will condense. Condensation is the phase change from gas to liquid.

57. The normal boiling point of substance Z is closest to

(A) 100 K
(B) 200 K
(C) 300 K
(D) 400 K
(E) 500 K

C is correct. *See pages 88–89.* The normal boiling point is the temperature at which the phase change from liquid to gas occurs at a pressure of 1 atm. If you extend a horizontal line from the 1.0 atm mark on the "pressure" axis and see where it intersects the liquid-gas boundary, you'll get the normal boiling point. Doing so on this phase diagram shows a normal boiling point of about 300K.

58. The shape of a PCl_3 molecule is described as

(A) bent
(B) trigonal pyramidal
(C) linear
(D) trigonal planar
(E) tetrahedral

B is correct. *See pages 73–74.* Phosphorus acts as the central atom in PCl_3. A phosphorus atom needs 3 electrons to complete its valence shell. It gets 3 electrons by forming covalent bonds with three chlorine atoms. The PCl_3 molecule has the following structure.

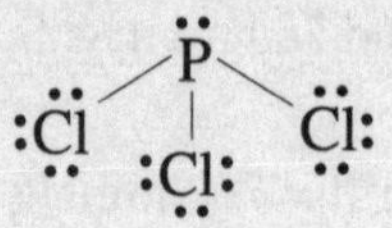

Of the four electron pair sites around phosphorus, one is a lone pair. This gives the PCl_3 molecule a trigonal pyramidal shape.

59. What volume of 0.4 M $Ba(OH)_2$ *(aq)* is needed to exactly neutralize 100 milliliters of 0.2 M HBr*(aq)*?

(A)   25 ml
(B)   50 ml
(C)   100 ml
(D)   200 ml
(E)   400 ml

A is correct. *See pages 119–120.* First consider the neutralization that occurs between HBr and $Ba(OH)_2$:

$$2HBr + Ba(OH)_2 \rightarrow BaBr_2 + 2H_2O$$

Notice that for every 2 moles of HBr, only one mole of $Ba(OH)_2$ is needed for neutralization. We have 0.1 liters (or 100 ml) of 0.2 M HBr. This means we have 0.1 liters × 0.2 moles/liter or 0.02 moles of HBr. We need 0.01 moles of $Ba(OH)_2$ to neutralize 0.02 moles of HBr. Twenty-five milliliters of 0.4 M $Ba(OH)_2$*(aq)* has 0.025 liters × 0.4 moles/liter or 0.01 moles of $Ba(OH)_2$. So A is right.

60. Which of the following is true regarding the aqueous dissociation of HCN, $K_a = 4.9 \times 10^{-10}$, at 25°C ?

    I. At equilibrium, $[H^+] = [CN^-]$
    II. At equilibrium, $[H^+] > [HCN]$
    III. HCN(aq) is a strong acid.

(A) I only
(B) II only
(C) I and II only
(D) II and III only
(E) I, II, and III

A is correct. *See page 118.* A small K_a indicates that an acid is weak. That means statement III is false and therefore we can eliminate choices D and E. It also means that most HCN remains as molecules, as opposed to H^+ and CN^- ions. So statement II is false. Process of elimination tells us that statement I must be true. And it is: $HCN \leftrightharpoons H^+ + CN^-$. Notice that the molar ratio of H^+ to CN^- is 1:1.

61. Which of the following atoms has the largest second ionization energy ?

(A) Aluminum, Al
(B) Calcium, Ca
(C) Chlorine, Cl
(D) Iron, Fe
(E) Sodium, Na

E is correct. *See page 66.* Ionization energies get very large once we try to remove core electrons, which are attracted more strongly to the nucleus than valence electrons. So an atom with a very high second ionization energy would be expected to have one valence electron. Thus the second electron to be removed from such an atom would be a core electron. Among the choices, only sodium atoms have a single valence electron.

62. $2Fe^{2+} + Cl_2 \rightarrow 2\,Fe^{3+} + 2Cl^-$
           $Fe^{3+} + e^- \rightarrow Fe^{2+}; E^0_{red} = {}^-0.77 \text{ volts}$
           $Cl_2 + 2e^- \rightarrow 2Cl^-; E^0_{red} = 1.36 \text{ volts}$

The standard potential difference of an electrochemical cell using the overall reaction above is

(A) 0.18 volts
(B) 0.59 volts
(C) 1.05 volts
(D) 2.13 volts
(E) 2.90 volts

D is correct. *See pages 129–130.* Fe^{2+} is oxidized in the redox reaction. To get the standard oxidation potential for $Fe^{2+} \rightarrow Fe^{3+} + e^-$, just take the opposite of the standard reduction potential. So E^0_{ox} for $Fe^{2+} \rightarrow Fe^{3+} + e^-$ is +0.77 volts. Cl_2 is reduced for the reduction half-reaction and E^0_{red} is 1.36 volts. The potential difference for the overall reaction (E^0_{cell}) is +0.77 volts + 1.36 volts = 2.13 volts.

63. The reaction of zinc metal, Zn, and hydrochloric acid, HCl, produces which of the following?

   I. H_2 (g)
   II. Cl_2 (g)
   III. Zn^{2+} (aq)

   (A) II only
   (B) III only
   (C) I and II only
   (D) I and III only
   (E) I, II and III

D is correct. *See page 115.* Remember that many metals react with acids to produce hydrogen gas. Your first step should be to write out the reaction that's going on. Here's the reaction of zinc and hydrochloric acid: $Zn(s) + 2HCl(aq) \rightarrow ZnCl_2(aq) + H_2(q)$. Notice that the products of this reaction are $Zn^{2+}(aq)$, $Cl^-(aq)$ (from $ZnCl_2$), and $H_2(g)$. So D is right.

64. $2H_2S(g) + 3O_2(g) \leftrightharpoons 2SO_2(g) + 2H_2O(g) + heat$

   For the above reaction, the equilibrium concentration of $SO_2(g)$ can be increased by

   (A) adding neon gas
   (B) increasing the temperature
   (C) adding a catalyst
   (D) increasing the concentration of $H_2O(g)$
   (E) increasing the concentration of $O_2(g)$

E is correct. *See pages 106–107.* This is a Le Chatelier's principle question. How can we produce crowding on the left side of the equation and drive equilibrium to the right (increasing the SO_2 concentration)? Don't be fooled by C: *Catalysts do not affect equilibrium.* Changing concentrations *do* influence equilibrium. Increasing the concentration of O_2 will produce crowding on the left side and lead to an increase in the concentration of SO_2.

65. Which of the following is increased by decreasing the volume of the reaction system?

   I. Rate of reaction
   II. Equilibrium concentration of reactants
   III. Value of K_{eq}

   (A) I only
   (B) III only
   (C) I and II only
   (D) II and III only
   (E) I, II, and III

A is correct. *See pages 102–103 and 108.* Decreasing the volume of the system will increase the concentration of reactants. Why? Because the same number of molecules in a smaller space increases the ratio of molecules per volume. How will this affect the reaction rate? It will increase it because decreasing the volume makes it easier for molecules to collide. What about equilibrium? Reducing the system volume will force the equilibrium to shift in the direction that produces fewer moles of gas. This means the equilibrium concentration of reactants will decrease because equilibrium will shift to the right (4 moles of gas on the right vs. 5 on the left). Only a temperature change will affect the value of K_{eq}, so this will stay the same. Among the three, only item I will increase, so the answer is A.

66. $Fe_2O_3(s) + 3CO(g) \rightarrow 2\,Fe(s) + 3CO_2(g)$

When 3.0 moles of Fe_2O_3 is allowed to completely react with 56 grams of CO according to the above equation, approximately how many moles of iron, Fe, are produced?

(A) 0.7
(B) 1.3
(C) 2.0
(D) 2.7
(E) 6.0

B is correct. *See pages 44–45.* When quantities are given for more than one reactant you must see which is limiting. Fifty-six grams of CO (molecular weight = 28 amu) is 2 moles of CO. Since the stoichiometric ratio of Fe_2O_3 to CO is 1:3 (based on coefficients from the balanced equation), we see that CO is limiting. (We would need more than 9 moles of CO based on the 1:3 ratio for Fe_2O_3 to be limiting in this case.) The ratio of CO to Fe is 3:2. So 2 moles of CO will produce about 1.3 moles of Fe. You could quickly estimate this as between 1 and 2 to save time and still get the answer.

67. $2Na_2O_2(s) + 2H_2O(l) \rightarrow 4\,NaOH(aq) + O_2(g)$

Sodium peroxide, Na_2O_2, and water react in the flask at 25 °C according to the equation and in the apparatus above. If water levels are equal inside and outside the beaker, then the gas pressure inside the beaker is equal to the

(A) pressure of oxygen gas collected
(B) vapor pressure of water at 25 °C
(C) sum of pressure of oxygen gas collected and atmospheric pressure
(D) sum of vapor pressure of water at 25 °C and atmospheric pressure
(E) sum of pressure of oxygen gas collected and vapor pressure of water at 25 °C

E is correct. *See pages 81–82 and 89.* Consider what gases are being collected in the beaker. Oxygen gas is flowing in from the reaction. Water vapor, $H_2O(g)$, is also entering the beaker from the evaporation of water. The pressure exerted by $H_2O(g)$ is equal to the vapor pressure of water. The total gas pressure in the beaker is, therefore, the sum of the pressure of oxygen gas collected and vapor pressure of water (at 25 °C in this particular problem).

68. Which of the following molecules has the strongest carbon-to-carbon bond?

(A) C_2H_2
(B) C_2H_4
(C) C_2H_6
(D) C_3H_8
(E) C_4H_{10}

A is correct. *See page 72.* If you try to draw the structure of acetylene, C_2H_2, you'll see that the carbon atoms must share three pairs of electrons to achieve octets:

$$H - C \equiv C - H$$

So C_2H_2 has a triple bond between carbon atoms. None of the other molecules has a carbon to carbon triple bond. Since this is the strongest type of carbon-to-carbon bond, A is right.

69. $$N_2O_4(g) \leftrightarrows 2\,NO_2(g)$$

The following concentration data were gathered for the above reaction at 5 minute intervals from the start of an experiment:

Time After Start of Experiment	$[N_2O_4]$	$[NO_2]$
0 min (start)	0.00 M	0.50 M
5 min	0.10 M	0.33 M
10 min	0.20 M	0.20 M
15 min	0.25 M	0.15 M
20 min	0.28 M	0.13 M
25 min	0.28 M	0.13 M

If the experiment was carried out in a closed system at constant temperature, then during which time interval (from the start of the experiment) did the reaction most likely achieve equilibrium?

(A) 0 min (start) to 5 min
(B) 5 min to 10 min
(C) 10 min to 15 min
(D) 15 min to 20 min
(E) 20 min to 25 min

D is correct. *See pages 104–105.* Equilibrium is attained when the concentrations of all species become constant. The concentrations of N_2O_4 and NO_2 stay the same from the 20 minute mark to the 25 minute mark. This means equilibrium was achieved before the 20 minute mark. Since the concentrations of N_2O_4 and NO_2 are different from the 15 minute mark to the 20 minute mark, equilibrium was not achieved at exactly 15 minutes from the start of the reaction. Thus, equilibrium was attained between 15 and 20 minutes after the start of the reaction.

17

The Princeton Review SAT II: Chemistry Subject Test II

CHEMISTRY
SUBJECT TEST II

You are about to take the second Princeton Review simulated SAT II: Chemistry Subject Test.

After answering questions 1–23, which constitute part A, you'll be directed to answer questions 101–116, which constitute part B. Then begin again at question 24. Questions 24–69 constitute Part C.

When you're ready to score yourself, refer to the scoring instructions and answer key on pages 184 and 185. Full explanations regarding the correct answers to all questions start on page 211.

Material in the following table may be useful in answering the questions in this examination.

PERIODIC CHART OF THE ELEMENTS

1 **H** 1.0																	2 **He** 4.0
3 **Li** 6.9	4 **Be** 9.0											5 **B** 10.8	6 **C** 12.0	7 **N** 14.0	8 **O** 16.0	9 **F** 19.0	10 **Ne** 20.2
11 **Na** 23.0	12 **Mg** 24.3											13 **Al** 27.0	14 **Si** 28.1	15 **P** 31.0	16 **S** 32.1	17 **Cl** 35.5	18 **Ar** 39.9
19 **K** 39.1	20 **Ca** 40.1	21 **Sc** 45.0	22 **Ti** 47.9	23 **V** 50.9	24 **Cr** 52.0	25 **Mn** 54.9	26 **Fe** 55.8	27 **Co** 58.9	28 **Ni** 58.7	29 **Cu** 63.5	30 **Zn** 65.4	31 **Ga** 69.7	32 **Ge** 72.6	33 **As** 74.9	34 **Se** 79.0	35 **Br** 79.9	36 **Kr** 83.8
37 **Rb** 85.5	38 **Sr** 87.6	39 **Y** 88.9	40 **Zr** 91.2	41 **Nb** 92.9	42 **Mo** 95.9	43 **Tc** (98)	44 **Ru** 101.1	45 **Rh** 102.9	46 **Pd** 106.4	47 **Ag** 107.9	48 **Cd** 112.4	49 **In** 114.8	50 **Sn** 118.7	51 **Sb** 121.8	52 **Te** 127.6	53 **I** 126.9	54 **Xe** 131.3
55 **Cs** 132.9	56 **Ba** 137.3	57 ***La** 138.9	72 **Hf** 178.5	73 **Ta** 180.9	74 **W** 183.9	75 **Re** 186.2	76 **Os** 190.2	77 **Ir** 192.2	78 **Pt** 195.1	79 **Au** 197.0	80 **Hg** 200.6	81 **Tl** 204.4	82 **Pb** 207.2	83 **Bi** 209.0	84 **Po** (209)	85 **At** (210)	86 **Rn** (222)
87 **Fr** (223)	88 **Ra** 226.0	89 **†Ac** 227.0															

*Lanthanum Series

58 **Ce** 140.1	59 **Pr** 140.9	60 **Nd** 144.2	61 **Pm** (145)	62 **Sm** 150.4	63 **Eu** 152.0	64 **Gd** 157.3	65 **Tb** 158.9	66 **Dy** 162.5	67 **Ho** 164.9	68 **Er** 167.3	69 **Tm** 168.9	70 **Yb** 173.0	71 **Lu** 175.0

†Actinium Series

90 **Th** 232.0	91 **Pa** 231.0	92 **U** 238.0	93 **Np** 237.0	94 **Pu** (244)	95 **Am** (243)	96 **Cm** (247)	97 **Bk** (247)	98 **Cf** (251)	99 **Es** (252)	100 **Fm** (258)	101 **Md** (258)	102 **No** (259)	103 **Lr** (260)

CHEMISTRY TEST II

<u>Note:</u> For all questions involving solutions and/or chemical equations, assume that the system is in water unless otherwise stated.

Part A

<u>Directions:</u> Each set of lettered choices below refers to the numbered statements or formulas immediately following it. Select the one lettered choice that best fits each statement or formula, and then fill in the corresponding oval on the answer sheet. A choice may be used once, more than once, or not at all in each set.

<u>Questions 1–4</u>

- (A) Molarity
- (B) Molality
- (C) Mole fraction
- (D) Density
- (E) Partial pressure

1. Has the units: atmospheres or millimeters of mercury

2. Has the units: moles/kilogram

3. Is a measure of mass per unit volume

4. Is the quantity used in the calculation of boiling point elevation

<u>Questions 5–9</u>

- (A) Hydrogen bonding
- (B) Ionic bonding
- (C) Network bonding
- (D) London dispersion force
- (E) Metallic bonding

5. Chiefly responsible for the relatively high boiling point of water

6. Is present in liquid oxygen

7. Is primarily responsible for the hardness of diamond

8. Allows copper to conduct electricity

9. Is present in solid KCl

GO ON TO THE NEXT PAGE →

Questions 10–13

   (A) Na^+
   (B) Al
   (C) F
   (D) Ti
   (E) Br^-

10. Has seven valence electrons

11. Has the electron configuration $1s^22s^22p^63s^23p^1$

12. Has the same electron configuration as neon atom

13. Has valence electrons in *d* orbitals

Questions 14–17

   (A) A 0.01-molar solution of HNO_3
   (B) A 0.01-molar solution of $HC_2H_3O_2$
   (C) A 0.01-molar solution of $Cu(NO_3)_2$
   (D) A 0.01-molar solution of $NaNO_3$
   (E) A 0.01-molar solution of NaOH

14. Will be colored blue

15. Will have a pH of 2

16. Will have the lowest freezing point

17. Will contain undissociated aqueous particles

GO ON TO THE NEXT PAGE

Questions 18–20

    (A) Enthalpy change
    (B) Entropy change
    (C) Gibbs free energy change
    (D) Activation energy
    (E) Specific heat capacity

18. Is the amount of energy that must be added to raise the temperature of 1 gram of a substance 1°C

19. Its value indicates the spontaneity of a reaction

20. Its value indicates whether a reaction is endothermic or exothermic

Questions 21–23

    (A) Ionization energy
    (B) Electronegativity
    (C) Atomic radius
    (D) Atomic number
    (E) Mass number

21. Is the measure of the pull of the nucleus of an atom on the electrons of other atoms bonded to it

22. Is the energy required to remove an electron from an atom

23. Is equal to the number of protons in an atom

GO ON TO THE NEXT PAGE

CHEMISTRY II—*Continued*

Part B

Directions: Each question below consists of two statements, I in the left-hand column and II in the right-hand column. For each question, determine whether statement I is true or false and whether statement II is true or false and fill in the corresponding T or F ovals on your answer sheet. Fill in oval CE only if statement II is a correct explanation of statement I.

	I		II
	EXAMPLES:		
	I		II
EX 1.	H_2SO_4 is a strong acid	BECAUSE	H_2SO_4 contains sulfur.
EX 2.	An atom of oxygen is electrically neutral	BECAUSE	an oxygen atom contains an equal number of protons and electrons.

SAMPLE ANSWERS

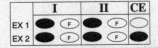

	I		II
101.	An ionic solid is a good conductor of electricity	BECAUSE	an ionic solid is composed of positive and negative ions joined together in a lattice structure held together by electrostatic forces.
102.	The bond in an O_2 molecule is nonpolar	BECAUSE	the oxygen atoms in an O_2 molecule share the bonding electrons equally.
103.	When a sample of water freezes, the process is exothermic	BECAUSE	ice is at a lower potential energy state than water.
104.	At 25 °C, an aqueous solution with a pH of 5 will have a pOH of 9	BECAUSE	the pH of a buffered solution is not greatly affected by the addition of a relatively small amount of acid or base.
105.	When a chlorine atom gains an electron, it becomes a positively charged ion	BECAUSE	a neutral atom has equal numbers of protons and electrons.
106.	Lithium has a larger first ionization energy than oxygen	BECAUSE	oxygen atoms have larger atomic radii than lithium atoms.
107.	Potassium chloride dissolves readily in water	BECAUSE	water is a polar solvent.
108.	Ammonia is a Lewis base	BECAUSE	ammonia can donate an electron pair to a bond.

GO ON TO THE NEXT PAGE

	I		**II**
109.	Elemental fluorine is more reactive than elemental neon	BECAUSE	neon has a larger atomic weight than fluorine.
110.	The addition of a catalyst will decrease the ΔH for a reaction	BECAUSE	a catalyst provides an alternate reaction pathway with a lower activation energy.
111.	The oxygen atom in a water molecule has a –2 oxidation state	BECAUSE	water molecules exhibit hydrogen bonding.
112.	When a salt sample dissolves in water, ΔS for the process is positive	BECAUSE	for a salt sample, aqueous ions have greater entropy than ions in a solid.
113.	When the temperature of a reaction at equilibrium is increased, the equilibrium will shift to favor the endothermic direction	BECAUSE	at equilibrium, all reactants have been converted into products.
114.	An atom of ^{12}C contains 12 protons	BECAUSE	the identity of an element is determined by the number of protons in the nuclei of its atoms.
115.	Water boils at a lower temperature at high altitude than at low altitude	BECAUSE	the vapor pressure of water is lower at higher altitude.
116.	Elemental sodium is a strong reducing agent	BECAUSE	an atom of elemental sodium gives up its valence electron readily.

RETURN TO THE SECTION OF YOUR ANSWER SHEET YOU STARTED FOR CHEMISTRY AND ANSWER QUESTIONS 24–69.

GO ON TO THE NEXT PAGE

Part C

Directions: Each of the questions or incomplete statements below is followed by five suggested answers or completions. Select the one that is best in each case and then fill in the corresponding oval on the answer sheet.

24. What is the oxidation state of bromine in $HBrO_3$?

    (A) −3
    (B) −1
    (C) +1
    (D) +3
    (E) +5

25. What is the percent by mass of silicon in a sample of silicon dioxide?

    (A) 21%
    (B) 33%
    (C) 47%
    (D) 54%
    (E) 78%

26. How many electrons does a ^{37}Cl ion with a charge of −1 contain?

    (A) 16
    (B) 17
    (C) 18
    (D) 37
    (E) 38

27. $CH_4(g) + 2\,O_2(g) \rightarrow CO_2(g) + 2H_2O(g) + 800$ kJ
    If 1 mole of $O_2(g)$ is consumed in the reaction given above, how much energy is produced?

    (A) 200 kJ
    (B) 400 kJ
    (C) 800 kJ
    (D) 1200 kJ
    (E) 1600 kJ

28. Which of the following is NOT true of the element sodium?

    (A) It takes the oxidation state +1.
    (B) It reacts with water to form a basic solution.
    (C) It forms metallic bonds in its solid uncombined form.
    (D) It is found in nature as a diatomic gas.
    (E) It reacts with a halogen to form an ionic salt.

29. What volume of a 0.200 molar solution of sodium hydroxide is required to neutralize 40.0 liters of a 0.300 molar hydrochloric acid solution?

    (A) 10 liters
    (B) 20 liters
    (C) 40 liters
    (D) 60 liters
    (E) 120 liters

30. ... PH_3 + ... O_2 → ... P_2O_5 + ... H_2O
    When the equation above is balanced and the coefficients are reduced to the lowest whole numbers the coefficient for H_2O is

    (A) 1
    (B) 2
    (C) 3
    (D) 4
    (E) 5

31. ... $H_2SO_4(aq)$ + ... $Ba(OH)_2(aq)$ →
    Which of the following are products of the reaction shown above?

    I. $O_2(g)$
    II. $H_2O(l)$
    III. $BaSO_4(s)$

    (A) I only
    (B) III only
    (C) I and II only
    (D) I and III only
    (E) II and III only

32. $2\,Mg(s) + O_2(g) \rightarrow 2\,MgO(s)$
    If 48.6 grams of magnesium is placed in a container with 64.0 grams of oxygen gas and the reaction above proceeds to completion, what is the mass of $MgO(s)$ produced?

    (A) 15.4 grams
    (B) 32.0 grams
    (C) 80.6 grams
    (D) 96.3 grams
    (E) 112 grams

GO ON TO THE NEXT PAGE

33. An ideal gas in a closed inflexible container has a pressure of 6 atmospheres and a temperature of 27 °C. What will be the new pressure of the gas if the temperature is decreased to –73 °C?

    (A) 2 atm
    (B) 3 atm
    (C) 4 atm
    (D) 8 atm
    (E) 9 atm

34. Equal molar quantities of hydrogen gas and oxygen gas are present in a closed container at a constant temperature. Which of the following quantities will be the same for the two gases?

    I. Partial pressure
    II. Average kinetic energy
    III. Average molecular velocity

    (A) I only
    (B) I and II only
    (C) I and III only
    (D) II and III only
    (E) I, II and III

35. Which of the following is a nonpolar molecule?

    (A) CO_2
    (B) H_2O
    (C) NH_3
    (D) NO
    (E) HI

36. What is the molar concentration of a 500 milliliter solution that contains 20 grams of $CaBr_2$ (formula weight = 200)?

    (A) 0.1 molar
    (B) 0.2 molar
    (C) 0.5 molar
    (D) 1 molar
    (E) 5 molar

37. The structure of $BeCl_2$ can best be described as

    (A) linear
    (B) bent
    (C) trigonal
    (D) tetrahedral
    (E) square

38. $2 NO(g) + 2 H_2(g) \rightarrow N_2(g) + 2 H_2O(g)$
    Which of the following statements is true regarding the reaction given above?

    (A) If 1 mole of H_2 is consumed, 0.5 mole of N_2 is produced.
    (B) If 1 mole of H_2 is consumed, 0.5 mole of H_2O is produced.
    (C) If 0.5 mole of H_2 is consumed, 1 mole of N_2 is produced.
    (D) If 0.5 mole of H_2 is consumed, 1 mole of NO is consumed.
    (E) If 0.5 mole of H_2 is consumed, 1 mole of H_2O is produced.

GO ON TO THE NEXT PAGE

Questions 39–40 pertain to the reaction represented by the following equation:

$$...Cu(s) + ...NO_3^-(aq) + ...H^+(aq) \rightarrow ...Cu^{2+}(aq) + ...NO_2(g) + ...H_2O(l)$$

39. When the equation above is balanced with lowest whole number coefficients, the coefficient for $H^+(aq)$ will be

(A) 1
(B) 2
(C) 3
(D) 4
(E) 5

40. Which of the following takes place during the reaction above?

(A) $Cu(s)$ is oxidized.
(B) $Cu(s)$ is reduced.
(C) $H^+(aq)$ is oxidized.
(D) $H^+(aq)$ is reduced.
(E) $NO_3^-(aq)$ is oxidized.

41. Which of the following could be the molecular formula for a molecule with an empirical formula of CH_2?

(A) CH
(B) CH_4
(C) C_2H_2
(D) C_2H_6
(E) C_3H_6

42. When CO_2 is bubbled through distilled water at 25 °C, which of the following is most likely to occur?

(A) Solid carbon will precipitate.
(B) An electrical current will be produced in an oxidation-reduction reaction.
(C) The pH of the solution will be reduced.
(D) The water will boil.
(E) Methane (CH_4) gas will be formed.

43. In which of the following processes is entropy increasing?

(A) $N_2(g) + 3\ Cl_2(g) \rightarrow 2\ NCl_3(g)$
(B) $H_2O(g) \rightarrow H_2O(l)$
(C) $2\ H_2O(l) \rightarrow 2\ H_2(g) + O_2(g)$
(D) $CO(g) + 2\ H_2(g) \rightarrow CH_3OH(l)$
(E) $2\ NO_2(g) \rightarrow N_2O_4(g)$

44.

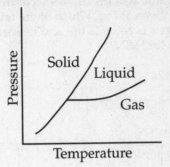

Based on the phase diagram above, which series of phase changes could take place as pressure is decreased at a constant temperature?

(A) solid to liquid to gas
(B) solid to gas to liquid
(C) gas to liquid to solid
(D) gas to solid to liquid
(E) liquid to gas to solid

45. Which of the following forms of radioactive decay has (have) no electrical charge?

I. Alpha decay
II. Beta decay
III. Gamma decay

(A) II only
(B) III only
(C) I and II only
(D) I and III only
(E) II and III only

46. Based on the solubility products given below, which of the following salts is the most soluble?

(A) $BaCO_3$ $K_{sp} = 5.1 \times 10^{-9}$
(B) $PbCrO_4$ $K_{sp} = 2.8 \times 10^{-13}$
(C) $AgCl$ $K_{sp} = 1.8 \times 10^{-10}$
(D) $CaSO_4$ $K_{sp} = 9.1 \times 10^{-6}$
(E) ZnC_2O_4 $K_{sp} = 2.7 \times 10^{-8}$

GO ON TO THE NEXT PAGE

47. $$HCN(aq) \rightarrow H^+(aq) + CN^-(aq)$$

Hydrocyanic acid dissociates according to the reaction given above. Which of the following expressions is equal to the acid dissociation constant for HCN?

(A) $\left[H^+\right]\left[CN^-\right]$

(B) $\left[H^+\right]\left[CN^-\right]\left[HCN\right]$

(C) $\dfrac{\left[HCN\right]}{\left[H^+\right]\left[CN^-\right]}$

(D) $\dfrac{\left[H^+\right]\left[CN^-\right]}{\left[HCN\right]}$

(E) $\dfrac{1}{\left[H^+\right]\left[CN^-\right]\left[HCN\right]}$

48. The reaction progress diagram of an uncatalyzed reaction is shown by the solid line. Which dotted line presents the same reaction in the presence of a catalyst?

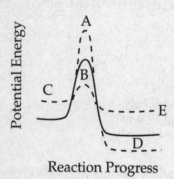

Reaction Progress

49. In a hydrogen atom, when an electron jumps from an excited energy state to a more stable energy state,

(A) electromagnetic radiation is emitted by the atom
(B) electromagnetic radiation is absorbed by the atom
(C) the atom becomes a positively charged ion
(D) the atom becomes a negatively charged ion
(E) the atom undergoes nuclear decay

Questions 50–52 pertain to the following situation:

A closed 5.0 liter vessel contains a sample of neon gas. The temperature inside the container is 25 °C and the pressure is 1.5 atmospheres. (The gas constant, R, is equal to 0.08 L-atm/mol-K.)

50. Which of the following expressions is equal to the molar quantity of gas in the sample?

(A) $\dfrac{(1.5)(5.0)}{(0.08)(25)}$ moles

(B) $\dfrac{(0.08)(25)}{(1.5)(5.0)}$ moles

(C) $\dfrac{(1.5)(25)}{(0.08)(5.0)}$ moles

(D) $\dfrac{(0.08)(298)}{(1.5)(5.0)}$ moles

(E) $\dfrac{(1.5)(5.0)}{(0.08)(298)}$ moles

51. If the neon gas in the vessel is replaced with an equal molar quantity of helium gas, which of the following properties of the gas in the container will be changed?

   I. Pressure
  II. Temperature
 III. Density

(A) I only
(B) II only
(C) III only
(D) I and II only
(E) II and III only

GO ON TO THE NEXT PAGE

52. The volume of the vessel was gradually changed while temperature was held constant until the pressure was measured at 1.6 atmospheres. Which of the following expressions is equal to the new volume?

(A) $5.0 \times \dfrac{1.5}{1.6}$ liters

(B) $5.0 \times \dfrac{1.6}{1.5}$ liters

(C) $25 \times \dfrac{1.5}{1.6}$ liters

(D) $0.08 \times \dfrac{1.6}{1.5}$ liters

(E) $0.08 \times \dfrac{1.5}{1.6}$ liters

53. An oxidation-reduction reaction takes place in a chemical cell and the flow of electrons is used to provide energy for a light bulb. Which of the following statements is true of the reaction?

(A) The reaction is non-spontaneous and has a positive voltage.
(B) The reaction is non-spontaneous and has a negative voltage.
(C) The reaction is at equilibrium and has a voltage of zero.
(D) The reaction is spontaneous and has a positive voltage.
(E) The reaction is spontaneous and has a negative voltage.

54. A solution containing which of the following pairs of species could be a buffer?

(A) H^+ and Cl^-
(B) H_2CO_3 and HCO_3^-
(C) Na^+ and NO_3^-
(D) Na^+ and OH^-
(E) HNO_3 and NO_3^-

55. Which of the following species is the conjugate acid of ammonia (NH_3)?

(A) N_2
(B) H_2
(C) NH^{2-}
(D) NH_2^-
(E) NH_4^+

56. A solution of H_2SO_3 is found to have a hydrogen ion concentration of 1×10^{-3} molar at 25 °C. What is the hydroxide ion concentration in the solution?

(A) 1×10^{-13} molar
(B) 1×10^{-11} molar
(C) 1×10^{-7} molar
(D) 1×10^{-4} molar
(E) 1×10^{-3} molar

57. Which of the following expressions is equal to the number of iron (Fe) atoms present in a pure sample of solid iron with a mass of 10.0 grams? (the atomic mass of iron is 55.9)

(A) $(10.0)(55.9)(6.02 \times 10^{23})$ atoms

(B) $\dfrac{(6.02 \times 10^{23})}{(10.0)(55.9)}$ atoms

(C) $\dfrac{(10.0)(6.02 \times 10^{23})}{(55.9)}$ atoms

(D) $\dfrac{(55.9)}{(10.0)(6.02 \times 10^{23})}$ atoms

(E) $\dfrac{(10.0)}{(55.9)(6.02 \times 10^{23})}$ atoms

GO ON TO THE NEXT PAGE

58. A radioactive material is undergoing nuclear decay. After 40 minutes, 25% of the sample remains. What is the half-life of the sample?

    (A) 10 minutes
    (B) 20 minutes
    (C) 40 minutes
    (D) 80 minutes
    (E) 160 minutes

59.

Element	First Ionization Energy (KJ/mol)
Lithium	520
Sodium	496
Rubidium	403
Cesium	376

Based on the table above, which of the following is most likely to be the first ionization energy for potasssium?

    (A) 536 kJ/mol
    (B) 504 kJ/mol
    (C) 419 kJ/mol
    (D) 391 kJ/mol
    (E) 358 kJ/mol

Questions 60–62 pertain to the reaction represented by the following equation:

$$2\ NOCl(g) \leftrightarrow 2\ NO(g) + Cl_2(g)$$

60. Which of the following expressions gives the equilibrium constant for the reaction above?

    (A) $\dfrac{[NOCl]}{[NO][Cl_2]}$

    (B) $\dfrac{[NO][Cl_2]}{[NOCl]}$

    (C) $\dfrac{[NOCl]^2}{[NO]^2[Cl_2]}$

    (D) $\dfrac{[NO]^2[Cl_2]}{[NOCl]^2}$

    (E) $\dfrac{[NOCl]^2}{[NO]^2[Cl_2]^2}$

61. Which of the following changes to the equilibrium above would serve to decrease the concentration of Cl_2?

    I.   The addition of $NOCl(g)$ to the reaction vessel.
    II. The addition of $NO(g)$ to the reaction vessel.
    III. A decrease in the volume of the reaction vessel.

    (A) I only
    (B) II only
    (C) I and II only
    (D) I and III only
    (E) II and III only

GO ON TO THE NEXT PAGE

62. Which of the following is true of the reaction above as it proceeds in the forward direction?

    (A) NO(g) is produced at the same rate that NOCl(g) is consumed.
    (B) NO(g) is produced at half the rate that NOCl(g) is consumed.
    (C) NO(g) is produced at twice the rate that NOCl(g) is consumed.
    (D) Cl₂(g) is produced at the same rate that NOCl(g) is consumed.
    (E) Cl₂(g) is produced at twice the rate that NOCl(g) is consumed.

63. Which of the following is an organic molecule?

    (A) SiO_2
    (B) NH_3
    (C) H_2O
    (D) CH_4
    (E) BeF_2

64.

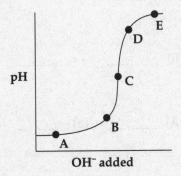

OH⁻ added

The graph above represents the titration of a strong acid with a strong base. Which of the points shown on the graph indicates the equivalence point in the titration?

    (A) A
    (B) B
    (C) C
    (D) D
    (E) E

65. Which of the following statements about fluorine is NOT true?

    (A) It is the most electronegative element.
    (B) It contains 19 protons in its nucleus.
    (C) Its compounds can engage in hydrogen bonding.
    (D) It takes the oxidation state –1.
    (E) It is found in nature as a diatomic gas.

66. The reactivity and chemical behavior of an atom is governed by many factors. The most important factor is

    (A) the number of protons in the atom's nucleus
    (B) the number of neutrons in the atom's nucleus
    (C) the number of protons and neutrons in the atom's nucleus
    (D) the ratio of protons to neutrons in the atom's nucleus
    (E) the number of electrons in the atom's valence shell

67. A beaker contains a saturated solution of copper(I) chloride, a slightly soluble salt with a solubility product of 1.2×10^{-6}. The addition of which of the salts listed below to the solution would cause the precipitation of copper(I) chloride?

    (A) Sodium chloride
    (B) Potassium bromide
    (C) Silver(I) nitrate
    (D) Lead(II) acetate
    (E) Magnesium iodide

68. Which of the following is true regarding a Ne atom with a mass number of 20 and and an O^{2-} ion with a mass number of 16?

    (A) They contain the same number of protons.
    (B) They contain the same number of neutrons.
    (C) They contain the same number of protons plus neutrons.
    (D) They are isoelectronic.
    (E) They are isomers.

69. Which of the following is necessarily true of a non-ionic substance with a high boiling point?

    (A) It has a large vapor pressure.
    (B) It has strong intermolecular attractive forces.
    (C) It has a low freezing point.
    (D) It has a low heat of vaporization.
    (E) It will be present in gas phase at very low temperatures.

STOP

IF YOU FINISH BEFORE TIME IS CALLED, YOU MAY CHECK YOUR WORK ON THIS TEST ONLY. DO NOT TURN TO ANY OTHER TEST IN THIS BOOK.

HOW TO SCORE THE PRINCETON REVIEW CHEMISTRY SUBJECT TEST

When you take the real exam, the proctors will collect your test booklet and bubble sheet and send your answer sheet to New Jersey where a computer (yes, a big, old-fashioned one that has been around since the '60s) looks at the pattern of filled-in ovals on your answer sheet and gives you a score. We couldn't include even a small computer with this book, so we are providing this more primitive way of scoring your exam.

DETERMINING YOUR SCORE

STEP 1 Using the answer key on the next page, determine how many questions you got right and how many you got wrong on the test. Remember, questions that you do not answer don't count as either right answers or wrong answers.

STEP 2 List the number of right answers here.

(A) _____

STEP 3 List the number of wrong answers here. Now divide that number by 4. (Use a calculator if you're feeling particularly lazy.)

(B) _____ ÷ 4 = _____

STEP 4 Subtract the number of wrong answers divided by 4 from the number of correct answers. Round this score to the nearest whole number. This is your raw score.

(A) _____ – (B) _____ = _____

STEP 5 To determine your real score, take the number from Step 4 above and look it up in the left column of the Score Conversion Table on page 186; the corresponding score on the right is your score on the exam.

ANSWERS TO THE PRINCETON REVIEW CHEMISTRY SUBJECT TEST II

Question Number	Correct Answer	Right	Wrong	Question Number	Correct Answer	Right	Wrong
1.	E	___	___	46.	D	___	___
2.	B	___	___	47.	D	___	___
3.	D	___	___	48.	B	___	___
4.	B	___	___	49.	A	___	___
5.	A	___	___	50.	E	___	___
6.	D	___	___	51.	C	___	___
7.	C	___	___	52.	A	___	___
8.	E	___	___	53.	D	___	___
9.	B	___	___	54.	B	___	___
10.	C	___	___	55.	E	___	___
11.	B	___	___	56.	B	___	___
12.	A	___	___	57.	C	___	___
13.	D	___	___	58.	B	___	___
14.	C	___	___	59.	C	___	___
15.	A	___	___	60.	D	___	___
16.	C	___	___	61.	E	___	___
17.	B	___	___	62.	A	___	___
18.	E	___	___	63.	D	___	___
19.	C	___	___	64.	C	___	___
20.	A	___	___	65.	B	___	___
21.	B	___	___	66.	E	___	___
22.	A	___	___	67.	A	___	___
23.	D	___	___	68.	D	___	___
24.	E	___	___	69.	B	___	___
25.	C	___	___				
26.	C	___	___				
27.	B	___	___	101.	F, T		
28.	D	___	___	102.	T, T, CE		
29.	D	___	___	103.	T, T, CE		
30.	C	___	___	104.	T, T		
31.	E	___	___	105.	F, T		
32.	C	___	___	106.	F, F		
33.	C	___	___	107.	T, T, CE		
34.	B	___	___	108.	T, T, CE		
35.	A	___	___	109.	T, T		
36.	B	___	___	110.	F, T		
37.	A	___	___	111.	T, T		
38.	A	___	___	112.	T, T, CE		
39.	B	___	___	113.	T, F		
40.	A	___	___	114.	F, T		
41.	E	___	___	115.	T, F		
42.	C	___	___	116.	T, T, CE		
43.	C	___	___				
44.	A	___	___				
45.	B	___	___				

THE PRINCETON REVIEW CHEMISTRY SUBJECT TEST
SCORE CONVERSION TABLE
Recentered scale as of April 1995

Raw Score	Scaled Score	Raw Score	Scaled Score	Raw Score	Scaled Score
85	800	45	620	5	390
84	800	44	620	4	390
83	800	43	610	3	380
82	800	42	610	2	380
81	800	41	600	1	370
80	800	40	590	0	370
79	800	39	590	−1	370
78	790	38	580	−2	360
77	780	37	580	−3	360
76	780	36	570	−4	350
75	780	35	560	−5	340
74	780	34	560	−6	340
73	780	33	550	−7	330
72	770	32	550	−8	330
71	770	31	540	−9	320
70	750	30	530	−10	310
69	750	29	530	−11	310
68	740	28	520	−12	300
67	740	27	520	−13	300
66	740	26	520	−14	290
65	730	25	510	−15	280
64	730	24	510	−16	280
63	710	23	500	−17	270
62	710	22	500	−18	270
61	710	21	490	−19	260
60	700	20	480	−20	250
59	700	19	480	−21	250
58	690	18	470		
57	690	17	470		
56	680	16	460		
55	680	15	450		
54	680	14	450		
53	670	13	440		
52	670	12	440		
51	660	11	430		
50	650	10	420		
49	650	9	420		
48	630	8	410		
47	630	7	410		
46	630	6	400		

18

Answers and Explanations

PART A

Questions 1–4

    (A) Molarity
    (B) Molality
    (C) Mole fraction
    (D) Density
    (E) Partial pressure

1. Has the units: atmospheres or millimeters of mercury

E is correct. *See page 81.* Atmospheres and millimeters of mercury (also written as mmHg or torr) are units of pressure used in the measurement of gas properties. Partial pressure is the only quantity listed that is measured in pressure units.

2. Has the units: moles/kilogram

B is correct. *See page 96.* Molality (*m*) is the measure of moles of solute present per kilogram of solvent. It is the only quantity listed that measures moles per kilogram. Molality differs from molarity (*M*) in that molarity is the measure of moles of solute per liter of solution, as opposed to kilograms of solvent.

3. Is a measure of mass per unit volume

D is correct. *See page 20.* Density is the measure of the mass of gas, liquid, or solid contained within a given volume. The densities of liquids and solids are relatively independent of their surroundings, while the density of a gas depends on the size of the container in which it is confined.

4. Is the quantity used in the calculation of boiling
    point elevation

B is correct. *See page 96.* Molality (*m*) is used in the calculation of boiling point elevation according to the formula: $\Delta T = k_b mi$, where k_b is the boiling point elevation constant for a solvent, *m* is the molality of the solution and *i* is the van't Hoff factor, which tells how many particles one unit of the solute will create when it dissociates. Molality is also used in the calculation of freezing point depression.

Questions 5–9

    (A) Hydrogen bonding
    (B) Ionic bonding
    (C) Network bonding
    (D) London dispersion force
    (E) Metallic bonding

5. Chiefly responsible for the relatively high boiling
    point of water

A is correct. *See page 85.* Water (H_2O) contains hydrogen bonds between the hydrogen atoms of each molecule and the oxygen atoms of neighboring molecules. Many of water's distinctive properties, such as its lower density as a solid than as a liquid and its relatively high boiling point, are due to hydrogen bonding.

6. Is present in liquid oxygen

D is correct. *See page 85.* Liquid oxygen is held together by London dispersion forces, which are very weak attractions between molecules. In nonpolar molecules, such as O_2, London dispersion forces are the only type of intermolecular attraction that exists. London dispersion forces occur because of instantaneous charge imbalances in molecules. Most substances that experience only London dispersion forces are gases at room temperature.

7. Is primarily responsible for the hardness of diamond

C is correct. *See page 86.* Diamond owes its great strength to the fact that its carbon atoms are bonded together in a tetrahedral network of covalent bonds. This tetrahedral structure means that diamonds have no natural breaking points and are thus very difficult to shatter.

8. Allows copper to conduct electricity

E is correct. *See page 72.* Solid copper is held together by metallic bonding, in which positively charged nuclei are present in a sea of mobile electrons. The electrons move freely from nucleus to nucleus. This electron mobility is responsible for the distinctive properties of metals, such as conductivity and malleability.

9. Is present in solid KCl

B is correct. *See page 70.* Solid KCl (potassium chloride) salt is held together by ionic bonds. The positively charged potassium ions and the negatively charged chloride ions are held together by the **electrostatic force** between them. Remember, the electrostatic force comes from the attraction between a positive and a negative ion, and is very strong.

Questions 10–13

(A) Na^+
(B) Al
(C) F
(D) Ti
(E) Br^-

10. Has seven valence electrons

C is correct. *See pages 53–55.* Fluorine (F) has seven electrons in its second shell, one short of a complete octet.

11. Has the electron configuration $1s^2 2s^2 2p^6 3s^2 3p^1$

B is correct. *See pages 53–55.* Aluminum (Al) has three electrons in its third shell, two in the s subshell and one in the p subshell.

12. Has the same electron configuration as a neon atom

A is correct. *See pages 53–55.* A positively charged sodium ion (Na^+) has given up the one electron in its third shell, so it has the same electron configuration as a neon atom, which has a completed second shell.

13. Has valence electrons in *d* orbitals

D is correct. *See pages 53–55.* Titanium (Ti) is a transition metal, with two electrons in its $3d$ subshell.

QUESTIONS 14–17

(A) A 0.01-molar solution of HNO_3
(B) A 0.01-molar solution of $HC_2H_3O_2$
(C) A 0.01-molar solution of $Cu(NO_3)_2$
(D) A 0.01-molar solution of $NaNO_3$
(E) A 0.01-molar solution of $NaOH$

14. Will be colored blue

C is correct. The solution containing the Cu^{2+} ion will be blue. Most solutions containing salts of transition metals will be distinctly colored because the *d* subshell electrons of transition metals absorb and emit electromagnetic radiation in the visible spectrum.

15. Will have a pH of 2

A is correct. *See page 118.* HNO_3 is a strong acid, so it will dissociate completely in solution. That means that a 0.01-molar solution of HNO_3 will have a hydrogen ion concentration of 0.01-molar. pH is $-\log[H^+]$, and $-\log(0.01) = 2$. So the pH of the solution will be 2.

16. Will have the lowest freezing point

C is correct. *See page 98.* Freezing point depression is a colligative property, which means that it depends only on the number of particles in a solution, not on their specific identities. For every unit of $Cu(NO_3)_2$ in a solution, 3 particles are produced: 1 Cu^{2+} and 2 NO_3^-. For all the other choices, each unit in solution produces only 2 particles.

17. Will contain undissociated aqueous particles

B is correct. *See page 98.* $HC_2H_3O_2$ (acetic acid) is a weak acid, which means that very little dissociation occurs when it is placed in solution. That means that most of the particles present in the acetic acid solution will be undissociated particles. All of the other solutions listed contain solutes that dissociate completely.

QUESTIONS 18–20

    (A) Enthalpy change
    (B) Entropy change
    (C) Gibbs free energy change
    (D) Activation energy
    (E) Specific heat capacity

18. Is the amount of energy that must be added to raise the temperature of 1 gram of a substance 1°C

E is correct. *See page 23.* The specific heat capacity is the amount of energy that must be added to raise the temperature of 1 gram of a substance 1°C. If a substance has a large value for its specific heat capacity, it can absorb a large amount of heat while undergoing a small temperature change.

19. Its value indicates the spontaneity of a reaction

C is correct. *See page 46.* The value of the Gibbs free energy change (ΔG) for a reaction indicates the spontaneity of the reaction. If ΔG is negative, the forward reaction is spontaneous. If ΔG is positive, the reaction is not spontaneous. If ΔG is zero, the forward reaction is at equilibrium.

20. Its value indicates whether a reaction is endothermic or exothermic

A is correct. *See page 45.* The value of the enthalpy change (ΔH) for a reaction indicates whether the reaction is endothermic or exothermic. If ΔH is positive, energy is absorbed over the course of the reaction and the reaction is endothermic. If ΔH is negative, energy is released over the course of the reaction and the reaction is exothermic.

QUESTIONS 21–23

    (A) Ionization energy
    (B) Electronegativity
    (C) Atomic radius
    (D) Atomic number
    (E) Mass number

21. Is the measure of the pull of the nucleus of an atom on the electrons of other atoms

B is correct. *See page 67.* Electronegativity indicates how strongly an atom will attract the electrons of another atom in a bond. The larger the electronegativity difference between two atoms in a bond, the more polar the bond will be.

22. Is the energy required to remove an electron from an atom

A is correct. *See page 66.* Ionization energy is the energy required to remove an electron from an atom or ion. The larger the ionization energy, the more difficult it is to remove the electron.

23. Is equal to the number of protons in an atom

D is correct. *See page 31.* The atomic number, which defines the identity of an element, is equal to the number of protons in the atom's nucleus. The mass number, by the way, is equal to the sum of the protons and neutrons in an atom's nucleus. Atoms with the same atomic number and different mass numbers are called isotopes.

PART B

101. An ionic solid is a good   BECAUSE   an ionic solid is composed of
      conductor of electricity   positive and negative ions joined
                                                        together in a lattice structure held
                                                        together by electrostatic forces.

F, T *See page 70.* Divide and conquer. The first statement is false. Neither the electrons nor the ions in an ionic solid are free to move about, so an ionic solid will not conduct electricity. The second statement is true. An ionic solid is composed of positive and negative ions joined in a lattice structure by electrostatic forces. The first statement is false and the second statement is true.

102. The bond in an O_2 molecule   BECAUSE   the oxygen atoms in an O_2
      is nonpolar   molecule share the bonding
                                                          electrons equally.

T, T, CE *See page 71.* Divide and conquer. Both statements are true. Since the oxygen atoms are identical to each other, they will have equal attraction for the bonding electrons. The second statement is a correct explanation for the first statement, so we fill in the oval marked CE.

103. When a sample of water freezes,   BECAUSE   ice is at a lower potential energy
      the process is exothermic   state than water.

T, T, CE *See page 45.* Divide and conquer. Both statements are true. Ice has stronger intermolecular forces and more stability than water, so when water freezes energy is released. The second statement is a correct explanation for the first statement, so we fill in the oval marked CE.

104. At 25 °C, an aqueous solution   BECAUSE   the pH of a buffered solution is not
      with a pH of 5 will have a pOH of 9   greatly affected by the addition of
      a

                                                          relatively small amount of
                                                          acid or base.

T, T *See page 119.* Divide and conquer. The first statement is true. For an aqueous solution at 25 °C, pH + pOH = 14. The second statement is also true. The definition of a buffer is a solution whose pH is not easily changed by the addition of an acid or base. Now we ask if the word "because" relates the two statements so that the second statement is an explanation for the first statement. The second statement does not explain the first statement, so we do not fill in the oval marked CE.

105. When a chlorine atom gains an ___ BECAUSE ___ a neutral atom has equal numbers
     electron, it becomes a positively   of protons and electrons.
     charged ion

F, T *See Chapter 4.* Divide and conquer. The first statement is false. When an atom gains an electron, it becomes a negatively charged ion. The second statement is true. Protons are positively charged and electrons are negatively charged, so an atom that has equal numbers of protons and electrons will be electrically neutral. The first statement is false and the second statement is true.

106. Lithium has a larger first ___ BECAUSE ___ oxygen atoms have larger atomic
     ionization energy than oxygen   radii than lithium atoms.

F, F Divide and conquer. The first statement is false. Within a period, elements on the left hand side of the periodic table generally have lower first ionization energies than elements on the right hand side. That's because as we move across a period, we are adding protons to the nucleus, which increases the pull of the nucleus on the valence electrons, making them more difficult to remove. The second statement is also false. The same reasoning applies here; oxygen's nucleus has more protons, so oxygen will exert greater pull on its electrons. As a result, oxygen's valence electrons will be closer to the nucleus on average, than lithium's, making the atomic radius smaller for oxygen. Both statements are false.

107. Potassium chloride dissolves ___ BECAUSE ___ water is a polar solvent.
     readily in water

T, T, CE *See page 97.* Divide and conquer. The first statement is true. Potassium chloride (KCl) is a soluble salt. The second statement is also true. The second statement is a correct explanation for the first statement because we know that like dissolves like, so an ionic solid is best dissolved by a polar solvent. Both statements are true and we fill in the oval marked CE.

108. Ammonia is a Lewis base ___ BECAUSE ___ ammonia can donate an
                                                 electron pair to a bond.

T, T, CE *See page 117.* Divide and conquer. Both statements are true because we know that ammonia (NH_3) is a Lewis base and that a Lewis base is an electron pair donor. The second statement is a correct explanation for the first statement because the two statements together give us the definition of a Lewis base. Both statements are true and we fill in the oval marked CE.

109. Elemental fluorine is more ___ BECAUSE ___ neon has a larger atomic
     reactive than elemental neon   weight than fluorine.

T, T Divide and conquer. The first statement is true. Fluorine is more reactive than neon because fluorine needs one electron to complete its valence shell while neon has a complete octet of electrons in its valence shell. The second statement is true. Neon has an atomic weight of 20.2 g/mol, while fluorine has an atomic weight of 19.0 g/mol. Now we ask if the second statement explains the first statement. Fluorine is more reactive than neon for the reason given above, *not* because of atomic weight, so the second statement does *not* explain the first. Both statements are true and we do *not* fill in the oval marked CE.

110. The addition of a catalyst will   BECAUSE   a catalyst provides an alternate
      decrease the ΔH for a reaction   reaction pathway with a
                                             lower activation energy.

F, T *See page 103.* Divide and conquer. The first statement is false. The enthalpy change (ΔH) for a reaction is unaffected by the addition of a catalyst. The second statement is true. A catalyst increases the rate of a reaction by decreasing the activation energy of the reaction. The first statement is false and the second statement is true.

111. The oxygen atom in a water   BECAUSE   water molecules exhibit
      molecule has a –2 oxidation   hydrogen bonding.
      state

T, T *See page 126.* Divide and conquer. The first statement is true. In water (H_2O), the oxygen atom gains two electrons and takes the –2 oxidation state while each of the two hydrogen atoms gives up an electron and takes the +1 oxidation state, making the molecule electrically neutral. The second statement is also true. Water does exhibit hydrogen bonding. Now we ask whether the second statement is an explanation for the first. The two statements are not related, so the word *because* is not appropriate here. Both statements are true and we do not fill in the oval marked CE.

112. When a salt sample dissolves   BECAUSE   for a salt sample, aqueous ions
      in water, ΔS for the   have greater entropy than
       process is positive   ions in a solid.

T, T, CE *See page 45.* Divide and conquer. Entropy is a measure of disorder, and aqueous ions have greater disorder than ions in a solid, so both statements are true. The second statement is a good explanation for the first statement because knowing that aqueous ions have greater entropy than ions in a solid we can see why entropy is increasing in the solution process. Both statements are true and we fill in the oval marked CE.

113. When the temperature of a   BECAUSE   at equilibrium, all reactants have
      reaction at equilibrium is   been converted into products.
      increased, the equilibrium will
      shift to favor the endothermic direction

T, F *See page 106.* Divide and conquer. The first statement is true. From LeChatelier's law we know that when temperature is increased, an equilibrium will move in the direction that will absorb the excess heat. That's the endothermic direction. The second statement is false. A reaction reaches equilibrium when the rate of the forward reaction is equal to the rate of the reverse reaction, not when all the reactants have been used up. The first statement is true and the second statement is false.

114. An atom of ^{12}C contains   BECAUSE   the identity of an element is
      12 protons   determined by the number of
                                             protons in the nuclei of its atoms.

F, T *See page 32.* Divide and conquer. The first statement is false. A carbon atom always contains 6 protons. The number 12 is the mass number, which is the sum of the protons and neutrons in the nucleus. The second statement is true. The number of protons in an atom gives the atomic number and the identity of the element. The first statement is false and the second statement is true.

115. Water boils at a lower   BECAUSE   the vapor pressure of water
     temperature at high altitude   is lower at higher altitude.
     than at low altitude

T, F *See page 89.* Divide and conquer. The first statement is true. Water's vapor pressure increases when heat is added and water boils when its vapor pressure is equal to the atmospheric pressure. At high altitudes, atmospheric pressure is decreased, so water will boil at a lower temperature. The second statement is false. The vapor pressure of water is unaffected by altitude. The first statement is true and the second statement is false.

116. Elemental sodium is a strong   BECAUSE   an atom of elemental sodium gives
     reducing agent   up its valence electron readily.

T, T, CE *See page 129.* Divide and conquer. Both statements are true. A strong reducing agent is readily oxidized. Remember LEO says GER: when something is oxidized, it loses electrons. A sodium atom has only one valence electron, which it gives up readily, so it is easily oxidized. Therefore, elemental sodium is a strong reducing agent. The second statement is a good explanation for the first statement. Both statements are true and we fill in the oval marked CE.

PART C

24. What is the oxidation state of bromine in $HBrO_3$?

    (A) −3
    (B) −1
    (C) +1
    (D) +3
    (E) +5

E is correct. *See page 126.* The oxidation states of all of the atoms in a neutral molecule have to add up to zero. We know that oxygen almost always takes the oxidation state −2 and that hydrogen is almost always +1, so we know that $(+1) + (Br) + (3)(-2) = 0$. That makes the oxidation state of bromine +5.

25. What is the percent by mass of silicon in a sample
    of silicon dioxide?

    (A) 21%
    (B) 33%
    (C) 47%
    (D) 54%
    (E) 78%

C is correct. *See page 39.* The molecular formula of silicon dioxide is SiO_2, so the molecular weight is $(28) + (2)(16) = (28) + (32) = 60$. The percent by mass of silicon is equal to $\frac{28}{60} \times 100$ which is slightly less than 50%, or 47% to be exact.

26. How many electrons does a ^{37}Cl ion with a charge of -1 contain?

(A) 16
(B) 17
(C) 18
(D) 37
(E) 38

C is correct. *See page 31.* The number of electrons in a chloride ion with a -1 charge will be one greater than the number of protons. A chlorine atom or ion always contains 17 protons, so a chloride ion with a -1 charge will contain 18 electrons.

27. $CH_4(g) + 2\,O_2(g) \rightarrow CO_2(g) + 2H_2O(g) + 800\ kJ$

If 1 mole of $O_2(g)$ is consumed in the reaction given above, how much energy is produced?

(A) 200 kJ
(B) 400 kJ
(C) 800 kJ
(D) 1200 kJ
(E) 1600 kJ

B is correct. *See page 46.* From the balanced equation we can see that when 2 moles of $O_2(g)$ are consumed, 800 kJ of energy are produced. So when half that number of moles of $O_2(g)$ (1 mole) are consumed, half as much energy is produced (400 kJ).

28. Which of the following is NOT true of the element sodium?

(A) It takes the oxidation state +1.
(B) It reacts with water to form a basic solution.
(C) It forms metallic bonds in its solid uncombined form.
(D) It is found in nature as a diatomic gas.
(E) It reacts with a halogen to form an ionic salt.

D is correct. All of the statements are true except choice D. Sodium is not found in nature as a diatomic gas; it is usually seen in nature in ionic salts.

29. What volume of a 0.200 molar solution of sodium hydroxide is required to neutralize 40.0 liters of a 0.300 molar hydrochloric acid solution?

(A) 10 liters
(B) 20 liters
(C) 40 liters
(D) 60 liters
(E) 120 liters

D is correct. *See page 119.* We need to add as many moles of hydroxide ions as there are moles of hydrogen ions in the solution. We use the relationship, moles = (molarity)(liters). We know that moles of hydroxide must equal moles of hydrogen ion and that we have a strong acid and a strong base that dissociate completely in solution. We also know that one unit of HCl gives one hydrogen ion and one unit of NaOH gives one hydroxide ion upon dissociation. So, we can just set moles of hydroxide ion equal to moles of hydrogen ion and use the following equation:

$(M_{HCl})(L_{HCl}) = (M_{NaOH})(L_{NaOH})$

$(0.300\ M)(40.0\ L) = (0.200\ M)(x)$

$x = 60.0\ L$

30. ... PH_3 + ... O_2 → ... P_2O_5 + ... H_2O

When the equation above is balanced and the coefficients are reduced to the lowest whole numbers the coefficient for H_2O is

(A) 1
(B) 2
(C) 3
(D) 4
(E) 5

C is correct. *See page 43.* Plug the answers into the equation. If the coefficient for H_2O is 3, that means that there are six hydrogens and the coefficient for PH_3 must be 2. That makes 1 the coefficient for P_2O_5. Now we have eight oxygens on the right, so the coefficient for O_2 on the left must be 4. Since we have 1 as a coefficient for one of the species in the reaction, these must be the lowest whole number coefficients and C is correct.

31. $H_2SO_4(aq)$ + $Ba(OH)_2(aq)$ →

Which of the following are products of the reaction shown above?

  I. $O_2(g)$
  II. $H_2O(l)$
  III. $BaSO_4(s)$

(A) I only
(B) III only
(C) I and II only
(D) I and III only
(E) II and III only

E is correct. *See page 42.* First, look at your reactants: You have an acid and a base, so you know they will neutralize one another when put together. Now write out the products:

$$H_2SO_4(aq) + Ba(OH)_2(aq) \rightarrow BaSO_4 + H_2O$$

Note that in this problem, you don't need to balance anything, just figure out the type of reaction and the products, and the answer is easy. The products of an acid-base neutralization (when the base is a metal hydroxide) are water and a salt. In this case the salt is barium sulfate.

32. $2 Mg(s) + O_2(g) \rightarrow 2 MgO(s)$

   If 48.6 grams of magnesium is placed in a container with 64.0 grams of oxygen gas and the reaction above proceeds to completion, what is the mass of MgO(s) produced?

   (A) 15.4 grams
   (B) 32.0 grams
   (C) 80.6 grams
   (D) 96.3 grams
   (E) 12 grams

C is correct. *See page 45.* We need to determine the limiting reagent. Magnesium has an atomic weight of about 24 g/mol, so 48 grams of magnesium is 2 moles. O_2 has a molecular weight of 32 g/mol, so 64 grams of O_2 is also about 2 moles. We need twice as much Mg for the reaction, so we'll run out of it first, and magnesium is the limiting reagant. Two moles of Mg will produce 2 moles of MgO, which has a molecular weight of 40.3 g/mol, so we end up with 80.6 grams of MgO.

33. An ideal gas in a closed inflexible container has a pressure of 6 atmospheres and a temperature of 27 °C. What will be the new pressure of the gas if the temperature is decreased to –73 °C?

   (A) 2 atm
   (B) 3 atm
   (C) 4 atm
   (D) 8 atm
   (E) 9 atm

C is correct. *See page 80.* We know that pressure and temperature of an ideal gas are related by the following equation (when the amount of gas and its volume are held constant): $\frac{P_1}{T_1} = \frac{P_2}{T_2}$. We also know that we need to convert Celsius to Kelvin, so 27 °C = 300 K and –73 °C = 200 K. Now we can calculate:

$$\frac{(6\ atm)}{(300\ K)} = \frac{x}{(200\ K)}$$

$x = 4$ atm

34. Equal molar quantities of hydrogen gas and oxygen gas are present in a closed container at a constant temperature. Which of the following quantities will be the same for the two gases?

    I. Partial pressure
    II. Average kinetic energy
    III. Average molecular velocity

(A) I only
(B) I and II only
(C) I and III only
(D) II and III only
(E) I, II and III

B is correct. *See page 81.* The partial pressures of the two gases will be the same because partial pressure of a gas is directly proportional to the number of moles of the gas present and we have equal numbers of moles of the two gases. The average kinetic energies of the two gases will be the same because the average kinetic energy of a gas is directly proportional to absolute temperature and the two gases are at the same temperature. The average molecular velocities will differ because when two gases have equal kinetic energies, the molecules of the gas with lower molecular weight must be moving faster on average.

35. Which of the following is a nonpolar molecule?

(A) CO_2
(B) H_2O
(C) NH_3
(D) NO
(E) HI

A is correct. *See page 75.* CO_2 is a nonpolar molecule even though it contains polar bonds. That's because carbon dioxide has its three atoms arranged in linear fashion with its negatively charged oxygen atoms on the ends. There is a partial positive charge on the carbon atom. Due to the symmetrical arrangement of two equivalent polar bonds, the overall molecule has no net charge.

$$O=C=O$$
$$\delta^- \quad \delta^+ \quad \delta^-$$

36. What is the molar concentration of a 500 milliliter solution that contains 20 grams of $CaBr_2$ (formula weight = 200)?

(A) 0.1 molar
(B) 0.2 molar
(C) 0.5 molar
(D) 1 molar
(E) 5 molar

B is correct. *See page 39.* Knowing that moles = $\dfrac{grams}{formula\ weight}$, we can calculate the number of moles of $CaBr_2$ in the solution:

$$\text{Moles of } CaBr_2 = \frac{(20g)}{(200\ g/mol)}\ 0.1 \text{ mole.}$$

Now we can calculate the molarity of the solution (don't forget to convert milliliters to liters):

$$\text{Molarity} = \frac{moles}{liters} = \frac{(0.1\ mol)}{(0.5\ L)} = 0.2 \text{ molar.}$$

37. The structure of $BeCl_2$ can best be described as

    (A) linear
    (B) bent
    (C) trigonal
    (D) tetrahedral
    (E) square

A is correct. *See page 75.* Be has two valence electrons to give up to Cl, so the two Cl atoms align themselves opposite each other and the molecule is linear. [Cl–Be–Cl]

38. $2\,NO(g) + 2\,H_2(g) \rightarrow N_2(g) + 2\,H_2O(g)$

    Which of the following statements is true regarding the reaction given above?

    (A) If 1 mole of H_2 is consumed, 0.5 mole of N_2 is produced.
    (B) If 1 mole of H_2 is consumed, 0.5 mole of H_2O is produced.
    (C) If 0.5 mole of H_2 is consumed, 1 mole of N_2 is produced.
    (D) If 0.5 mole of H_2 is consumed, 1 mole of NO is consumed.
    (E) If 0.5 mole of H_2 is consumed, 1 mole of H_2O is produced.

A is correct. *See page 43.* From the balanced equation, there will be twice as much H_2 consumed as there is N_2 produced.

Questions 39–40 pertain to the reaction represented by the following equation:

$$...Cu(s) + ...NO_3^-(aq) + ...H^+(aq) \rightarrow$$
$$...Cu^{2+}(aq) + ...NO_2(g) + ...H_2O(l)$$

39. When the equation above is balanced with lowest whole number coefficients, the coefficient for $H^+(aq)$ will be

    (A) 1
    (B) 2
    (C) 3
    (D) 4
    (E) 5

B is correct. *See page 43.* Plug the answers into the reaction and see which one works. Let's start at choice C, because it's in the middle. If there are 3 H^+, then there can't be a whole number coefficient for H_2O, so the answer can't be an odd number. So the answer must be B or D. Try D. If there are 4H^+, then there are 2H_2O. The coppers are in balance if each has a coefficient of 1. Notice that this makes the net charge on the right side +2. With 4H^+, the charge on the left is +4. Since charges must be in balance, the charge on the left must be reduced. If the coefficient of NO_3^- is 2, this will balance charges. NO_2 will need a coefficient of 2 to balance nitrogens and oxygens. The equation is now balanced with the lowest whole number terms.

40. Which of the following takes place during the re-
    action above?

    (A) Cu(s) is oxidized.
    (B) Cu(s) is reduced.
    (C) H⁺(aq) is oxidized.
    (D) H⁺(aq) is reduced.
    (E) NO₃⁻(aq) is oxidized.

A is correct. *See page 125.* During the reaction, Cu^0 is converted to Cu^{2+}. Remember LEO says GER; Cu has lost electrons, so it has been oxidized. By the way, NO_3^- is reduced in this reaction and the oxidation state of H^+ is not changed.

41. Which of the following could be the molecular
    formula for a molecule with an empirical formula
    of CH_2?

    (A) CH
    (B) CH_4
    (C) C_2H_2
    (D) C_2H_6
    (E) C_3H_6

E is correct. *See page 38.* The empirical formula is the molecular formula with the numbers reduced to lowest whole numbers, so if the molecular formula is C_3H_6, then the empirical formula is CH_2.

42. When CO_2 is bubbled through distilled water at
    25 °C, which of the following is most likely to oc-
    cur?

    (A) Solid carbon will precipitate.
    (B) An electrical current will be produced in an
         oxidation-reduction reaction.
    (C) The pH of the solution will be reduced.
    (D) The water will boil.
    (E) Methane (CH_4) gas will be formed.

C is correct. *See page 118.* CO_2 combines with water to form carbonic acid (H_2CO_3).

$$CO_2 + H_2O \rightleftharpoons H_2CO_3 \rightleftharpoons H^+ + HCO_3^-$$

Carbonic acid is a weak acid which will release H^+ ions into the solution. When the concentration of H^+ increases, the pH decreases.

43. In which of the following processes is entropy
    increasing?

    (A) $N_2(g) + 3 Cl_2(g) \rightarrow 2 NCl_3(g)$
    (B) $H_2O(g) \rightarrow H_2O(l)$
    (C) $2 H_2O(l) \rightarrow 2 H_2(g) + O_2(g)$
    (D) $CO(g) + 2 H_2(g) \rightarrow CH_3OH(l)$
    (E) $2 NO_2(g) \rightarrow N_2O_4(g)$

C is correct. *See page 45.* Entropy is the measure of randomness and gases are more random than liquids. Also, the more molecules, the greater the randomness. In choice C, a liquid is being converted into gases and the number of molecules is increasing, so entropy must be increasing.

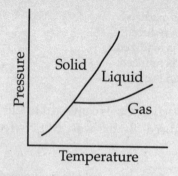

44. Based on the phase diagram above, which series of phase changes could take place as pressure is decreased at a constant temperature?

(A) solid to liquid to gas
(B) solid to gas to liquid
(C) gas to liquid to solid
(D) gas to solid to liquid
(E) liquid to gas to solid

A is correct. *See page 88.* As pressure is decreased at constant temperature, phase changes will occur as shown in the diagram below:

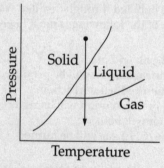

45. Which of the following forms of radioactive decay has (have) no electrical charge?

   I. Alpha decay
  II. Beta decay
 III. Gamma decay

(A) II only
(B) III only
(C) I and II only
(D) I and III only
(E) II and III only

B is correct. *See page 59.* Gamma decay involves the release of electromagnetic radiation, which has no electrical charge. Alpha particles are positively charged and beta particles are negatively charged.

46. Based on the solubility products given below, which of the following salts is the most soluble?

(A) $BaCO_3$ $K_{sp} = 5.1 \times 10^{-9}$
(B) $PbCrO_4$ $K_{sp} = 2.8 \times 10^{-13}$
(C) $AgCl$ $K_{sp} = 1.8 \times 10^{-10}$
(D) $CaSO_4$ $K_{sp} = 9.1 \times 10^{-6}$
(E) ZnC_2O_4 $K_{sp} = 2.7 \times 10^{-8}$

D is correct. *See page 109.* The solubility product (K_{sp}) is a measure of the concentrations of dissolved particles present in solution at equilibrium. Since all of these salts will ionize into two ions per unit, the salt with the largest value of K_{sp} will be the most soluble.

47. $$HCN(aq) \rightarrow H^+(aq) + CN^-(aq)$$

Hydrocyanic acid dissociates according to the reaction given above. Which of the following expressions is equal to the acid dissociation constant for HCN?

(A) $\left[H^+\right]\left[CN^-\right]$

(B) $\left[H^+\right]\left[CN^-\right]\left[HCN\right]$

(C) $\dfrac{\left[HCN\right]}{\left[H^+\right]\left[CN^-\right]}$

(D) $\dfrac{\left[H^+\right]\left[CN^-\right]}{\left[HCN\right]}$

(E) $\dfrac{1}{\left[H^+\right]\left[CN^-\right]\left[HCN\right]}$

D is correct. *See page 105.* The acid dissociation constant is an equilibrium constant, with the concentrations of the products in the numerator and the concentrations of the reactants in the denominator.

48. The reaction progress diagram of an uncatalyzed reaction is shown by the solid line. Which dotted line presents the same reaction in the presence of a catalyst?

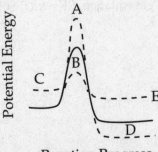

Reaction Progress

B is correct. A catalyst lowers the activation energy of a reaction, but does not change the potential energy of the starting materials or products. Choice A actually raises the activation energy, and C, D, and E change the reactant or product energies. So choice B is right.

49. In a hydrogen atom, when an electron jumps from an excited energy state to a more stable energy state,

(A) electromagnetic radiation is emitted by the atom
(B) electromagnetic radiation is absorbed by the atom
(C) the atom becomes a positively charged ion
(D) the atom becomes a negatively charged ion
(E) the atom undergoes nuclear decay

A is correct. *See page 54.* When an electron jumps from an excited state to a more stable state, energy must be released by the atom. This energy is released in the form of electromagnetic radiation. This process can also be seen in reverse when an atom absorbs electromagnetic radiation and its electrons jump to excited energy levels.

Questions 50–52 pertain to the following situation:

A closed 5.0 liter vessel contains a sample of neon gas. The temperature inside the container is 25 °C and the pressure is 1.5 atmospheres. (The gas constant, R, is equal to 0.08 L-atm/mol-K.)

50. Which of the following expressions is equal to the molar quantity of gas in the sample?

(A) $\dfrac{(1.5)(5.0)}{(0.08)(25)}$ moles

(B) $\dfrac{(0.08)(25)}{(1.5)(5.0)}$ moles

(C) $\dfrac{(1.5)(25)}{(0.08)(5.0)}$ moles

(D) $\dfrac{(0.08)(5.0)}{(1.5)(25)}$ moles

(E) $\dfrac{(1.5)(5.0)}{(0.08)(298)}$ moles

E is correct. *See page 81.* Use the ideal gas equation, $PV = nRT$. Solve for n, the number of moles of gas. Don't forget to convert 25 °C to 298 K.

$$n = \frac{PV}{RT} = \frac{(1.5)(5.0)}{(0.08)(298)} \text{ moles}$$

51. If the neon gas in the vessel is replaced with an equal molar quantity of helium gas, which of the following properties of the gas in the container must be changed?

    I. Pressure
    II. Temperature
    III. Density

(A) I only
(B) II only
(C) III only
(D) I and II only
(E) II and III only

C is correct. *See page 81.* Pressure and temperature will not be changed as long as the number of moles of gas in the vessel doesn't change. The density of the gas will decrease because equal numbers of moles of helium and neon will have different masses, and density is the measure of mass per unit volume.

52. The volume of the vessel was gradually changed while temperature was held constant until the pressure was measured at 1.6 atmospheres. Which of the following expressions is equal to the new volume?

(A) $5.0 \times \dfrac{1.5}{1.6}$ liters

(B) $5.0 \times \dfrac{1.6}{1.5}$ liters

(C) $25 \times \dfrac{1.5}{1.6}$ liters

(D) $0.08 \times \dfrac{1.6}{1.5}$ liters

(E) $0.08 \times \dfrac{1.5}{1.6}$ liters

A is correct. *See page 81.* From the ideal gas equation, we can derive that volume is related to pressure by the following relationship (when n and T are kept constant):

$$P_1 V_1 = P_2 V_2$$

Solve for the new volume, V_2

$$V_2 = V_1 \frac{P_1}{P_2} = 5.0 \times \frac{1.5}{1.6} \, \text{L}$$

53. An oxidation-reduction reaction takes place in a
    chemical cell and the flow of electrons is used to
    provide energy for a light bulb. Which of the fol-
    lowing statements is true of the reaction?

    (A) The reaction is non-spontaneous and has a
        positive voltage.
    (B) The reaction is non-spontaneous and has a
        negative voltage.
    (C) The reaction is at equilibrium and has a
        voltage of zero.
    (D) The reaction is spontaneous and has a
        positive voltage.
    (E) The reaction is spontaneous and has a
        negative voltage.

D is correct. *See page 45.* If the reaction is being used to provide energy to electrons, it must have a positive reaction potential, or voltage. In the same way, if the reaction is being used to provide energy to a circuit, it must be spontaneous (ΔG is negative).

54. A solution containing which of the following
    pairs of species could be a buffer?

    (A) H^+ and Cl^-
    (B) H_2CO_3 and HCO_3^-
    (C) Na^+ and NO_3^-
    (D) Na^+ and OH^-
    (E) HNO_3 and NO_3^-

B is correct. *See page 118.* A buffered solution contains both a weak acid and its conjugate base (or weak base and its conjugate acid). Carbonic acid (H_2CO_3) and bicarbonate ion (HCO_3^-) are the only examples of this in the answer choices. Choices A and E contain strong acids and their conjugates. Choice C contains a salt. Choice D contains a strong base.

55. Which of the following species is the conjugate
    acid of ammonia (NH_3)?

    (A) N_2
    (B) H_2
    (C) NH^{2-}
    (D) NH_2^-
    (E) NH_4^+

E is correct. *See page 116.* Ammonia is a base, which means it can accept a proton, or H^+ ion. So NH_3 accepts a proton to become NH_4^+.

56. A solution of H_2SO_3 is found to have a hydrogen ion concentration of 1×10^{-3} molar at 25 °C. What is the hydroxide ion concentration in the solution?

(A) 1×10^{-13} molar
(B) 1×10^{-11} molar
(C) 1×10^{-7} molar
(D) 1×10^{-4} molar
(E) 1×10^{-3} molar

B is correct. *See page 115.* We know that pH + pOH = 14 and that $[H^+][OH^-] = 1 \times 10^{-14}$ at 25 °C.

So $[OH^-] = \dfrac{(1 \times 10^{-14})}{[H^+]} M = \dfrac{(1 \times 10^{-14})}{1 \times 10^{-3}} M = 1 \times 10^{-11} M$

57. Which of the following expressions is equal to the number of iron (Fe) atoms present in a pure sample of solid iron with a mass of 10.0 grams? (the atomic mass of iron is 55.9)

(A) $(10.0)(55.9)(6.02 \times 10^{23})$ atoms

(B) $\dfrac{(6.02 \times 10^{23})}{(10.0)(55.9)}$ atoms

(C) $\dfrac{(10.0)(6.02 \times 10^{23})}{(55.9)}$ atoms

(D) $\dfrac{(55.9)}{(10.0)(6.02 \times 10^{23})}$ atoms

(E) $\dfrac{(10.0)}{(55.9)(6.02 \times 10^{23})}$ atoms

C is correct. *See page 39.* The number of moles of iron in the sample is given by the following

expression: moles $= \dfrac{\text{grams}}{\text{atomic mass}} = \dfrac{(10.0)}{(55.9)}$

Now we can use Avogadro's number (6.02×10^{23}) to find the number of atoms in the sample.

atoms $= (\text{moles})(6.02 \times 10^{23}) = \dfrac{(10.0)}{(55.9)}(6.02 \times 10^{23}) = \dfrac{(10.0)(6.02 \times 10^{23})}{55.9}$

58. A radioactive material is undergoing nuclear decay. After 40 minutes, 25% of the sample remains. What is the half-life of the sample?

(A) 10 minutes
(B) 20 minutes
(C) 40 minutes
(D) 80 minutes
(E) 160 minutes

B is correct. *See page 59.* The half-life of a radioactive material is the time that it takes for half of the sample to decay. After 1 half-life 50% remains, after 2 half lives 25% remains. If two half lives take 40 minutes, then 1 half-life takes 20 minutes.

59.

Element	First Ionization Energy (KJ/mol)
Lithium	520
Sodium	496
Rubidium	403
Cesium	376

Based on the table above, which of the following is most likely to be the first ionization energy for potasssium?

(A) 536 kJ/mol
(B) 504 kJ/mol
(C) 419 kJ/mol
(D) 391 kJ/mol
(E) 358 kJ/mol

C is correct. *See page 66.* Potassium (K) is in Group IA of the periodic table between sodium (Na) and rubidium (Rb). We know from our knowledge of periodic trends that the value of potassium's first ionization energy will fall between that of sodium and rubidium.

Questions 60–62 pertain to the reaction represented by the following equation:

$$2\,NOCl(g) \leftrightarrow 2\,NO(g) + Cl_2(g)$$

60. Which of the following expressions gives the equilibrium constant for the reaction above?

(A) $\dfrac{[NOCl]}{[NO][Cl_2]}$

(B) $\dfrac{[NO][Cl_2]}{[NOCl]}$

(C) $\dfrac{[NOCl]^2}{[NO]^2[Cl_2]}$

(D) $\dfrac{[NO]^2[Cl_2]}{[NOCl]^2}$

(E) $\dfrac{[NOCl]^2}{[NO]^2[Cl_2]^2}$

D is correct. *See page 104–108.* In the expression for the equilibrium constant, the products are in the numerator, the reactants are in the denominator and the coefficients become exponents. So the correct expression is $K = \dfrac{[NO]^2[Cl_2]}{[NOCl]^2}$.

61. Which of the following changes to the equilibrium above would serve to decrease the concentration of Cl_2?

 I. The addition of $NOCl(g)$ to the reaction vessel.
 II. The addition of $NO(g)$ to the reaction vessel.
 III. A decrease in the volume of the reaction vessel.

(A) I only
(B) II only
(C) I and II only
(D) I and III only
(E) II and III only

E is correct. *See page 106.* According to Le Chatelier's principle, an equilibrium will shift to relieve any stress placed on it. If NOCl is added, the equilibrium will shift to the right and increase the concentration of Cl_2, so I is wrong. If NO is added, the equilibrium will shift to the left and decrease the concentration of Cl_2, so II is correct. If the volume is decreased, the equilibrium will shift to the left, which has fewer moles of gas, and the concentration of Cl_2 will be decreased, so III is correct.

62. Which of the following is true of the reaction above as it proceeds in the forward direction?

    (A) NO(g) is produced at the same rate that NOCl(g) is consumed.
    (B) NO(g) is produced at half the rate that NOCl(g) is consumed.
    (C) NO(g) is produced at twice the rate that NOCl(g) is consumed.
    (D) Cl2(g) is produced at the same rate that NOCl(g) is consumed.
    (E) Cl2(g) is produced at twice the rate that NOCl(g) is consumed.

A is correct. *See page 44.* We can see from the balanced equation that for every mole of NOCl consumed, we get one mole of NO, so NO is appearing at the same rate that NOCl is disappearing.

63. Which of the following is an organic molecule?

    (A) SiO_2
    (B) NH_3
    (C) H_2O
    (D) CH_4
    (E) BeF_2

D is correct. Organic chemistry is the study of carbon compounds. Methane (CH_4) is the only compound listed that contains carbon.

64.

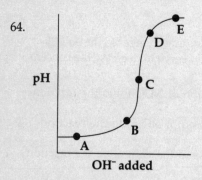

OH⁻ added

The graph above represents the titration of a strong acid with a strong base. Which of the points shown on the graph indicates the equivalence point in the titration?

    (A) A
    (B) B
    (C) C
    (D) D
    (E) E

C is correct. *See page 119.* The equivalence point is the point when enough base has been added to neutralize all the acid that was initially present in the solution. This point is in the middle of the steep part of a titration curve. In this case, when a strong acid is titrated by a strong base, the pH at the equivalence point will be 7 and the solution will be neutral.

65. Which of the following statements about fluorine is NOT true?

(A) It is the most electronegative element.
(B) It contains 19 protons in its nucleus.
(C) Its compounds can engage in hydrogen bonding.
(D) It takes the oxidation state –1.
(E) It is found in nature as a diatomic gas.

B is correct. *See page 31.* The atomic *mass* of fluorine is 19, the atomic *number*, which is the number of protons in the nucleus, is 9. All of the other statements are true.

66. The reactivity and chemical behavior of an atom is governed by many factors. The most important factor is

(A) the number of protons in the atom's nucleus
(B) the number of neutrons in the atom's nucleus
(C) the number of bonds it can form
(D) the type of nuclear decay it undergoes
(E) the number of electrons in the atom's valence shell

E is correct. *See page 32.* Atoms react with other atoms in order to fill their valence electron shells so the single most important factor in determining the reactivity of an atom is the makeup of its valence electron shell.

67. A beaker contains a saturated solution of copper(I) chloride, a slightly soluble salt with a solubility product of 1.2×10^{-6}. The addition of which of the salts listed below to the solution would cause the precipitation of copper(I) chloride?

(A) Sodium chloride
(B) Potassium bromide
(C) Silver(I) nitrate
(D) Lead(II) acetate
(E) Magnesium iodide

A is correct. *See page 106–108.* The addition of sodium chloride (NaCl) will introduce Cl^- ions to the solution. Because of the common ion effect, these Cl^- ions will affect the equilibrium of the copper(I) chloride (CuCl) with its dissociated ions. The addition of extra Cl^- ions causes the reformation and precipitation of CuCl.

68. Which of the following is true regarding a Ne atom with a mass number of 20 and an O^{2-} ion with a mass number of 16?

   (A) They contain the same number of protons.
   (B) They contain the same number of neutrons.
   (C) They contain the same number of protons plus neutrons.
   (D) They are isoelectronic.
   (E) They are isomers.

D is correct. *See page 54.* An O_2^- ion has gained two electrons to fill its outer shell. This gives an O^{2-} ion the same electron configuration as Ne. That is, the two are **isoelectronic**.

69. Which of the following is necessarily true of a non-ionic substance with a high boiling point?

   (A) It has a large vapor pressure.
   (B) It has strong intermolecular attractive forces.
   (C) It has a low freezing point.
   (D) It has a low heat of vaporization.
   (E) It will be present in gas phase at very low temperatures.

B is correct. If a nonionic substance has a high boiling point, that means that a large amount of energy is required to overcome its intermolecular attractions in converting it to the gas phase. So a high boiling point is an indication of very strong intermolecular attractive forces.

The
Princeton
Review

1.

YOUR NAME: _____
(Print)   Last   First   M.I.

SIGNATURE: _____ DATE: ___ / ___ / ___

HOME ADDRESS: _____
(Print)   Number and Street

_____
City   State   Zip Code

PHONE NO.: _____
(Print)

IMPORTANT: Please fill in these boxes exactly as shown on the back cover of your test book.

2. TEST FORM

_____

6. DATE OF BIRTH

Month		Day		Year	
⊂ ⊃ JAN					
⊂ ⊃ FEB					
⊂ ⊃ MAR	⊂0⊃	⊂0⊃	⊂0⊃	⊂0⊃	
⊂ ⊃ APR	⊂1⊃	⊂1⊃	⊂1⊃	⊂1⊃	
⊂ ⊃ MAY	⊂2⊃	⊂2⊃	⊂2⊃	⊂2⊃	
⊂ ⊃ JUN	⊂3⊃	⊂3⊃	⊂3⊃	⊂3⊃	
⊂ ⊃ JUL		⊂4⊃	⊂4⊃	⊂4⊃	
⊂ ⊃ AUG		⊂5⊃	⊂5⊃	⊂5⊃	
⊂ ⊃ SEP		⊂6⊃	⊂6⊃	⊂6⊃	
⊂ ⊃ OCT		⊂7⊃	⊂7⊃	⊂7⊃	
⊂ ⊃ NOV		⊂8⊃	⊂8⊃	⊂8⊃	
⊂ ⊃ DEC		⊂9⊃	⊂9⊃	⊂9⊃	

3. TEST CODE   **4. REGISTRATION NUMBER**

⊂0⊃ ⊂A⊃ ⊂0⊃ ⊂0⊃ ⊂0⊃ ⊂0⊃ ⊂0⊃ ⊂0⊃ ⊂0⊃ ⊂0⊃ ⊂0⊃
⊂1⊃ ⊂B⊃ ⊂1⊃ ⊂1⊃ ⊂1⊃ ⊂1⊃ ⊂1⊃ ⊂1⊃ ⊂1⊃ ⊂1⊃ ⊂1⊃
⊂2⊃ ⊂C⊃ ⊂2⊃ ⊂2⊃ ⊂2⊃ ⊂2⊃ ⊂2⊃ ⊂2⊃ ⊂2⊃ ⊂2⊃ ⊂2⊃
⊂3⊃ ⊂D⊃ ⊂3⊃ ⊂3⊃ ⊂3⊃ ⊂3⊃ ⊂3⊃ ⊂3⊃ ⊂3⊃ ⊂3⊃ ⊂3⊃
⊂4⊃ ⊂E⊃ ⊂4⊃ ⊂4⊃ ⊂4⊃ ⊂4⊃ ⊂4⊃ ⊂4⊃ ⊂4⊃ ⊂4⊃ ⊂4⊃
⊂5⊃ ⊂F⊃ ⊂5⊃ ⊂5⊃ ⊂5⊃ ⊂5⊃ ⊂5⊃ ⊂5⊃ ⊂5⊃ ⊂5⊃ ⊂5⊃
⊂6⊃ ⊂G⊃ ⊂6⊃ ⊂6⊃ ⊂6⊃ ⊂6⊃ ⊂6⊃ ⊂6⊃ ⊂6⊃ ⊂6⊃ ⊂6⊃
⊂7⊃ ⊂7⊃ ⊂7⊃ ⊂7⊃ ⊂7⊃ ⊂7⊃ ⊂7⊃ ⊂7⊃ ⊂7⊃ ⊂7⊃
⊂8⊃ ⊂8⊃ ⊂8⊃ ⊂8⊃ ⊂8⊃ ⊂8⊃ ⊂8⊃ ⊂8⊃ ⊂8⊃ ⊂8⊃
⊂9⊃ ⊂9⊃ ⊂9⊃ ⊂9⊃ ⊂9⊃ ⊂9⊃ ⊂9⊃ ⊂9⊃ ⊂9⊃ ⊂9⊃

7. SEX
⊂ ⊃ MALE
⊂ ⊃ FEMALE

The
Princeton
Review

5. YOUR NAME

First 4 letters of last name					FIRST INIT	MID INIT
⊂A⊃	⊂A⊃	⊂A⊃	⊂A⊃		⊂A⊃	⊂A⊃
⊂B⊃	⊂B⊃	⊂B⊃	⊂B⊃		⊂B⊃	⊂B⊃
⊂C⊃	⊂C⊃	⊂C⊃	⊂C⊃		⊂C⊃	⊂C⊃
⊂D⊃	⊂D⊃	⊂D⊃	⊂D⊃		⊂D⊃	⊂D⊃
⊂E⊃	⊂E⊃	⊂E⊃	⊂E⊃		⊂E⊃	⊂E⊃
⊂F⊃	⊂F⊃	⊂F⊃	⊂F⊃		⊂F⊃	⊂F⊃
⊂G⊃	⊂G⊃	⊂G⊃	⊂G⊃		⊂G⊃	⊂G⊃
⊂H⊃	⊂H⊃	⊂H⊃	⊂H⊃		⊂H⊃	⊂H⊃
⊂I⊃	⊂I⊃	⊂I⊃	⊂I⊃		⊂I⊃	⊂I⊃
⊂J⊃	⊂J⊃	⊂J⊃	⊂J⊃		⊂J⊃	⊂J⊃
⊂K⊃	⊂K⊃	⊂K⊃	⊂K⊃		⊂K⊃	⊂K⊃
⊂L⊃	⊂L⊃	⊂L⊃	⊂L⊃		⊂L⊃	⊂L⊃
⊂M⊃	⊂M⊃	⊂M⊃	⊂M⊃		⊂M⊃	⊂M⊃
⊂N⊃	⊂N⊃	⊂N⊃	⊂N⊃		⊂N⊃	⊂N⊃
⊂O⊃	⊂O⊃	⊂O⊃	⊂O⊃		⊂O⊃	⊂O⊃
⊂P⊃	⊂P⊃	⊂P⊃	⊂P⊃		⊂P⊃	⊂P⊃
⊂Q⊃	⊂Q⊃	⊂Q⊃	⊂Q⊃		⊂Q⊃	⊂Q⊃
⊂R⊃	⊂R⊃	⊂R⊃	⊂R⊃		⊂R⊃	⊂R⊃
⊂S⊃	⊂S⊃	⊂S⊃	⊂S⊃		⊂S⊃	⊂S⊃
⊂T⊃	⊂T⊃	⊂T⊃	⊂T⊃		⊂T⊃	⊂T⊃
⊂U⊃	⊂U⊃	⊂U⊃	⊂U⊃		⊂U⊃	⊂U⊃
⊂V⊃	⊂V⊃	⊂V⊃	⊂V⊃		⊂V⊃	⊂V⊃
⊂W⊃	⊂W⊃	⊂W⊃	⊂W⊃		⊂W⊃	⊂W⊃
⊂X⊃	⊂X⊃	⊂X⊃	⊂X⊃		⊂X⊃	⊂X⊃
⊂Y⊃	⊂Y⊃	⊂Y⊃	⊂Y⊃		⊂Y⊃	⊂Y⊃
⊂Z⊃	⊂Z⊃	⊂Z⊃	⊂Z⊃		⊂Z⊃	⊂Z⊃

1 ⊂A⊃ ⊂B⊃ ⊂C⊃ ⊂D⊃ ⊂E⊃
2 ⊂A⊃ ⊂B⊃ ⊂C⊃ ⊂D⊃ ⊂E⊃
3 ⊂A⊃ ⊂B⊃ ⊂C⊃ ⊂D⊃ ⊂E⊃
4 ⊂A⊃ ⊂B⊃ ⊂C⊃ ⊂D⊃ ⊂E⊃
5 ⊂A⊃ ⊂B⊃ ⊂C⊃ ⊂D⊃ ⊂E⊃
6 ⊂A⊃ ⊂B⊃ ⊂C⊃ ⊂D⊃ ⊂E⊃
7 ⊂A⊃ ⊂B⊃ ⊂C⊃ ⊂D⊃ ⊂E⊃
8 ⊂A⊃ ⊂B⊃ ⊂C⊃ ⊂D⊃ ⊂E⊃
9 ⊂A⊃ ⊂B⊃ ⊂C⊃ ⊂D⊃ ⊂E⊃
10 ⊂A⊃ ⊂B⊃ ⊂C⊃ ⊂D⊃ ⊂E⊃
11 ⊂A⊃ ⊂B⊃ ⊂C⊃ ⊂D⊃ ⊂E⊃
12 ⊂A⊃ ⊂B⊃ ⊂C⊃ ⊂D⊃ ⊂E⊃
13 ⊂A⊃ ⊂B⊃ ⊂C⊃ ⊂D⊃ ⊂E⊃
14 ⊂A⊃ ⊂B⊃ ⊂C⊃ ⊂D⊃ ⊂E⊃
15 ⊂A⊃ ⊂B⊃ ⊂C⊃ ⊂D⊃ ⊂E⊃
16 ⊂A⊃ ⊂B⊃ ⊂C⊃ ⊂D⊃ ⊂E⊃
17 ⊂A⊃ ⊂B⊃ ⊂C⊃ ⊂D⊃ ⊂E⊃
18 ⊂A⊃ ⊂B⊃ ⊂C⊃ ⊂D⊃ ⊂E⊃
19 ⊂A⊃ ⊂B⊃ ⊂C⊃ ⊂D⊃ ⊂E⊃
20 ⊂A⊃ ⊂B⊃ ⊂C⊃ ⊂D⊃ ⊂E⊃
21 ⊂A⊃ ⊂B⊃ ⊂C⊃ ⊂D⊃ ⊂E⊃
22 ⊂A⊃ ⊂B⊃ ⊂C⊃ ⊂D⊃ ⊂E⊃
23 ⊂A⊃ ⊂B⊃ ⊂C⊃ ⊂D⊃ ⊂E⊃

24 ⊂A⊃ ⊂B⊃ ⊂C⊃ ⊂D⊃ ⊂E⊃
25 ⊂A⊃ ⊂B⊃ ⊂C⊃ ⊂D⊃ ⊂E⊃
26 ⊂A⊃ ⊂B⊃ ⊂C⊃ ⊂D⊃ ⊂E⊃
27 ⊂A⊃ ⊂B⊃ ⊂C⊃ ⊂D⊃ ⊂E⊃
28 ⊂A⊃ ⊂B⊃ ⊂C⊃ ⊂D⊃ ⊂E⊃
29 ⊂A⊃ ⊂B⊃ ⊂C⊃ ⊂D⊃ ⊂E⊃
30 ⊂A⊃ ⊂B⊃ ⊂C⊃ ⊂D⊃ ⊂E⊃
31 ⊂A⊃ ⊂B⊃ ⊂C⊃ ⊂D⊃ ⊂E⊃
32 ⊂A⊃ ⊂B⊃ ⊂C⊃ ⊂D⊃ ⊂E⊃
33 ⊂A⊃ ⊂B⊃ ⊂C⊃ ⊂D⊃ ⊂E⊃
34 ⊂A⊃ ⊂B⊃ ⊂C⊃ ⊂D⊃ ⊂E⊃
35 ⊂A⊃ ⊂B⊃ ⊂C⊃ ⊂D⊃ ⊂E⊃
36 ⊂A⊃ ⊂B⊃ ⊂C⊃ ⊂D⊃ ⊂E⊃
37 ⊂A⊃ ⊂B⊃ ⊂C⊃ ⊂D⊃ ⊂E⊃
38 ⊂A⊃ ⊂B⊃ ⊂C⊃ ⊂D⊃ ⊂E⊃
39 ⊂A⊃ ⊂B⊃ ⊂C⊃ ⊂D⊃ ⊂E⊃
40 ⊂A⊃ ⊂B⊃ ⊂C⊃ ⊂D⊃ ⊂E⊃
41 ⊂A⊃ ⊂B⊃ ⊂C⊃ ⊂D⊃ ⊂E⊃
42 ⊂A⊃ ⊂B⊃ ⊂C⊃ ⊂D⊃ ⊂E⊃
43 ⊂A⊃ ⊂B⊃ ⊂C⊃ ⊂D⊃ ⊂E⊃
44 ⊂A⊃ ⊂B⊃ ⊂C⊃ ⊂D⊃ ⊂E⊃
45 ⊂A⊃ ⊂B⊃ ⊂C⊃ ⊂D⊃ ⊂E⊃
46 ⊂A⊃ ⊂B⊃ ⊂C⊃ ⊂D⊃ ⊂E⊃

47 ⊂A⊃ ⊂B⊃ ⊂C⊃ ⊂D⊃ ⊂E⊃
48 ⊂A⊃ ⊂B⊃ ⊂C⊃ ⊂D⊃ ⊂E⊃
49 ⊂A⊃ ⊂B⊃ ⊂C⊃ ⊂D⊃ ⊂E⊃
50 ⊂A⊃ ⊂B⊃ ⊂C⊃ ⊂D⊃ ⊂E⊃
51 ⊂A⊃ ⊂B⊃ ⊂C⊃ ⊂D⊃ ⊂E⊃
52 ⊂A⊃ ⊂B⊃ ⊂C⊃ ⊂D⊃ ⊂E⊃
53 ⊂A⊃ ⊂B⊃ ⊂C⊃ ⊂D⊃ ⊂E⊃
54 ⊂A⊃ ⊂B⊃ ⊂C⊃ ⊂D⊃ ⊂E⊃
55 ⊂A⊃ ⊂B⊃ ⊂C⊃ ⊂D⊃ ⊂E⊃
56 ⊂A⊃ ⊂B⊃ ⊂C⊃ ⊂D⊃ ⊂E⊃
57 ⊂A⊃ ⊂B⊃ ⊂C⊃ ⊂D⊃ ⊂E⊃
58 ⊂A⊃ ⊂B⊃ ⊂C⊃ ⊂D⊃ ⊂E⊃
59 ⊂A⊃ ⊂B⊃ ⊂C⊃ ⊂D⊃ ⊂E⊃
60 ⊂A⊃ ⊂B⊃ ⊂C⊃ ⊂D⊃ ⊂E⊃
61 ⊂A⊃ ⊂B⊃ ⊂C⊃ ⊂D⊃ ⊂E⊃
62 ⊂A⊃ ⊂B⊃ ⊂C⊃ ⊂D⊃ ⊂E⊃
63 ⊂A⊃ ⊂B⊃ ⊂C⊃ ⊂D⊃ ⊂E⊃
64 ⊂A⊃ ⊂B⊃ ⊂C⊃ ⊂D⊃ ⊂E⊃
65 ⊂A⊃ ⊂B⊃ ⊂C⊃ ⊂D⊃ ⊂E⊃
66 ⊂A⊃ ⊂B⊃ ⊂C⊃ ⊂D⊃ ⊂E⊃
67 ⊂A⊃ ⊂B⊃ ⊂C⊃ ⊂D⊃ ⊂E⊃
68 ⊂A⊃ ⊂B⊃ ⊂C⊃ ⊂D⊃ ⊂E⊃
69 ⊂A⊃ ⊂B⊃ ⊂C⊃ ⊂D⊃ ⊂E⊃

101 ⊂A⊃ ⊂B⊃ ⊂C⊃ ⊂D⊃ ⊂E⊃
102 ⊂A⊃ ⊂B⊃ ⊂C⊃ ⊂D⊃ ⊂E⊃
103 ⊂A⊃ ⊂B⊃ ⊂C⊃ ⊂D⊃ ⊂E⊃
104 ⊂A⊃ ⊂B⊃ ⊂C⊃ ⊂D⊃ ⊂E⊃
105 ⊂A⊃ ⊂B⊃ ⊂C⊃ ⊂D⊃ ⊂E⊃
107 ⊂A⊃ ⊂B⊃ ⊂C⊃ ⊂D⊃ ⊂E⊃
108 ⊂A⊃ ⊂B⊃ ⊂C⊃ ⊂D⊃ ⊂E⊃
109 ⊂A⊃ ⊂B⊃ ⊂C⊃ ⊂D⊃ ⊂E⊃
110 ⊂A⊃ ⊂B⊃ ⊂C⊃ ⊂D⊃ ⊂E⊃
111 ⊂A⊃ ⊂B⊃ ⊂C⊃ ⊂D⊃ ⊂E⊃
112 ⊂A⊃ ⊂B⊃ ⊂C⊃ ⊂D⊃ ⊂E⊃
113 ⊂A⊃ ⊂B⊃ ⊂C⊃ ⊂D⊃ ⊂E⊃
114 ⊂A⊃ ⊂B⊃ ⊂C⊃ ⊂D⊃ ⊂E⊃
115 ⊂A⊃ ⊂B⊃ ⊂C⊃ ⊂D⊃ ⊂E⊃
116 ⊂A⊃ ⊂B⊃ ⊂C⊃ ⊂D⊃ ⊂E⊃

The Princeton Review

1.

YOUR NAME: _____
(Print)   Last   First   M.I.

SIGNATURE: _____ DATE: ___ / ___ / ___

HOME ADDRESS: _____
(Print)   Number and Street

_____
City   State   Zip Code

PHONE NO.: _____
(Print)

IMPORTANT: Please fill in these boxes exactly as shown on the back cover of your test book.

2. TEST FORM

3. TEST CODE

4. REGISTRATION NUMBER

⊂0⊃	⊂A⊃	⊂0⊃	⊂0⊃	⊂0⊃	⊂0⊃	⊂0⊃	⊂0⊃	⊂0⊃	⊂0⊃	⊂0⊃
⊂1⊃	⊂B⊃	⊂1⊃	⊂1⊃	⊂1⊃	⊂1⊃	⊂1⊃	⊂1⊃	⊂1⊃	⊂1⊃	⊂1⊃
⊂2⊃	⊂C⊃	⊂2⊃	⊂2⊃	⊂2⊃	⊂2⊃	⊂2⊃	⊂2⊃	⊂2⊃	⊂2⊃	⊂2⊃
⊂3⊃	⊂D⊃	⊂3⊃	⊂3⊃	⊂3⊃	⊂3⊃	⊂3⊃	⊂3⊃	⊂3⊃	⊂3⊃	⊂3⊃
⊂4⊃	⊂E⊃	⊂4⊃	⊂4⊃	⊂4⊃	⊂4⊃	⊂4⊃	⊂4⊃	⊂4⊃	⊂4⊃	⊂4⊃
⊂5⊃	⊂F⊃	⊂5⊃	⊂5⊃	⊂5⊃	⊂5⊃	⊂5⊃	⊂5⊃	⊂5⊃	⊂5⊃	⊂5⊃
⊂6⊃	⊂G⊃	⊂6⊃	⊂6⊃	⊂6⊃	⊂6⊃	⊂6⊃	⊂6⊃	⊂6⊃	⊂6⊃	⊂6⊃
⊂7⊃		⊂7⊃	⊂7⊃	⊂7⊃	⊂7⊃	⊂7⊃	⊂7⊃	⊂7⊃	⊂7⊃	⊂7⊃
⊂8⊃		⊂8⊃	⊂8⊃	⊂8⊃	⊂8⊃	⊂8⊃	⊂8⊃	⊂8⊃	⊂8⊃	⊂8⊃
⊂9⊃		⊂9⊃	⊂9⊃	⊂9⊃	⊂9⊃	⊂9⊃	⊂9⊃	⊂9⊃	⊂9⊃	⊂9⊃

6. DATE OF BIRTH

Month	Day		Year	
⊂ ⊃ JAN				
⊂ ⊃ FEB				
⊂ ⊃ MAR	⊂0⊃	⊂0⊃	⊂0⊃	⊂0⊃
⊂ ⊃ APR	⊂1⊃	⊂1⊃	⊂1⊃	⊂1⊃
⊂ ⊃ MAY	⊂2⊃	⊂2⊃	⊂2⊃	⊂2⊃
⊂ ⊃ JUN	⊂3⊃	⊂3⊃	⊂3⊃	⊂3⊃
⊂ ⊃ JUL		⊂4⊃	⊂4⊃	⊂4⊃
⊂ ⊃ AUG		⊂5⊃	⊂5⊃	⊂5⊃
⊂ ⊃ SEP		⊂6⊃	⊂6⊃	⊂6⊃
⊂ ⊃ OCT		⊂7⊃	⊂7⊃	⊂7⊃
⊂ ⊃ NOV		⊂8⊃	⊂8⊃	⊂8⊃
⊂ ⊃ DEC		⊂9⊃	⊂9⊃	⊂9⊃

7. SEX
⊂ ⊃ MALE
⊂ ⊃ FEMALE

The Princeton Review

5. YOUR NAME

First 4 letters of last name				FIRST INIT	MID INIT
⊂A⊃	⊂A⊃	⊂A⊃	⊂A⊃	⊂A⊃	⊂A⊃
⊂B⊃	⊂B⊃	⊂B⊃	⊂B⊃	⊂B⊃	⊂B⊃
⊂C⊃	⊂C⊃	⊂C⊃	⊂C⊃	⊂C⊃	⊂C⊃
⊂D⊃	⊂D⊃	⊂D⊃	⊂D⊃	⊂D⊃	⊂D⊃
⊂E⊃	⊂E⊃	⊂E⊃	⊂E⊃	⊂E⊃	⊂E⊃
⊂F⊃	⊂F⊃	⊂F⊃	⊂F⊃	⊂F⊃	⊂F⊃
⊂G⊃	⊂G⊃	⊂G⊃	⊂G⊃	⊂G⊃	⊂G⊃
⊂H⊃	⊂H⊃	⊂H⊃	⊂H⊃	⊂H⊃	⊂H⊃
⊂I⊃	⊂I⊃	⊂I⊃	⊂I⊃	⊂I⊃	⊂I⊃
⊂J⊃	⊂J⊃	⊂J⊃	⊂J⊃	⊂J⊃	⊂J⊃
⊂K⊃	⊂K⊃	⊂K⊃	⊂K⊃	⊂K⊃	⊂K⊃
⊂L⊃	⊂L⊃	⊂L⊃	⊂L⊃	⊂L⊃	⊂L⊃
⊂M⊃	⊂M⊃	⊂M⊃	⊂M⊃	⊂M⊃	⊂M⊃
⊂N⊃	⊂N⊃	⊂N⊃	⊂N⊃	⊂N⊃	⊂N⊃
⊂O⊃	⊂O⊃	⊂O⊃	⊂O⊃	⊂O⊃	⊂O⊃
⊂P⊃	⊂P⊃	⊂P⊃	⊂P⊃	⊂P⊃	⊂P⊃
⊂Q⊃	⊂Q⊃	⊂Q⊃	⊂Q⊃	⊂Q⊃	⊂Q⊃
⊂R⊃	⊂R⊃	⊂R⊃	⊂R⊃	⊂R⊃	⊂R⊃
⊂S⊃	⊂S⊃	⊂S⊃	⊂S⊃	⊂S⊃	⊂S⊃
⊂T⊃	⊂T⊃	⊂T⊃	⊂T⊃	⊂T⊃	⊂T⊃
⊂U⊃	⊂U⊃	⊂U⊃	⊂U⊃	⊂U⊃	⊂U⊃
⊂V⊃	⊂V⊃	⊂V⊃	⊂V⊃	⊂V⊃	⊂V⊃
⊂W⊃	⊂W⊃	⊂W⊃	⊂W⊃	⊂W⊃	⊂W⊃
⊂X⊃	⊂X⊃	⊂X⊃	⊂X⊃	⊂X⊃	⊂X⊃
⊂Y⊃	⊂Y⊃	⊂Y⊃	⊂Y⊃	⊂Y⊃	⊂Y⊃
⊂Z⊃	⊂Z⊃	⊂Z⊃	⊂Z⊃	⊂Z⊃	⊂Z⊃

1 ⊂A⊃ ⊂B⊃ ⊂C⊃ ⊂D⊃ ⊂E⊃
2 ⊂A⊃ ⊂B⊃ ⊂C⊃ ⊂D⊃ ⊂E⊃
3 ⊂A⊃ ⊂B⊃ ⊂C⊃ ⊂D⊃ ⊂E⊃
4 ⊂A⊃ ⊂B⊃ ⊂C⊃ ⊂D⊃ ⊂E⊃
5 ⊂A⊃ ⊂B⊃ ⊂C⊃ ⊂D⊃ ⊂E⊃
6 ⊂A⊃ ⊂B⊃ ⊂C⊃ ⊂D⊃ ⊂E⊃
7 ⊂A⊃ ⊂B⊃ ⊂C⊃ ⊂D⊃ ⊂E⊃
8 ⊂A⊃ ⊂B⊃ ⊂C⊃ ⊂D⊃ ⊂E⊃
9 ⊂A⊃ ⊂B⊃ ⊂C⊃ ⊂D⊃ ⊂E⊃
10 ⊂A⊃ ⊂B⊃ ⊂C⊃ ⊂D⊃ ⊂E⊃
11 ⊂A⊃ ⊂B⊃ ⊂C⊃ ⊂D⊃ ⊂E⊃
12 ⊂A⊃ ⊂B⊃ ⊂C⊃ ⊂D⊃ ⊂E⊃
13 ⊂A⊃ ⊂B⊃ ⊂C⊃ ⊂D⊃ ⊂E⊃
14 ⊂A⊃ ⊂B⊃ ⊂C⊃ ⊂D⊃ ⊂E⊃
15 ⊂A⊃ ⊂B⊃ ⊂C⊃ ⊂D⊃ ⊂E⊃
16 ⊂A⊃ ⊂B⊃ ⊂C⊃ ⊂D⊃ ⊂E⊃
17 ⊂A⊃ ⊂B⊃ ⊂C⊃ ⊂D⊃ ⊂E⊃
18 ⊂A⊃ ⊂B⊃ ⊂C⊃ ⊂D⊃ ⊂E⊃
19 ⊂A⊃ ⊂B⊃ ⊂C⊃ ⊂D⊃ ⊂E⊃
20 ⊂A⊃ ⊂B⊃ ⊂C⊃ ⊂D⊃ ⊂E⊃
21 ⊂A⊃ ⊂B⊃ ⊂C⊃ ⊂D⊃ ⊂E⊃
22 ⊂A⊃ ⊂B⊃ ⊂C⊃ ⊂D⊃ ⊂E⊃
23 ⊂A⊃ ⊂B⊃ ⊂C⊃ ⊂D⊃ ⊂E⊃

24 ⊂A⊃ ⊂B⊃ ⊂C⊃ ⊂D⊃ ⊂E⊃
25 ⊂A⊃ ⊂B⊃ ⊂C⊃ ⊂D⊃ ⊂E⊃
26 ⊂A⊃ ⊂B⊃ ⊂C⊃ ⊂D⊃ ⊂E⊃
27 ⊂A⊃ ⊂B⊃ ⊂C⊃ ⊂D⊃ ⊂E⊃
28 ⊂A⊃ ⊂B⊃ ⊂C⊃ ⊂D⊃ ⊂E⊃
29 ⊂A⊃ ⊂B⊃ ⊂C⊃ ⊂D⊃ ⊂E⊃
30 ⊂A⊃ ⊂B⊃ ⊂C⊃ ⊂D⊃ ⊂E⊃
31 ⊂A⊃ ⊂B⊃ ⊂C⊃ ⊂D⊃ ⊂E⊃
32 ⊂A⊃ ⊂B⊃ ⊂C⊃ ⊂D⊃ ⊂E⊃
33 ⊂A⊃ ⊂B⊃ ⊂C⊃ ⊂D⊃ ⊂E⊃
34 ⊂A⊃ ⊂B⊃ ⊂C⊃ ⊂D⊃ ⊂E⊃
35 ⊂A⊃ ⊂B⊃ ⊂C⊃ ⊂D⊃ ⊂E⊃
36 ⊂A⊃ ⊂B⊃ ⊂C⊃ ⊂D⊃ ⊂E⊃
37 ⊂A⊃ ⊂B⊃ ⊂C⊃ ⊂D⊃ ⊂E⊃
38 ⊂A⊃ ⊂B⊃ ⊂C⊃ ⊂D⊃ ⊂E⊃
39 ⊂A⊃ ⊂B⊃ ⊂C⊃ ⊂D⊃ ⊂E⊃
40 ⊂A⊃ ⊂B⊃ ⊂C⊃ ⊂D⊃ ⊂E⊃
41 ⊂A⊃ ⊂B⊃ ⊂C⊃ ⊂D⊃ ⊂E⊃
42 ⊂A⊃ ⊂B⊃ ⊂C⊃ ⊂D⊃ ⊂E⊃
43 ⊂A⊃ ⊂B⊃ ⊂C⊃ ⊂D⊃ ⊂E⊃
44 ⊂A⊃ ⊂B⊃ ⊂C⊃ ⊂D⊃ ⊂E⊃
45 ⊂A⊃ ⊂B⊃ ⊂C⊃ ⊂D⊃ ⊂E⊃
46 ⊂A⊃ ⊂B⊃ ⊂C⊃ ⊂D⊃ ⊂E⊃

47 ⊂A⊃ ⊂B⊃ ⊂C⊃ ⊂D⊃ ⊂E⊃
48 ⊂A⊃ ⊂B⊃ ⊂C⊃ ⊂D⊃ ⊂E⊃
49 ⊂A⊃ ⊂B⊃ ⊂C⊃ ⊂D⊃ ⊂E⊃
50 ⊂A⊃ ⊂B⊃ ⊂C⊃ ⊂D⊃ ⊂E⊃
51 ⊂A⊃ ⊂B⊃ ⊂C⊃ ⊂D⊃ ⊂E⊃
52 ⊂A⊃ ⊂B⊃ ⊂C⊃ ⊂D⊃ ⊂E⊃
53 ⊂A⊃ ⊂B⊃ ⊂C⊃ ⊂D⊃ ⊂E⊃
54 ⊂A⊃ ⊂B⊃ ⊂C⊃ ⊂D⊃ ⊂E⊃
55 ⊂A⊃ ⊂B⊃ ⊂C⊃ ⊂D⊃ ⊂E⊃
56 ⊂A⊃ ⊂B⊃ ⊂C⊃ ⊂D⊃ ⊂E⊃
57 ⊂A⊃ ⊂B⊃ ⊂C⊃ ⊂D⊃ ⊂E⊃
58 ⊂A⊃ ⊂B⊃ ⊂C⊃ ⊂D⊃ ⊂E⊃
59 ⊂A⊃ ⊂B⊃ ⊂C⊃ ⊂D⊃ ⊂E⊃
60 ⊂A⊃ ⊂B⊃ ⊂C⊃ ⊂D⊃ ⊂E⊃
61 ⊂A⊃ ⊂B⊃ ⊂C⊃ ⊂D⊃ ⊂E⊃
62 ⊂A⊃ ⊂B⊃ ⊂C⊃ ⊂D⊃ ⊂E⊃
63 ⊂A⊃ ⊂B⊃ ⊂C⊃ ⊂D⊃ ⊂E⊃
64 ⊂A⊃ ⊂B⊃ ⊂C⊃ ⊂D⊃ ⊂E⊃
65 ⊂A⊃ ⊂B⊃ ⊂C⊃ ⊂D⊃ ⊂E⊃
66 ⊂A⊃ ⊂B⊃ ⊂C⊃ ⊂D⊃ ⊂E⊃
67 ⊂A⊃ ⊂B⊃ ⊂C⊃ ⊂D⊃ ⊂E⊃
68 ⊂A⊃ ⊂B⊃ ⊂C⊃ ⊂D⊃ ⊂E⊃
69 ⊂A⊃ ⊂B⊃ ⊂C⊃ ⊂D⊃ ⊂E⊃

101 ⊂A⊃ ⊂B⊃ ⊂C⊃ ⊂D⊃ ⊂E⊃
102 ⊂A⊃ ⊂B⊃ ⊂C⊃ ⊂D⊃ ⊂E⊃
103 ⊂A⊃ ⊂B⊃ ⊂C⊃ ⊂D⊃ ⊂E⊃
104 ⊂A⊃ ⊂B⊃ ⊂C⊃ ⊂D⊃ ⊂E⊃
105 ⊂A⊃ ⊂B⊃ ⊂C⊃ ⊂D⊃ ⊂E⊃
107 ⊂A⊃ ⊂B⊃ ⊂C⊃ ⊂D⊃ ⊂E⊃
108 ⊂A⊃ ⊂B⊃ ⊂C⊃ ⊂D⊃ ⊂E⊃
109 ⊂A⊃ ⊂B⊃ ⊂C⊃ ⊂D⊃ ⊂E⊃
110 ⊂A⊃ ⊂B⊃ ⊂C⊃ ⊂D⊃ ⊂E⊃
111 ⊂A⊃ ⊂B⊃ ⊂C⊃ ⊂D⊃ ⊂E⊃
112 ⊂A⊃ ⊂B⊃ ⊂C⊃ ⊂D⊃ ⊂E⊃
113 ⊂A⊃ ⊂B⊃ ⊂C⊃ ⊂D⊃ ⊂E⊃
114 ⊂A⊃ ⊂B⊃ ⊂C⊃ ⊂D⊃ ⊂E⊃
115 ⊂A⊃ ⊂B⊃ ⊂C⊃ ⊂D⊃ ⊂E⊃
116 ⊂A⊃ ⊂B⊃ ⊂C⊃ ⊂D⊃ ⊂E⊃

ABOUT THE AUTHOR

Theodore Silver holds a medical degree from the Yale University School of Medicine, a Bachelor's degree from Yale University, and a law degree from the University of Connecticut.

Dr. Silver has been intensely involved in the field of education, testing, and test preparation since 1976 and has written several books and computer tutorials pertaining to those fields. He became affiliated with The Princeton Review in 1988 and is chief author and architect of The Princeton Review MCAT preparatory course.

Dr. Silver is Associate Professor of Law at Touro College Jacob D. Fuchsberg Law Center where he teaches the law of medical practice and malpractice, contracts, and federal income taxation.

NOTES

NOTES

FIND US...

International

Hong Kong
4/F Sun Hung Kai Centre
30 Harbour Road, Wan Chai,
Hong Kong
Tel: (011)85-2-517-3016

Japan
Fuji Building 40, 15-14
Sakuragaokacho, Shibuya Ku,
Tokyo 150, Japan
Tel: (011)81-3-3463-1343

Korea
Tae Young Bldg, 944-24,
Daechi- Dong, Kangnam-Ku
The Princeton Review—ANC
Seoul, Korea 135-280,
South Korea
Tel: (011)82-2-554-7763

Mexico City
PR Mex S De RL De Cv
Guanajuato 228 Col. Roma
06700 Mexico D.F., Mexico
Tel: 525-564-9468

Montreal
666 Sherbrooke St.
West, Suite 202
Montreal, QC H3A 1E7 Canada
Tel: 514-499-0870

Pakistan
1 Bawa Park - 90 Upper Mall
Lahore, Pakistan
Tel: (011)92-42-571-2315

Spain
Pza. Castilla, 3 - 5º A, 28046
Madrid, Spain
Tel: (011)341-323-4212

Taiwan
155 Chung Hsiao East Road
Section 4 - 4th Floor,
Taipei R.O.C., Taiwan
Tel: (011)886-2-751-1243

Thailand
Building One, 99 Wireless Road
Bangkok, Thailand 10330
Tel: 662-256-7080

Toronto
1240 Bay Street, Suite 300
Toronto M5R 2A7 Canada
Tel: 800-495-7737
Tel: 716-839-4391

Vancouver
4215 University Way NE
Seattle, WA 98105
Tel: 206-548-1100

National (U.S.)
We have more than 60 offices around the U.S. and run courses at over 400 sites. For courses and locations within the U.S. call 1-800-2-Review and you will be routed to the nearest office.

The Princeton Review

Find the Right School

BEST 331 COLLEGES
2001 EDITION
The Smart Buyer's Guide to College
0-375-75633-7 • $20.00

THE COMPLETE BOOK OF COLLEGES
2001 EDITION
0-375-76152-7 • $26.95

THE GUIDE TO PERFORMING ARTS PROGRAMS
Profiles of Over 600 Colleges, High Schools and Summer Programs
0-375-75095-9 • $24.95

POCKET GUIDE TO COLLEGES
2001 EDITION
0-375-75631-0 • $9.95

AFRICAN AMERICAN STUDENT'S GUIDE TO COLLEGE
Making the Most of College:
Getting In, Staying In, and Graduating
0-679-77878-0 • $17.95

Get in

CRACKING THE SAT & PSAT
2001 EDITION
0-375-75621-3 • $18.00

CRACKING THE SAT & PSAT WITH SAMPLE TESTS ON CD-ROM
2001 EDITION
0-375-75622-1 • $29.95

SAT MATH WORKOUT
2ND EDITION
0-375-76177-7 • $14.95

SAT VERBAL WORKOUT
2ND EDITION
0-375-76176-4 • $14.95

CRACKING THE ACT WITH SAMPLE TESTS ON CD-ROM
2001 EDITION
0-375-76180-2 • $29.95

CRACKING THE ACT
2001 EDITION
0-375-76179-9 • $18.00

CRASH COURSE FOR THE ACT
10 Easy Steps to Higher Score
0-375-75376-5 • $9.95

CRASH COURSE FOR THE SAT
10 Easy Steps to Higher Score
0-375-75324-9 • $9.95

Get Help Paying for it

DOLLARS & SENSE FOR COLLEGE STUDENTS
How <u>Not</u> to Run Out of Money by Midterms
0-375-75206-4 • $10.95

PAYING FOR COLLEGE WITHOUT GOING BROKE
2001 EDITION
Insider Strategies to Maximize Financial Aid
and Minimize College Costs
0-375-76156-X • $18.00

THE SCHOLARSHIP ADVISOR
2001 EDITION
0-375-76160-8 • $25.00

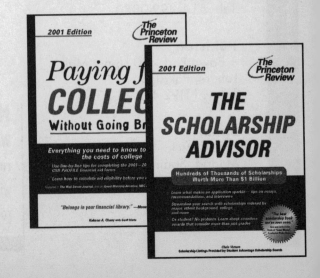

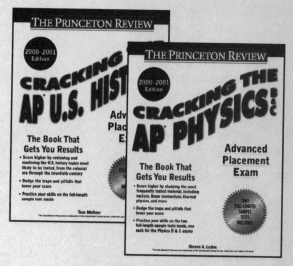

think
scholarships
are just
for scholars?

think again.

Do you have a hidden talent? Or maybe an interesting last name? Perhaps you're ambidextrous? Whatever your unique characteristic is, we've probably got a scholarship for you. **studentadvantage.com/scholaraid** is an online database with 17,000 scholarships available, totaling 2.5 million awards. That's $21.6 billion worth of scholarships! It's confidential, easy to use and best of all free. Go to **studentadvantage.com/scholaraid** and cash in for just being you!

 studentadvantage.com

discounts | scholarships | news | entertainment | career | health | travel | research